N

Proce

The Tools, Practices And Habits Used To Make Music
You're Happy With
By Jesse Cannon

By Jesse Cannon
noisecreators.com
processingcreativitybook.com
Copyright @ 2017 by Jesse Cannon
This work is licensed under a Creative Commons Attribution-
Noncommercial-ShareAlike 4.0 Unported License.

Published by Noise Creators, 540 39th Street #1, Union City, NJ 07087
For more information visit processingcreativitybook.com

Library of Congress Cataloging-in-Publication Data

Cannon, Jesse
Processing creativity : The tools, practices and habits used to make great
music / by Jesse Cannon
p.cm
ISBN-13: 978-0-9885613-3-5
ISBN-10: 0-9885613-3-6
1. Popular music—Production and direction 2. Creative Thinking 3.
Sound Recording Industry I. Title

Manufactured in the USA

Credits:
Author: Jesse Cannon
Editor: Ashley Aron
Cover Art: Jesse Cannon
Cover Design and Additional Cover Art Direction: Todd Thomas
Additional Editing and Insight: Todd Thomas and Mike Oettinger

Table Of Contents

Introduction: Why Write A Book On Creativity In Music?

There's a constant discussion going on in every circle of the internet as well as bars and clubs across the world about why a record fails to live up to expectations:

"Why is this record not as good as the last one?"

"This record should've been the same as their first."

"They've been making the same record forever."

"I liked the demo better!"

When looking at the creative process from the outside, most fans don't understand why the musicians they love can't see what's so clear to them — *make the album the fans want.* It seems so obvious to them what the musician should do. What they don't understand is these musicians aren't making their decisions based on cash grabs, trend jumping, phoning it in or the other assumptions commonly made by fans. While these are the common assumptions, the reasons an album's vision succeeds or falls flat are usually more practical.

Contrary to what's usually discussed, these pitfalls stem from musicians' lack of knowledge about what they should be doing to make music that both they and their fans want to hear. There's a treacherous path of decisions, ego checks, bad advice and skills that plague musicians when they try to make a great record. To get through it, they need extensive consideration of these plagues along with a resilient drive to authentically express what they feel. While modern technology has given musicians the most amazing tools to make music with, no one tool can show them how to consistently release great album after great album. Instead, they stumble into sophomore slumps *(aka making a disappointing second record)* or inauthentic, career-killing records that alienate fans.

This Book Exists To Fill A Void Of Mentorship
Look no further than the ramblings of countless music business veterans over the past fifteen years on how "the music business no longer develops artists." For the uninitiated, from the seventies through the nineties, musicians that had the potential to develop into a great artist were signed to big budget record deals. The hope was they'd eventually make a great record after learning a few lessons from recording some lackluster early albums. It was expected that on their first records they'd be "finding their sound," yielding a small fanbase and hopefully, by the third or fourth record, they'd become a creative force with a large fanbase that would justify the early investment. David Bowie, Kate Bush, Fleetwood Mac, Bruce Springsteen and The Who are all legendary acts whose early records fell on deaf ears, but their label kept investing in them until they became the classic artists we know today. Today, this nurturing comes in the form of indie labels. However, the idea that musicians can receive a consistent paycheck that would enable them to devote their full attention to this artistic growth is nearly extinct, as few indie artists are cash-flush enough to forgo a day job.

The importance of this artistic development has been abandoned after years of humility-lacking record label executives (aka A&R) continually being confused when an artist gains success yet they fail to resonate with the A&R's jaded ears – after all, if they don't understand how a musician got popular, it must be luck? Not really. We all have different emotional needs we look to comfort with music. Instead of acknowledging that it's impossible to have a universal taste that understands what's emotionally appealing about every artist, this lack of humility leads A&R to only sign "sure things" that need minimal development to recoup an investment. This turns record labels into banks with a marketing department instead of patrons of creative mentorship, polluting the music business with a practice that rarely yields lasting artists and places favor on short-term investments.

While some of the best music is being made today, the ability for musicians to sustain their creativity has suffered. Since this mentorship has declined over the past two decades, the decisions of A&R, management and artists are commonly based off poorly thought-out assumptions instead of research and practices that develop great music. While researching this book, I witnessed countless records fall short of their expectations. I was able to trace back these failures to a belief in a few creative "wives' tales" that, had they been assessed properly, would have led to a much better record.

Due to the lack of investment from labels, the responsibility to seek out mentors who can guide musicians to avoid creative downfalls is placed solely on the artist and their management. Today, this mentorship is typically done by studying the endless amount of articles, documentaries and sound bites that litter the web. While the internet has brought a vast democratization of information, the knowledge of how to make good creative decisions is kept behind closed doors or spills out in so many sparse sources that loopholes in this knowledge are inevitable.

While nearly every musician greatly values creativity, they do little to no research on how to do it effectively. They want a highly creative result but have little know-how of how to gain one, outside of taking in small pieces of advice while imitating stories they've heard of those they admire. When I decided to write this book, I felt the need to take in every bit of the advice musicians would need to achieve these results and assemble it in a single source.

Record Labels Don't Put Their Money Where Their Mouths Are

Despite everyone in the music business beating to death the advice "good music is the best marketing tool," the overwhelming majority of their practices shows they don't practice what they preach. Record budgets are shrinking year after year and little to no thought is put into how to nurture an artist's musical output. Producers are hired based on poor assumptions of repeated performance despite every artist having different blanks to be filled in by a producer. Even worse, minimal research and favors-for-favors deals lead to producers with connections getting a job instead of the right producer, which doesn't put the artist first. Those involved with an artist's development treat their music like a meal that needs to be cooked quickly then served to get the next product sold instead of an expression they claim to value nurturing.

One of the more telling stories to illustrate this point was told to me on a podcast I did with Riley Breckenridge of Thrice. When the band made their first album for indie Hopeless Records, they were able to write two songs a month in a two weeks on, two weeks off schedule. These thirteen songs resulted in their sophomore record, *The Illusion of Safety*.

The record catapulted the band from playing to twenty people a night to 1,000+ seat venues, all on a small indie budget.

Thrice was quickly snatched up by a major label, where they were thrown into a model that puts profits before artistic nurture. With the grueling tour schedule of their debut LP, they were left with three months to rest and write their major label debut, which would see countless dollars devoted to promotion. The result left the band feeling lackluster about the record despite its success, as their previous record had delivered new emotional colors to a genre that was largely stagnant. Their major label debut, *The Artist In The Ambulance*, was a reiteration on their previous release, sharing many of the same traits. Instead of continuing to exceed their hopes of developing their sound, they made the safe record that was expected of them since they were left with a minimal amount of time to devote to this development.

For their next record, they didn't succumb to the pressures of the label and devoted the needed time to reach the artistic heights they wanted to achieve. The result is *Vheissu*, the record that Breckenridge says is the reason he still has a career playing music more than a decade later. The record exceeded creative expectations, being commonly cited as one of the most influential works in the genre.

Today, artists are expected to write a record in a single month in between tours and deliver exceptional results. Just a decade ago they commonly had more time than that to get inspired, never mind write an album's worth of material. They get handed a budget that's hardly worthy of reaching the heights labels claim to believe the artist has in them. Little evaluation is given when demos are finished or to even listen to tracking rough mixes before going to a mixer. As long as a final product is pumped out quickly, hopefully, the public will buy it. After all, the artist needs to get back on the road immediately since the only way the booking agent, manager and label will make money is sales of more albums and merchandise.

There's a better way to harness songs from artists that allows creativity to flourish while not costing much more money but may take some time away from the content-machine-work-ethic that's pushed on musicians today. With proper consideration, they can make more emotionally resonant music that affects listeners at a deeper level. Since there's been no clear answer on how to get musicians paid more fairly for their work, allocating resources to get a greater creative result can help musicians get past the tough hand they get dealt in today's music business by establishing a deeper emotional bond with listeners.

Righting The Wrongs Of The Creativity Industrial Complex

There's a massive creative self-help industrial complex that pumps out articles of half-truths all day. This book is written to correct many of the misconstrued quotations in these articles each day by applying them to a musical context. I've read far too many articles that oversimplify creative dilemmas to "this is the cure for every problem" or butcher quotes from famous people. Instead, it's time to discuss what the common advice really means for musicians' decisions. Since the word creativity didn't come along until 1870 and wasn't in widespread use until the 1950s, we're still only beginning to get good at discussing it.

Most of what musicians are taught about the subject ranges from flat-out false to lacking a crucial detail that gets overlooked, resulting in many of the toxic relationships and unfulfilled visions littered throughout musicians' lives. I found remedies for the most common breakdowns in the creative process while gaining insight into how to see them more accurately. I hope this book gives greater deliberation to your creative decisions as well as understanding how to cultivate an environment that makes you happier with the music you make. The thoughts in this book aren't here to tell you what to do; they're to help you consider decisions that may benefit from more evaluation.

In the internet age, the web content vultures circle to find an article to write about every exception to a rule, ignoring the common rules where most artists achieve the creative result they're looking for. The story of what works most of the time is rarely as interesting as the exception that makes an amazing creation in spite of the "rules." There's no doubt there will be times you can find an exception to some of the ideas in this book. Every example in this book has an exception, but I try to focus on best practices along with how science can help us improve ourselves. **There are no rules to creativity, but knowing science, best practices and common rules can help you find the best ways to get the results you want.**

A No-BS Approach

Popular books on creativity regularly talk about intangible concepts such as angels, muses and gods. Too often in the past, authors of these books have equated what they don't understand or haven't researched to be intangible with an uncontrollable mystique instead of concepts that can be discovered, enhanced or influenced by applying emerging scientific research or common psychological techniques. Even worse, what authors don't understand or sufficiently research, they chalk up to unknown mysteries with no rational explanation. Sadly, the subject isn't thoroughly researched by those who traffic in it, since by nature they'd rather be creating than researching.

I pored over scientific papers, thousands of interviews, a hundred some-odd books, documentaries and years of active practice to draw correlations and actionable ways you can get past blocks to get an outcome you're happy with. I've written these ideas in a simple way that leaves little guessing about intangible concepts and instead gives you actionable methods to get the creative results you want.

What To Consider Throughout Your Reading

Some information in this book is bound to be obvious to you. I'm a deep believer that any book you read is a decision to prioritize time on a subject you wish to explore further. During that time, you should consider how you further your thoughts on the subject. As long as the book spurs growth on the subject, your time was used wisely, making your consumption of the book a success. Contrary to what many bad teachers tell you, non-fiction books are made for you to consider how you feel about a subject, not just for memorizing quotes. The research shows that contemplation in your creative endeavors leads to a better output.

If you don't find certain parts of this book to be true, that doesn't mean you should find the rest of the book invalid. **I hope you disagree with me at times.** In any conversation you have, there are moments of consensus as well as disagreements. Books are written to further a conversation that allows a subject to evolve and extract conclusions from. Creative processes are an ever-evolving subject, changing faster than ever as we see more dilemmas presented with the countless technological innovations released every day. Please break the rules, find a better way and then share it with me. In fact, if you disagree with me, let's have an exchange over Skype or email.

It's also important to note that I'm not telling you how to make records out of a belief that I'm the greatest record producer to walk the Earth. I'm far from it, but what I'm very good at is translating great ideas into an easy to understand language. This book isn't how I think you should work; it's thoughts to help figure out the decisions that work best for you.

Creativity And Me

For nearly two decades, I've spent about three hundred days a year helping musicians fulfill their creative vision. I was lucky enough to get into the music business during the last days of big budget analog tape recording as the business turned to the early days of scrappy Pro Tools DIY recording, allowing me to learn lessons from both worlds. I've had the chance to work with some of the greatest minds in music on down to the most novice musicians. Sadly, this means I've also watched countless musicians struggle through many unneeded fights and existential crises caused by creative frustration. Whether it's not knowing how to get the best out of a composition, harboring a toxic environment that creates a vacuum of ideas or not knowing what order to work in to get the best results, I've seen it all. I'm compelled to rid musicians of these unnecessary struggles, and it gave me an urgency to get this book out into the world.

When I finished my last book, *Get More Fans: The DIY Guide To The New Music Business* — a 700+ page exploration of how musicians promote their music — the most dismissive comment I received was: "All you need to do is make great music and it'll promote itself." While there's no better marketing tool than great music, this oversimplifies a vast landscape that's hard to navigate, where you still need a deep pool of knowledge to get through once people like your music. Conversely, even if a musician did a great job promoting their music and it wasn't that good, it would still fail since doing great advertising for a bad product is the fastest way to give it a horrible reputation. Since I agree that great music is the best marketing tool for itself, I figured the next book I should write is about how you make great music.

Processing Creativity

Writing *Get More Fans* was some of the most fulfilling work I've ever done. Hearing from thousands of readers on how it helped them fulfill their dreams filled me with a joy far greater than helping a single band make a successful record. This time around, I wanted to assemble a book that could do the same for musicians looking to make great music. I've seen musicians show ambition towards getting the most out of their creative vision and subsequently fail by ignoring key practices that get the most out of their work. It pains me to see creators being tortured by their art, so I hope anyone who reads this book will be happier with the songs they make as well as any other creative work they do.

My passion to rid people of their creative frustration stems from knowing it in my own life. I was a depressed, even suicidal teenager, experiencing the frustration of creative hurdles that would send me into depression, along with the extreme happiness I felt when I could overcome them. I had no map of how to get around these blocks to know that this struggle was normal. As I got older, I learned how to get past these hurdles to become the extremely happy person I am today. I hope this book helps to rid the world of the misery I went through as a teenager by giving a better idea of how to get over the creative hurdles you experience throughout your growth as a creator.

During those teen years experimenting with recording equipment, I attracted the notice of America's largest and most esteemed freeform radio station, WFMU. I stayed there for nearly a decade working with groups such as The Magnetic Fields, The Sea and Cake, Spoon and countless other creative musicians making the most interesting music of the day. This job gave me the daily experience of speaking with many great minds in up-and-coming groups that would eventually go on to influence millions of musicians. It also exposed me to the biggest music nerds around who would play me the great minds of underground music such as Can, Neu, Steve Reich and much more at a young age.

As I entered my twenties, I experienced the defeat of trying to make music on a computer that could occasionally record four tracks at a time, clunky Akai samplers and early MIDI synthesizers. As bands other than my own hired me to produce their records, I got to work in various NYC studios where I began to learn how to work this complicated equipment and express myself. I then took a job at Alan Douches' West West Side Music, the top mastering studio for indie labels in America for the past three decades. Every day I got to talk with music business veterans who were responsible for running the careers of the biggest indie musicians out there. I got to see their process while picking their brains about music. Getting to be in the same room as many of the most respected brains in music allowed me to become hyper-aware of the thoughts that go into making great music. Being able to converse with a wide variety of artists as they're making the final decisions of their creative works while they're fresh in their head taught me invaluable lessons about the consideration that goes into crafting classic albums.

Over this time, I've had a hand in the production, engineering, mixing and mastering of well over 1,000 records. I've been lucky enough to sit in the room with legends like Joey & Dee Dee Ramone, Stephen Merritt, John McEntire, Robert Smith and Darryl McDaniels (DMC. This fortune has also allowed me to work on records as a producer, engineer, mixer or mastering engineer for groups such as Animal Collective, "Weird Al" Yankovic, Brand New, The Misfits, The Menzingers, Bad Books, NOFX, Dalek, Northstar and Lifetime. I got to work with producer Steve Evetts, making records with Say Anything, Saves The Day, Senses Fail and The Dillinger Escape Plan. I traveled the world with producer Ross Robinson to work on records with The Cure, Limp Bizkit and Chase Pagan.

On the business side, I've been able to see the creative breakdowns from the perspective of those who need artists to make money. I've been part of record labels such as Go Kart, Lost Tape Collective and Drug Front Records. I managed the groups Man Overboard and Transit, who signed to one of the largest indie labels in the world, Rise Records. I co-founded a service called Noise Creators, which connects musicians with the best producers in music. I also teach courses on recording music for the amazing service CreativeLive.

I've been lucky enough to see the creative process from countless angles and hope you enjoy what I've learned. I'm fortunate to keep meeting amazing musicians who I make great music with each day. Along the way, I found countless correlations between the research I did for this book and what I've witnessed in my work. As I learned these lessons, I found myself doing the most creative work I've ever done and am extremely thankful for the time I put in learning it all.

Not A Producer But Instead A Creative Director

A thought I've had for the past decade is that my job title of record producer might be inaccurate. In nearly any other profession where the term "producer" is used it's applied to someone charged with overseeing or clerical work. What the modern record producer does is more similar to what's called a creative director in the graphic design, film, fashion, advertising, media or entertainment industries. I know this well since my father held this job title in the advertising world for over forty years.

Most record producers spend each day helping musicians get past creative hurdles while establishing a process that'll help get the best song from an artist. We figure out how to convey the artist's vision while staying within their limitations (budget, musicians, technology, etc.). Since producers commonly make more music than the artists, it's their job to have experience figuring out the best practices that lead to better creative outcomes, while avoiding commonly made mistakes. In my practice as a record producer, the work has been much more than budget allocation and hiring duties that producers in film, advertising and many other fields get charged with. The creative development record producers do each day sounds much more like the job title of a creative director.

Getting On The Same Page

Before we get to the fun part, it's important to quickly establish some working definitions, since these words are used in poor context throughout the content farms of the internet today. There are also some terms that are academic or only used in the music business that may be helpful to understand.

Creativity - The use of the imagination, especially in the production of a new artistic work.

Emotional Resonance - The amount of emotion we feel when reacting to a performance of a song. This resonance can be a feeling of apathy when hearing a badly performed cover of a song you enjoy or a dancing frenzy when a song compels you.

Epiphany - A sudden realization of great truth that connects concepts you didn't see a connection between before.

Fluency - The ability to express oneself easily and articulately.

Innovation - A new method, idea or product that's commonly accepted to possess new traits and purposes.

Intent - A purpose you're pursuing, such as the expression of an emotion or idea.

Trusting Your Gut - When you hear a flaw in a song, you'll feel a slight lack of comfort about it. Trusting to listen to that lack of comfort is trusting your gut.

Perspire/Perspiration - The opposite of inspiration; this is what you create from your inspiration.

Resistance - This is a catchall term for what holds you back from creating.

Riffs (or Beats) - A small part of a song that's commonly a hook or the basis for further building.

Suits - A&R, record label employees, managers, booking agents and all the other business types who have a concern for your art making money.

Team - As someone with no interest in sports or corporate lingo, this term can be a bit cringeworthy. Trust me, there will be no falling backward so your drummer can catch you in this book. We know how that'll turn out. Sadly, the use of the word team is the best way to describe those you collaborate with, whether it's band members, studio musicians, your management, producer or A&R, those you discuss your music with are a team, so you should all be on the same side. I use this word since I can't find a better one. If you can find one, please help me out, I'll rewrite this whole book just to get this bad taste out of my mouth.

You're Good Enough, Smart Enough And Doggone It, People Like You

There's a wide variety of myths that have been perpetuated about those who are good at being creative that don't line up with the facts. These myths make amateurs feel they shouldn't even try to create since their dreams will get squashed by their overwhelming mediocrity. They believe they don't have what it takes from reading stories about outliers that make for good clickbait stories on blogs.

Doubt, insecurity and fear embody huge parts of the resistance many artists go through, and these myths are commonly the cause. As we grow up, we begin to believe stories that tell us we're not creative. In kindergarten over 50% of children identify as being creative, but by the time they're teenagers that number drops to 10%. While I don't believe everyone is a creative genius, it's a bad idea to paint this picture so black and white. While some of the drop in creative pursuits comes from children who decide to go into less creative fields, a lot of this doubt is from myths we tell ourselves about who can and cannot be creative. Let's dispel some myths:

Myth: Creativity Is Inherited - Any evidence that creativity is inherited is purely anecdotal. Instead, many think that being around an environment where creative best practices are abundant leads to this enhanced ability. There's much more evidence that it's developed by acquiring a set of traits. Scientists have found that at most genetics contribute only 10% of someone's creativity.

Myth: Those With High IQs Are More Creative - Donald MacKinnon surveyed creators such as architects and scientists, finding that those who were most creative showed little correlation to their creative output and IQ. Instead, the greatest creators of any IQ developed a process that allowed them to stumble upon the best ideas. He found that once you cross an IQ of 120, intelligence has absolutely no bearing on whether you'll be more creative. Neuroscience has proven countless times that unless your brain is severely damaged, you have the potential to be creative.

Myth: You Need To Be Depressed To Be Highly Creative - Nancy C. Andreassen did a famous study on The Iowa Writers Workshop (considered to be the best writing program in the world) focusing on depression in artists. She found that 80% of the attendees suffered from mental health issues, a common thread being an inability to create in the darkest throes of their depression. Social psychologist Joseph Forgas says melancholia (often considered depression's less overbearing cousin) can help creativity, yet sadness diminishes insight. Comfort in melancholia allows creators to focus with a painstaking refinement on their works.

While depression isn't a necessary ingredient for creativity, there's something to be said for the sadness stemming from a significant loss as a creative accelerator. A study of great creators shows they often suffer a huge loss at an early age where the pain from this loss becomes creative inspiration as well as a motivator.

Myth: You Need To Be Insane To Be Highly Creative - Schizophrenia or being clinically insane doesn't enhance creativity. The evidence doesn't bear scrutiny since most of those diagnosed aren't functional enough to create. Every study has proven that mental illness in hyper-creatives is the exception, not the rule. Psychologists say instead that creativity is part of a fully functioning personality.

Science continually finds highly creative people are walking contradictions. They're more introspective and high functioning in many ways but may contain attributes of depression or what is viewed as being crazy. The myth that creators are crazy stems from being more sensitive than others, which gets described as crazy by those not experienced in diagnosing mental illness. They're usually blind to a crippling trait or belief that continually alienates others, which gets categorized as being cuckoo.

Myth: You Need To Pass A Personality Test - No personality test can determine if someone's creative or not. This goes especially for any test a high school guidance counselor administers. If you've been told you're not creative after taking a test, scientists have proven time and time again these personality tests lack the nuance needed to test creativity. Charlie Kaufman, who wrote some of the most creative movies of recent years such as *Eternal Sunshine of the Spotless Mind*, *Adaptation* and *Human Nature*, has said "we're all great writers when we're dreaming." In our minds, there's always the potential to be creative – it just needs to be nurtured.

One of the most common contradictions creative people display is qualities of both introversion and extroversion. They're hard to pin down because their personalities are more complex than others. A study of heavy metal musicians showed they're both bold and brash while being sensitive and shy. They possess a plethora of traits that contradict stereotypes, which is why they make for great stories since it's hard for us to understand the complexity of their personalities.

Myth: If You're Not An Amazing Creator As A Teenager, You Won't Be One As An Adult - If you've ever listened to Marc Maron's WTF podcast, you've probably noticed a trend — many of the most accomplished creative guests on the show weren't that way as children. It's a common discussion that there may have been a small part of them that was a seed for the great creator they would become, but it wasn't fully nurtured until later in life. Every study on the subject shows that there's no correlation between being a great creator as a child and later as an adult. The over-representation of stories of creators who were great in their childhood stems from the story not being very interesting if that creativity doesn't amount to anything in adulthood. Only the success stories are told. While being creative at a young age can give you a head start, dedication to the pursuit of your craft at any age is much more important. Who you are as a creator today can be dramatically different after a few years of creating regularly.

Myth: You Need To Have Natural Talent To Excel At Creativity - By definition, the word talent is a "natural aptitude or skill." So when we discuss talent, it's implied that you're born with these skills. Which brings us to why I avoid using the word talent throughout this book. Anyone who's worked in music long enough has come to see that being good at a skill comes easily to some who are seemingly "born with it" whereas others work hard to acquire that skill. What's not discussed is that of those two roads you can take, how you get there doesn't matter as long as you get there. Great music is made by both those who it comes to naturally and to those who worked hard to get there.

What's commonly perceived as inherited is actually that the children of creators are nurtured by being given more time to create. By gaining that practice at an earlier age than those who work hard to become highly creative, they're perceived as superior. When it comes time to make creative work throughout our life, neither group creates superior work as long as they've put in the time to learn the dynamics of creating. This is why I discuss proficiency instead of talent, since that's what makes someone great regardless of how they got there.

Creative Weight Training

The idea that creativity should come easily to those who go on to do great things discourages many would-be creators from pursuing their endeavors since they don't immediately have the attention span or the skills to create great work. This thought neglects the fact that many of the skills you need to be highly creative take an immense amount of practice. Much like exercise or weight training, creative skills need to be used regularly and built upon continuously to be able to be used proficiently. Nearly every part of creativity takes practice that eventually gets you in shape to create easily and effectively.

Time - When I first started working in a recording studio, doing a six-hour session felt like an eternity. Within a year I could do a fourteen-hour day with no problem; fifteen years later, sustaining an eighteen-hour day isn't hard for me as long as I don't do too many in a row. Expecting to jump into ten-hour days in the studio without losing your attention span or getting exhausted is unrealistic. Most of us need to build up a stamina for long days of creation.

Arrangements - Most musicians start out learning simple three-chord pop songs building up to the ability to remember long, complex melodies. To get good at complex arrangements, you need to first learn the basics. Don't expect "Bohemian Rhapsody" to come out of you before you've learned "Basket Case."

Commitment - Committing to decisions is a practice that takes time. At first, musicians are uneasy about commitment in case they need to revisit an element of a song. In time, as you become confident the decisions you make are right, it becomes progressively easier to commit.

Ego Depletion - This unfortunately named term is the idea that every time you navigate through a creative crossroad throughout your day, you get more exhausted. Dr. Roy Baumeister discovered this in a study where he stated, "your finite willpower becomes depleted with each decision you have to make and each unfamiliar interaction you have to have." This relates to creativity in that every person only has so many decisions they can make without taking a break before they make poor decisions or give up on making good decisions.

Building up your resistance to ego depletion not only takes time by going through the creative practice, but it also takes strategy. By committing to production choices and utilizing templates, you spend less time making decisions, which frees your brain to sustain its creative fuel. Many "life hackers" take this to the extreme, where they'll have the same breakfast every day to save their brains for making more pressing decisions. While this example is excessive, the practice of ridding your life of pensive decisions before creating can help you use your creative power as effectively as possible. Making decisions during pre-production instead of long studio days can make the process of deep reconsideration in the studio more effective.

 **Cancer**

As I began work on this book I was diagnosed with papillary thyroid cancer. This book only exists from the past developments of previous cancer research. Being in remission from cancer today, I give a portion of every sale to cancer research since I wouldn't be here to share these thoughts without past research. Hopefully more research will help to stop cancer from taking so many lives away from us that would have otherwise gone on to share great, creative ideas.

Reading This Book

I decided to tinker with normal book formats by giving you a musical accompaniment. Every musician mentioned in this book is linked on a Spotify playlist I made. I figured it may be helpful to illustrate the book by easily ingesting the many musical references. Since you bought this book in it's physical form, I want you to get the benefits of the eBook as well, any underlined text is a link which you can click on by going to processingcreativitybook.com/extras. I link every source I thought a reader may want to investigate further. If the source is a book, I link to it on Amazon to support the authors of the book. If you're interested in digging deeper on a subject, their work is a click away and there's a section on further reading at the end of the book, as well as a clickable version available on the book's website.

Legal Disclaimer:

Even though I've occasionally worn a cheap suit, I'm not a lawyer. Nothing in this book should be taken as legal, health or business advice. Please consult with a lawyer to make sure anything you may be thinking of doing that was inspired by this book is in fact within the bounds of the law. Please consult the proper counsel before experimenting with any food, drink or drug mentioned in this book.

The author has exhaustively researched their sources to the best of their abilities to ensure accuracy and comprehensiveness. I assume no responsibility for errors, inaccuracies, omissions or inconsistency herein. Any slight against any of the subjects contained is unintentional. Readers should consult an attorney or accountant for any specific matter since many ideas in this book are spoken in generality and don't always refer to the exhaustive permission, laws and regulations you may need to abide by.

Thank You:

I'd like to send a special thank you to my parents, Joanne and David Cannon, who provide constant inspiration and support to do everything I've done in my life. I'd also like to thank Alan Douches, Ashley Aron, Ashley Cannon, Ben Weinman, Christine Hawkins, David Ahuja, Dean Rispler, Finn McKenty, Greg Ross, Jackie Brennan, Jerry Only, John Cafiero, Johnny Minardi, Jonathan Snyder, Ken Shadford, Marissa Dockery, Mike Gallucci, Mike Oettinger, Pat King, Ross Robinson, Sam Goldman, Shannon O'Neill Loyola, Spencer Ackerman, Steve Evetts, Thomas Nassiff, Todd Thomas and Zack Zarrillo.

Chapter 1: Making The Music You Love Is The Only Way To Make Music Other People Love

Aspiring musicians are always looking for a common trait in the musicians they love that enables them to make such great music. They figure if they can find this secret trait, they can emulate it to write music millions of people love just like those they admire. Within the first paragraph of this book, I'm going to give away the secret that every musician I know with a huge fanbase understands: **They make the music they want to hear, not the music they think their audience wants to hear.** They don't say clichés like:

"This is what's popular and it'll make us rich."

"This is what everyone will be into next year."

"Everyone is doing this now so we gotta start doing it."

The great musicians of any genre or era let their emotions guide them by making music that fills an emotional need inside of them. After they've expressed that emotion, listeners then connect with it when they need an emotional void filled. Don't get me wrong, not every song that's made by musicians making what they love gets popular. If it were that simple, this would be an essay, not a book. There are tons more moving parts to this puzzle, but this is both the first and most important part of the songwriting process that musicians get wrong. It's a linchpin that if left missing causes the wheels to fall off since emotionally vacant music fails to have any emotional impact to connect with listeners.

In my experience, every single act that's made music to "cash in" or "get popular" has failed, and every producer I've ever discussed this with has said the same thing. The musicians we've seen passionately working to perfect what they need to hear, go on to have at the very least a small but passionate fanbase (*as long as they put in the work to get others to hear it*).

Whereas the acts who disingenuously make music to please others can't even get their significant others to buy a record to support their music. Getting through a song that's made to please the masses is a painful experience. It's emotionless since it's not guided by authentic emotions. The musical chameleons that imitate someone else write songs with no feeling since it's only a diluted emulation of another person's authentic emotions. Instead, this watered down music fills in the blanks of a coloring book, which is the least emotionally resonant art form possible. When you're creating to please others, you always guess at what will be resonant since you can't know what others want to hear. This guessing game leads you down a rabbit hole that makes writing consistently great songs nearly impossible.

No One Wants To Hear Music Made To Please Others

Those who make music with motives of achieving commercial success as opposed to making the music they want to hear don't even want to hear their own music. There's a mind-boggling statistic that 20% of the songs on Spotify have never been listened to once. Just as awful, a large percentage of the songs on iTunes have never even been purchased. There are many reasons for this, but one culprit is there's no feeling to be found in the countless emotionally vacant songs, so even the writers or their loved ones would never subject themselves to another listen to this insincere garbage. Sadly, we've all had this commodity in music form pushed on us at some point in our lives as they strike a pose through music instead of trying to connect with us emotionally.

Whether it's a country music documentary on Johnny Cash or the excellent Stretch and Bobbito documentary on 90s hip-hop, those interviewed talk about "music that speaks from the heart." This music authentically comes from what the musician loves instead of trying to do what someone else wants them to do. There's a reason one of the most overused lyrical clichés is "my heart's a compass" right behind "follow your heart." Every artist creating great music is expressing an emotion, which they let guide them to a sound that makes them feel that emotion in a stronger way.

Processing Creativity

I know the idea that you need to love the music you make is counterintuitive to the stigma that listening to your music is for narcissistic, self-absorbed douchebags. In 2015, Apple even shamed Jamie Foxx for enjoying his own song in an iPhone commercial. But this trait is the commonality in everyone who makes great music. However, we shouldn't confuse this with musicians never wanting to hear their song again after it's recorded. Writing, rehearsing and recording, along with the paralysis of creative decisions you make along the way, is enough to have a sore spot towards a song for a lifetime.

When Making The Music You Love Collides With Expectations

The love a musician has for the music they make gets complicated with success. Artists suddenly have to keep the money coming in to support their team, who holds a financial interest in their music. To make matters worse, fans have expectations and musicians think they should live up to them in order to sustain their success. Sophomore slumps are often caused by giving in to the expectations of fans, money or commercial success instead of the artist listening to what their heart wants to do, just as they did when no one was expecting anything from them on their debut record.

Humans develop emotionally, as well as the naturally occurring development of what inspires them. Therefore, the music that's emotionally resonant with you changes as your emotions change. Inevitably, you experience different parts of life, evolving along the way. This is why you see your favorite bands struggle after they become successful and continue to grow further from their original sound. They know they get a paycheck by making music they no longer emotionally feel resonance towards. This payday is at risk if they follow their emotions by changing their sound to one that's emotionally resonant to them. This is why you see musicians make big changes to their sound instead of making the record their fans want to hear. They're listening to their heart instead of the sounds of those throwing money at them.

One of the most overused thoughts in rock criticism is that you have your whole life to write your first album, which is why debuts are often the most impressive work in an artist's catalog. This thought ignores that the artist probably made releases with other bands or wrote all of the songs in the past six months, disregarding older material that wasn't presently resonating with them. The main thought this neglects is that external forces haven't begun to tug at the songwriter, which is the much more common culprit for a poor showing on a second album.

Whether it's financial gain, writing hookier songs, having a hit or following whatever trend a clueless suit thinks will lead to success, the advice to not follow your most emotionally resonant instincts gets hurled at you the second your music receives acclaim. Instead of being advised to "just keep getting better at doing what you do," an army of "professionals" tries to influence the musician instead of letting them continue the authentic expression of what they feel, which is what made their music connect with an audience in the first place. Time and time again the musicians who resist outside pressures by writing their most emotionally potent truth allows them to sustain writing great songs.

It's not just the financial gains that tug at musicians after they become successful. As a musician grows emotionally past their old self, an illusion of a catch-22 occurs: they can make their fans happy by making a record of their old sound that's no longer emotionally resonant to them, or they can follow their musical inclinations that their fans may find alienating. Most great musicians know there's no choice but to follow their heart. For example, Blink-182 could no longer do songs about dog farts in their thirties, so they had great success with their huge sound departure self-titled record. Radiohead had to make music outside of the confines of a guitar after *OK Computer* since they had mastered that expression. Daft Punk can't make another *Homework* or *Discovery* since that's not what's emotionally resonant to them. They're all following their emotions by making the music they want to hear.

> *"If there's no feeling there can be no great art ... If there's no feeling, just forget it." – **Ray Bradbury***

The choice between doing what the fanbase wants versus what your heart is telling you to do is often framed as safe versus risky, but defying what the heart wants is the riskiest move of them all. Fans will say "just make part two of your last album" or "make more songs like ____." These critiques are regularly seen through the prism of business advice where "the customer is always right." But what's definitely not right is trying to make an emotional connection with someone when your heart isn't present. The only directional concern for a musician should be fulfilling an authentic, emotional expression of what's inside them since anything else leads to music no one wants to hear.

Badly navigating this concept has doomed many musicians' careers. When they make the music the fans want to hear without it being emotionally resonant to them, the fans call it hollow and soulless. You can make a list longer than the pages of this book of musicians who make the experimental record they want to make, fans revolt, so they return with an uninspired version of their fan-preferred-sound that never has the emotional impact of when that sound was emotionally resonant to them. To the listener, there's something missing they can't place their finger on that doesn't feel right. This missing element is the emotional connection between the artist and listener.

However, when the band makes the music they want to hear, they either come up with a record that alienates fans or a record that's celebrated. The "safe option" of a crowd-pleasing record only works when that sound is still emotionally resonant to a musician. The only "safe option" is doing what your heart wants since that's the only way your music will continue to be resonant to your audience.

This choice can also lead to musicians regretting their decisions. When I interview musicians who made a record inspired by making more money or what a suit told them to do, they're always regretful they didn't trust their heart by doing what they knew was right. They learn the lesson, but it's too late and their career is done. When the musician does what their heart wanted and it doesn't connect with their audience, they always have a more peaceful demeanor as they don't regard it as a regret. They accept it was all they could do and for whatever reason, their audience wasn't in the same place as them. **There's no choice but to make the music you want to hear since the other option is always regret and failure.**

This extends past my experience as well. If you watch any documentary on someone who made a great work, the most common correlation between all of them is an artist saying "I made it for myself, there was a void." They wanted a flavor they weren't tasting or an emotion they weren't feeling in other artists' work. Despite the excessive vacuousness of many stars today, you never hear that they made music to get "made, paid and laid." Even the dumbest genre-defining hair metal bands or pop stars will talk about how no one was doing what they were so they had to make it for the rest of the world to hear.

When Natalie Maines of the Dixie Chicks talks about working with Rick Rubin, she says he lets music be "discovered not manufactured," which is an artful way of describing the origins of great music. Rubin, being one of the most successful producers in music history with an unparalleled track record that spans both unknown acts and established artists across nearly every genre, has an undeniable understanding of how to craft a great song. He says, "any commercial considerations get in the way. If you think about music that gets on the radio, you won't be using your own voice in its most potent form. Competing and concern about what others think gets in the way of good music."

It's not hard to figure out why writing songs about your passions results in songs that sound passionate to others. Inherently, these passions are what we feel strongest about, so they'll evoke the strongest response inside us. They compel us to work tirelessly at getting our expression right. When we follow the compass of our emotions, we gain the added benefit that anything we're passionate about puts wind in our sails, which makes any endeavor easier. Ask anyone who has fallen in love as they describe the intense feelings of when someone understands them. When we connect with each other through the emotions in a song, it's very much the same.

Creativity In Music Is Different Than Creativity In Other Fields

As someone known for producing "emo" (short for emotional) music, I need to make the distinction that all music is emotional. When we listen to music, we're solely concerned with feeling an emotional reaction. Even in genres where technical prowess is rewarded, those who make emotional music coupled with proficient musical performance are the ones who connect with listeners. We've all heard thousands of songs that listeners judge on whether they elicit a strong emotional reaction. When they inspire no reaction, we have no interest in hearing them again.

While this is largely true of cinema, fine art, photography and a handful of other fields, it's not always the case in every field where creativity is discussed. In science, utility and innovation are the only qualities that are rewarded. In business, creativity is almost exclusively used for problem solving and only occasionally emotional. In advertising, all that matters is if you get users to change their behavior to consume the product you're advertising. While that may be done by manipulating emotions, creativity is only rewarded if you get the desired behavior from the ad. While design can often be emotional, it's mostly determined by function; it can spark emotion, but emotion isn't the most determinative factor in what's rewarded in design.

Sadly, creative advice in today's content farms is lumped together to be as broadly applicable as possible to gain the maximum amount of clicks from readers. The advice that's dispensed about creativity is given as if it applies to every field when music is often an exception since it's ruled by emotion. Since different creative fields have different objectives, the advice dispensed lacks the broad appeal they hope to achieve and falls flat when an audience takes it in.

Despite the views of money-hungry suits, music is only commodified when it has emotional potency. When we discuss creativity in music, it's often judged by playing complex scales or making sounds that've never been heard before. But since music's goal is to inspire an emotional reaction, creativity in the field is actually about finding an alignment with your musical ideas to craft an emotionally resonant song. **Creativity should be applied to the alignment of all the elements in a musical composition so they're working together to make the most emotionally potent version of your song possible.**

A Lack Of Concern For Being Judged

When you consider the judgment of your music by others, it makes it less potent. Judging which artists make great or creative work is called a "systems model." Van Gogh, The Velvet Underground, Goblin and Refused along with countless other artists weren't appreciated in their time, but it doesn't make them any less artistic or take away their vast influence on the world. This is not to say music criticism is useless; the discussion of any craft is beneficial to furthering an understanding of the deeper thought communicated that's not always said out loud by the artist. But to judge an artist's creativity based on groupthink or a systems model misses out that creative work needs to stimulate the creator first, then the world around them next.

In this book, I focus on you being happy with what you create since you can control that. Sadly, the tastes of the world won't always be aligned with your emotional expression. If you make polka-infused atonal piano treatments to express your emotions, the world may never come around since they probably find that rhythm annoying and out of key notes hard to listen to. You can never control whether the world finds you creative or not, so start by making music you love and ignore the world's judgments until you do. Let's instead discuss how you develop a process to make the best creative version of your song. If you devote yourself to finding how you make the most emotionally resonant music you can, I'm sure you can come up with music that both you and others enjoy.

Chapter 2: What We Enjoy About Music

Before we get any further, I think it's important to examine what we enjoy about music. If we understand what makes us react positively to it, it becomes far easier to make ourselves happy with the music we make.

Music Is Like A Mood-Altering Drug

Music is an emotional drug that listeners use to change their mood to one they would rather feel. To clarify, at a neurological level, certain songs give us a change in the chemicals in our brain that can help get us to an emotion we would rather feel than the one we are currently feeling. Emotionally, some people medicate up and others medicate down while some even do both. Some listeners put on a sad song when they're sad to feel better, finding comfort in it, whereas others put on a happy song to forget their pain. While it's argued that humans use music as filler to hold their attention or keep their thoughts quiet, every song also carries emotional stimulation that goes beyond the view of music as background noise for life. **The most common use of music in our lives is to alter the way we're feeling, bringing us an emotion we'd rather feel than the one we presently feel.**

The moods music alters within us are much more complicated than simply "happy" or "sad" while being highly subjective from person to person. The Dead Kennedys' "California Uber Alles" is a fun song to bounce around the room to for one person but, to another, is the soundtrack for smashing windows. The Magnetic Fields' lyrics in "100,000 Fireflies" can make someone feel less alone in the world or depress the living hell out of someone else. Bassnectar's "You & Me" is a beautiful love song to one person that provides comfort or another person's anthem to go crazy on the dancefloor. The song "All Right Now" by Free is constantly played at conservative political rallies as a motivational song, yet its subject is about <u>having sex with a meter maid you met an hour before</u>, which runs quite contrary to conservative values. The intent of a song doesn't need to correspond to a listener's reaction since as long as an emotional resonance exists, listeners will feel that resonance and interpret their reaction according to their own emotional makeup.

It's not always easy to understand why we're drawn to certain songs' emotional content. The world has a hard time understanding how a rich suburban brat craves hearing a gangster rap song about the lifestyle of extreme poverty when the biggest crime this privileged dweeb has committed is taking a under-aged pull off a cigarette. One of the reasons we find a song outside of our normal tastes or lifestyle to be resonant is the artist found a way to make it exceptionally emotionally potent. We can't help but get drawn into the extremely vivid picture they paint by showing us their authentic emotions; the power of it inspires a reaction in us. Just as we can enjoy the fun of pretending to be someone else by acting or performing, these songs elicit a change in us that helps enhance an act we want to embody that fills an emotional void we would rather feel for a moment.

When creators make highly resonant music, listeners make exceptions to what they normally enjoy; they feel so much emotional power that normal reservations get put aside. These cravings are primal, just as dancing to music has existed for as long as human history has been recorded. These reactions are subconscious, which is why we see addictive behavior in music consumption.

When we wonder why we enjoy music that seems to have little commonality with the emotions we regularly have each day, we ignore that we all have a wide span of feelings, so a song from outside our normal listening confines can be a highly resonant expression that we want to explore. When we hear music, we're usually meditating upon what the musicians are emotionally expressing. Just as you can read a book about someone's life that exists in a far different way than you do, exploring the emotions in a song is often the same. We explore these emotions as we latch on to the meaningful passages of wisdom, accompanied by a resonance-strengthening sound that helps make it more aligned to our current emotional state. As we focus on these emotions, we devote the time we need to get clarity on how we're feeling.

Just Because It Gets In Your Head Doesn't Mean It's Emotionally Resonant

It's commonly assumed that a song is successful at its job as long as it gets stuck in your head. This is a half-truth, since songs need to posses both emotional potency and a repetitive hook that keeps revisiting your thoughts so that you are reminded to listen to the song and continue to bond with it. Any song that employs repetition in a simple way can get in your head if you hear it enough. **What's much more important than hooks that stick with you are the songs that emotionally impact you, which you return to time and time again when you're looking to feel a different emotion than the one you're presently feeling.** The difference between the two is stark in that many songs can get in your head after minimal exposure, but this doesn't mean you'll form a decades-long relationship with them when you seek an emotional accompaniment to moments in your life. That takes an emotional resonance coupled with a memorable melody.

The cute hooks of annoying melodies we get in our head are short flings instead of the deep, meaningful relationships we form with the songs we love. Music without the added depth of emotional resonance doesn't have the potency to make a lasting impact on your life. You can get any song in your head if you hear it enough, but it doesn't mean you feel anything from it. These are two entirely different traits since songs that make you feel a strong emotion are repeatedly reached for, whereas hooks that get in your head are played just to rid you of an annoying earworm that won't go away.

The lack of potency that can be found in music is most apparent when you hear the soulless music that comes from ad agency jingle houses. The sole goal of jingles is to stick in your head to remind you of a product that you may need at some point. Their bland lack of emotion is a feature, not a bug. When music is dictated towards what a boardroom wants compared to what an artist wants to express, it's always missing the authenticity that makes resonance for a listener to connect with. There's a reason musicians turn to jingles in their career as a last resort, not out of passion. They lack emotion in favor of infecting you with an annoying hook you'll constantly be reminded about.

This is why you'll hear a melody that's catchy but devoid of emotion referred to as sounding "too-Disney!" The children Disney target with their music aren't emotionally sentient enough to find emotional resonance in music the way adults do, so they only respond to the catchiest melodies possible. This hollow lack of passion is optimized for humans who don't yet have the problems that breed emotional complexity that you develop as you experience life. The goal of a classic Disney tune (as opposed to the modern optimized songs like the ones in *Frozen*, which are written to appeal to both adults and children) is to infect the listener with a hook, so they repeatedly come back to the product for repeated viewings. Ask any adult with young children how successful they are at this and you're bound to get an exhausted eye roll.

You can get the 1877 K A R S 4 K I D S jingle in your head from the repeated bludgeoning the ad campaign brings, but would you ever put it on to accompany an emotion you're feeling in life? There's a reason no one turns to the terrible theme songs for TV shows or jingles when they need an emotional void filled since there's none to be found.

Pop Music Isn't The Same As A Product

One of the biggest mistakes cynics make when discussing what succeeds on the pop charts is the belief that those producing the music are optimizing it for what "the public wants to hear." I've yet to meet anyone among the producers and songwriters I've spent time with that knows what the public wants to hear. While many buffoons claim they can hear it — even the world's biggest hitmakers like Dr. Luke admit they can't tell. Instead, they try to make the best version of a song to their own ears. When we talk about commercial music being optimized to appeal to the masses, it's actually an evolution of musical development that has lead to concise pop formats that appeal to the majority of people.

Cynics frown on pop stars since they claim to be "artists" yet they monetize this art in the most ridiculous ways. The common misconception is producers like Pharrell, Max Martin and Dr. Luke have these labs where they do market research on how to make masses swallow fluffy pop songs whole. These producers are just artists making songs that feel emotionally resonant to them. Read any account of working with them and it's far less evil than imagined in the deep dark corners of the internet discussions of pop-hating underground music nerds. I love a good conspiracy, but you need to go to the major label boardroom where these songs get played for the real evil of the business: the ego-filled executives who push artistic compromise to appease focus groups since they believe they have formulas for mass success. Note that this evil happens after the artists are done with the song. To make matters worse, songs can rarely be tweaked to make algorithms or focus groups happy. Instead, the executives abandon the song, moving on to one of the hundreds of others vying for their marketing budget. These discarded songs are the ultimate proof that these producers aren't crafting to a focus group, since otherwise there wouldn't be thousands of them never released by the major labels each year.

Music is an evolving art where we continually discover new ways to make songs more resonant to the changing world we live in. As we observe adaptations that make songs more resonant, we adapt our creations to the resonances we've observed in others' work we enjoy. It's commonly thought a focus group study brought about the advent of <u>a hook appearing in a pop song within seven seconds</u>, when really, pop producers are just trusting their instincts and that's what appeals to those instincts. Trust me, if you ever hang out with most pop producers, their attention span wouldn't get through a three-page study.

Those who're successful at making pop are successful since they make the music they want to hear and have tastes that align with the public. This is why careers in pop are rarely sustained. These hitmakers often evolve too far ahead of the public's taste, becoming too advanced for mass consumption. This is why you'll also see the demise of some artists as they get too progressive for pop tastes or fail to evolve with the public by continuously releasing an emotional expression the public is no longer interested in, after moving on to more resonant emotional expressions. Tastes evolve fast in the mainstream. If you chase them, you end up failing – unless you happen to evolve simultaneously and enjoy the direction they're headed. Songwriters don't predict trends and put them in their songs. Their musical fluency is inspired by those making cutting-edge work, which inspires them to apply their own spin on genres that will be tomorrow's trends.

The misunderstood art of pop has always been that it's a format that has rules you have to work within but can still have progressive tendencies. Kanye West put it this way: "The concept of commercialism in the fashion and art world is looked down upon. You know, just to think, 'What amount of creativity does it take to make something that masses of people like?'" Many poptimists would argue that despite the vacuous message of most pop today, it's the most difficult genre to create great work in since it's the most competitive and needs to include an overlapping intersection of both fresh and familiar. For pop music to work, it needs to have a freshness to the masses that's both innovative and somewhat new, while not being too adventurous. This balance needs to be struck while crafting concise hooks that are effective in a format optimized for what the majority of listeners like.

When a song from left field enters the top 40 charts, many ignorant blowhards say it's from "the right palms being greased." While it's factually true that some palms need to be greased to get songs on top 40 radio, there're hundreds of songs that get the same grease as the hits that never make the top 200 since the public doesn't take to them. The public needs to respond to the song once it's played; if they don't, the palm-greasing is money down the drain as the stations stop playing it. This is evidenced every time the top 40 charts get a leftfield hit like Gotye's "Somebody That I Used To Know," Fun's "We Are Young" or any of the countless other songs that sound like nothing else in the mainstream at the moment.

Hipster Music Is Pretentious, Contrived, Blah, Blah, Blah

Now that I'm done apologizing for pop, I'll shower and go back to listening to my favorite punk records. Speaking of those punk records, on the other side of the argument is the ridicule that indie hipster acts get for their overly wrought concepts of making old-timey, sea chanty-filled music or whatever other ridiculously exaggerated micro-genre you can think of that hipsters are worshipping. While on the surface their music can seem pretentious, when you look closer it's formed by being intensely interested in a micro-genre of music where they've become fluent in how to craft a unique emotion that appeals to others interested in this niche emotion. Just the same as any other genre, only their fashion choices are more ripe for ridicule from being more nerdy, weird or cringe-worthy.

Trust me, I've mocked Mumford & all of his sons as well as whatever seapunk ridiculousness we're laughing at on Twitter each day. But I've also lived in the same neighborhood as the hipster musicians for long enough to have discussed their work over beers and they're simply fulfilling the emotion they want to hear. It's argued that they've contrived a weird image to get attention, but usually it's simply an interest they've pursued long enough to become good at embodying it. How they got to that interest may have been highly suspect, but by exploring their influences thoroughly and authentically expressing them, they've crafted a sound others enjoy.

That's Nice, But I Need To Make Some Money

Now that I've talked about how all of your friends' get-rich-in-music schemes are bound to fail, as you probably guessed by now, this book isn't about "getting rich in music quickly." Inevitably, right after I finish explaining that, I get accused of hating the monetization of music. I believe in making money off music! I've made my sole living off of monetizing music since I was a teenager. In fact, I've never had a job that wasn't music-related since I left high school. I even like money, so I spent years writing this book to get more of it. If you enjoy this book or my last one, I've applied the same philosophies to these endeavors. I made what I'd want to read first and it hopefully connects with you. So let's get this out of the way: **I don't blame you for wanting to make money off your music. There's no conflict in monetizing your music unless you put money before your music being emotionally resonant to you, but you need to be guided by what you feel in order to make music that will make you any money.**

Wanting Validation And Writing For Yourself Aren't A Contradiction

Usually, after someone argues with me about the entanglement of money & creativity, the next argument I hear is that humans want validation for what they create, so doing this all for yourself isn't realistic. Craving validation is embedded in most of us and, if anything, it's more common than in most other creative fields with attention-seeking musicians who are peacocking around town in eye-catching outfits. It's human nature that our brains enjoy being appreciated, and it's also completely valid that humans feel beaten down when we're underappreciated.

Validation occurs after the fact for artists who make what they love. When I make music or books, I do it to keep myself entertained, along with a feeling that my work needs to be in the world. But I won't be upset if you tweet how great this book is — in fact, it'll probably make my day. It isn't mutually exclusive to want praise for what you do and to create for yourself, but there's a sequence — **you need to be happy** with your work first so then others can be happy with it after the fact.

What Makes Music Resonant

How Emotion Is Communicated In A Song

Figuring out how to convey emotion is one of the secrets of great songwriters. Artists are compelled to make music that incites an emotional reaction. Reacting to the chords, tempos, arrangements, sound effects, tones and other variables of a song all goes into how you craft a song you want to hear. When writing a song, the writer will think of the emotion they want to convey until it's fully realized.

The subtlest changes in tempo, rhythm and the thousands of other variables in performance can all accentuate or diminish the level of emotion that's felt from a song. This accumulation of subtleties is what leads to the song's resonance. Look no further than the way great producers and songwriters talk about how they compose music. One of the best examples of this is an episode of the podcast Song Exploder, where producer Ariel Rechtshaid (Adele, Vampire Weekend, Charli XCX) talks about developing a Carly Rae Jepsen song, describing how each choice affects the emotion of a song. Every synth pad and arpeggiation expresses an emotion that's either closer to or further from the intended emotion. Each choice made, whether it's a tone knob, rhythm or single note modulation, either brings you further or closer to an emotion you're trying to convey.

Accumulating the subtleties of these emotions compositionally to exactly where they should fall on the emotional spectrum applies to every single genre. The choices of every detail – from the velocities of the synth hits, to how much compression is used, to how many vocal flaws are left in, to how organic the production is – will greatly determine the emotional reaction both you and listeners get from your song. No matter how quantized the beats and melody are, emotion is still conveyed.

Authenticity Is Potent

Authenticity has always been what draws listeners into songs, but today it's even more important. As I write this book throughout 2016, we see reality TV and YouTube stars on the rise, plus musicians who show their authentic, vulnerable emotions as opposed to the badly acted, implausible scenarios comprising the majority of TV and movies of yesteryear. The public has responded to two politicians who are perceived as authentic while those who are scripted are regularly derided for it, since we've grown to disdain those who think we can't see past their act. Bret Easton Ellis calls this a post-Empire world where when we fake our emotions to the public, everyone can see it since we now know what real, genuine emotion looks like. The veil of covering how we really feel with contrived, polite, PG-rated versions of ourselves has been lifted, and there's no going back.

Those in the public eye can no longer hide behind press releases or sanctioned interviews if they want to connect with an audience. Instead, they need to be honest to make connections through relatability on social media each day. The audience has grown callous to the fake facades of the past through the massive democratization of celebrity that's occurred in a world where gatekeepers have been thwarted by avenues such as YouTube that elevate authentic expression. Today, authenticity is currency; the more you expose, the more you're rewarded.

Music is pulling back that veil each year, and the evidence is seen as lyrics get more honest. Instead of obscuring depression and drug use in lyrical code, the nuance has been stripped, leaving no cover for songwriters to deny what everyone can see in plain sight. Talk of drug use and depression grace the red carpet of the MTV VMAs instead of the "everything's fine" poses of yesteryear, which would then be proved to be untrue, just as our instincts told us. What used to leak out in rare behind-the-scenes exposé is now front and center as the basis of what artists share to the world.

We've all experienced a friend wearing clothing that doesn't fit who they are — we sense the lack of authenticity as we stare with a questioning eye. Just the same, when a song lacks authenticity, our BS meters have been honed to react poorly to the frauds that litter our world. When we hear an imitation of the elements of another song, it confirms a lack of authenticity we already sensed. It clues listeners into an act that isn't expressing their own emotions by trying to gain fame through imitation.

Since we're making music for ourselves first, it's important to understand that when you hold back from your authentic expression, it's less resonant inside of you as well. You are your own first audience member, which is why finding new ways to make music resonant within you is the only way it will connect with others.

A lack of authenticity is heard when a singer delivers a stale performance lacking resonance. One of the reasons we need to write from a place of vulnerability is because without it, the singer won't have an emotion to express when they sing. **By imitating someone else, you aren't focusing on translating what you feel into music; you're focused on copying someone, which has no emotional resonance.** Jake Bugg talks of having to revisit the emotions he's felt when he performs a song to give it resonance. This practice gets confusing since singers can be singing another writer's lyrics, but the only way a song is delivered with resonance is when that singer can find a connection to the lyrics to emote with.

Vulnerability Allows Us To Connect With Others
*"Vulnerability is the essence of connection and connection is the essence of existence." — **Leo Christopher***

An important part of this equation is the importance of vulnerability. When we inaccurately portray our emotions, we hinder our ability to connect with others. Being able to say what you truly feel in its full, uncensored feeling allows that connection. Just as listeners can perceive when you're inauthentic, when you lack the ability to be vulnerable, it can be sensed that you're not saying what you're really feeling in its entirety. Writing about an emotion that's safe to express or not telling the whole truth of your feeling out of fear of others' reactions hinders the ability to connect with others who are feeling the same as you. When we become vulnerable by sharing our truth without fear, there's more to connect with by expressing the very real emotions we're scared to communicate.

For those who don't understand the power of vulnerability, it's how we form deep connections with one another. When you talk with someone and hold back the truth, it usually leads to small talk that you forget in no time. When you allow yourself to be vulnerable by saying a deeper truth with someone else that understands it, this leads to great conversations. You may even remember that conversation for years to come as it gives you a new understanding of your own life.

To connect with listeners, they must be able to empathize with the emotion you're expressing. The only way to make a listener feel emotional resonance is connecting with them, and this connection is only made deeper when you bring vulnerability into your music. We can only connect with emotions we've had ourselves and the joy of connection is this understanding of each other. With vulnerability we allow ourselves to say an emotion that's relatable. How often have we heard a song and found the way someone expresses a familiar emotion with a new genius twist that emotionally hits us? If you sing a song where you're hiding what you feel, how will that resonate with anyone?

This connection is why some songs don't resonate with some people yet resonate highly with others. The connection to a song is only formed if the listener understands the emotion that's conveyed. Friends can be puzzled when they love a song, yet their best friend who they connect with on so many levels doesn't understand it. Most of the time the answer lies in that the person who doesn't feel it doesn't experience the emotion the way the song is conveying it. The tools the musician uses to express that emotion may not be the way a friend feels that same emotion. Since we don't all have the same experiences of feeling different colors of emotions as our friends, our connections to the emotions expressed in songs won't always be the same.

Emotionally Painful Inspiration

Charles Maggio is not only a member of Rorschach, one of the most influential metal/hardcore bands ever, but he also runs one of the best indie labels to ever release music, Gern Blandsten. There's a great quote from him that's stuck with me for over a decade and a half. Someone asked him why he no longer sings for a band and he replied, "I'm healthy, my parents love me and have a great family, what do I have to write about?" While there are plenty of great writers that experience the same stability that still manage to make great art, he has a point. A great deal of the most emotionally resonant art is about a painful or passionate experience in the creator's life. One of the songs Charles is most known for is called "Bone Marrow Biopsy" after having to undergo the procedure twice during a battle with Hodgkin's disease during the early years of the band.

There's a reason Kurt Cobain, Amy Winehouse and Janis Joplin are some of the most emotionally resonant artists we've ever known. If you watched any of the recent documentaries about them, you could see that they felt more pain than the average person. It's often said the greatest creators are more sensitive than others, and these sensitivities allow them to hone in on how to express this deep feeling. Their translation of their sensitivity to pain was so extreme that anyone could empathize, but not from feeling the same as them. Instead, their pain is so much greater than most that it spans a wide breadth of relatability. We're able to connect with them since when we've felt pain, it's often a grain of salt compared to the authentic emotional resonance they express. We return to their songs consistently because when we feel pain, theirs is so much more intense than ours, so it's easy to connect with their painful expression of vulnerability. They have so much emotional resonance; we can easily find ways to connect to the broad and powerful way they feel.

As Natalie Maines said of Rick Rubin, finding what's "emotionally potent" will be the best arrow for your emotional bow. The pain in our lives becomes what's forcing itself out of us when it comes time to express ourselves since it's constantly on our mind. Author Bret Easton Ellis says, "pain drives many of the great artists much more than joy." When we feel passionate about a thought, we get flooded with the need to perspire, which is the clue that we should be letting this spill over into our music. The reason the most intense emotions we experience make for the most potent subjects for our music is because they're authentic experiences that motivate a passion that guides us to create. With that said, plenty of songwriters in healthy relationships can observe others' troubles and feel passion towards them that turn it into emotionally resonant perspiration.

Being Brave Enough To Say Your Most Emotionally Potent Truth

If you want to hide how you feel yet still talk to an audience about it, there's never been a greater way to disguise it than song lyrics. But this veiling in the name of covering how you feel doesn't allow others to relate to you. Writing about what's comfortable or veiled in complexity so that you can be safe from critique isn't relatable. The lack of authenticity when you hide what you really feel is the ultimate dilution of the potency of emotional resonance. Ambiguity can feel safe, but it hinders you from authentically expressing yourself to make a connection through music. If you want to express yourself, you need to do so without fear of judgment from your audience, friends, family or anyone else.

The evidence of having to write about what you feel most passionate about can be found throughout all genres of music in your record collection if you take the time to find it. James Alex of Beach Slang talks about this being the change he made in his music before starting the band. Seeing as he is the only example I know of a musician who appeals to teens on up to those in their forties, who found success with a new band at 38 years old, the example speaks volumes.

For those looking for a less niche example, take Beyoncé's *Lemonade.* The emotionally potent subject in her life was Jay Z's infidelity. While it would be far easier to keep this grievance out of the public eye, she needed to voice what was most resonant within her by making *Lemonade* when life handed her lemons. Songwriter Bonnie McKee, who's co-written a number of Katy Perry's hits, tells it like this: "When we're writing with her, we sit down and talk to her and try to find out what's going on in her life and find out the kernel of truth. I want her to sing about something she cares about, so we talk about her life and what she's going through and try to weave it into something powerful and visual." Ne-Yo has said when he hears the right song for him to sing it has to be an emotion he's already been feeling.

Mark Ronson says when it came time to write "Rehab" for Amy Winehouse, "We were walking down the street, we had just started working, we were three days in and she was telling me a story about some stuff that had gone down in her life. She said, 'Yeah my family came over and they tried to make me go to rehab and I was like, pffff! No, no, no.' And I thought, oh shit, that's quite hooky how you said that, if you're not opposed to it, we should go back to the studio and mess around with it." For many artists, talking about something so personal can be scary, but this is only one of countless examples of it paying off with a song that connected with millions of people.

What About Subjects That Aren't Pain And Love?

*"It's good to start with something that's true… If you start with something
that's false, you're always covering your tracks."*
— Paul Simon

Our own troubles commonly inspire the most resonant
expression, yet there are also thousands of powerful songs written about
subjects that aren't pain or love. The first argument I hear about writing
what's resonant to you is, "what about all the rappers who only rap about
money." At times the most emotionally resonant thought someone can
express is their lust for money, since the struggle of being poor is <u>all
that's on their minds</u> – and if that's all you think about, you need to
express it. Oneohtrix Point Never <u>writes songs to envision a sci-fi film
through music</u> since that's what he's most passionate about. Grimes <u>says
she imagines making a trailer for a fictitious movie</u>. On White Lung's
Paradise, Mish Way said she had little to purge in the way of relationship
struggles since she's now happily married, so she adapted her obsession
with serial killers by writing from their perspective. In 2017 it's easy to find
many people who are inspired by politics and bringing it into their music
with great resonance. Plenty of songwriters adapt the stories that are told
to them by others or read in books as they feel a resonance with them.
As long as that's what's trying to get out of them, they can do it in a way
that's resonant to them and others.

Just as we discussed before, listeners can only identify with
emotions they understand; love, loss and loneliness are the most intense
emotions we feel and therefore easy to connect with. This doesn't mean
there aren't important songs to be written about a variety of subjects
since love has been expressed in so many shapes and forms. While
more listeners can relate to unrequited love than serial killers, it's
shocking what can resonate with a listener when it's authentically
expressed. You can even be most passionate about partying. As
vacuous as that sounds, that's some musician's truth. Morrissey was able
to sustain half a dozen albums by writing passionately about "feeling
nothing at all." You must not force your passion towards a subject that's
not what you authentically feel. What matters is the passion to pursue
your ideas along with fearlessness of showing others how you feel and
your authentic need to have something to say on the subject.

Processing Creativity
The Intricacies Of What We Enjoy In Music

The Myth That Originality Is What Makes The Best Music
"Authenticity is invaluable, originality is non-existent" — **Jim Jarmusch**

Those in hipster music critics' circles usually celebrate music that appears to be "original" or "creative." Only the most brazen music listeners judge music on a scale of how derivative it is. If you're one of them, I challenge you to look through your record collection to find if what you actually enjoy is the music that contains as little derivative material as possible. Instead, I bet you'll find a lot of records that feel emotionally resonant that contain a common emotion you crave.

If you enjoy Elliott Smith, Public Enemy, Deadmau5, The Menzingers or Black Sabbath, I bet you also enjoy other artists that are derivative of them. You've also probably heard a few artists with that same influence, but you don't enjoy their records. This is a reaction to the artist being unable to do the sound with as much emotional resonance as you're used to. We don't react emotionally to the most original music we've ever heard; we react to songs that use new tools to bring us a new level of resonance in an emotion we desire. **What's often perceived as originality is actually creating a more resonant version of an emotion we enjoy in music than what we've heard in the past. The musicians we perceive as original find new ways of communicating an emotion that bring these songs a greater resonance than we've heard from those before them.**

Cynics frequently degrade certain genres as derivative, generic or "all sounding the same." This derision often comes from an outsider's perspective that lacks an understanding of the intricacies of a genre that the audience finds great depths to explore emotionally. When a classical music fan hears Converge or The Replacements, they think it all sounds the same and vice versa for a rock fan who's uneducated in classical music. The perception of whether music is derivative, generic or whatever we want to call it is based on the familiarity a listener has within a genre. Pop punk is widely derided for being one of the most generic genres, yet you can meet pop punk fans who will be fully ignorant of other sub-genres within the genre they enjoy since there's so much variety within it to listen to. Most music can be divided into niches of niches, and those who consume it are often boroughing down a well of an emotion they constantly crave a fix of.

What usually makes someone think a song is "original" is they haven't yet heard the influences the artist is drawing from. An ignorance of Pink Floyd would lead you to believe Radiohead's *OK Computer* redefined rock, and an ignorance of Autechre would lead you to think Clark invented a new genre, although none of these thoughts help music to be more emotionally resonant. However, if you're ignorant of the past influences, these sounds can be far more resonant since you've never experienced the emotion found within the songs they're deriving inspiration from.

Anyone who's ever watched one of those YouTube videos that show nearly every pop song is the same four-chord progression or enjoyed a three-chord techno or punk song should be able to pick up that originality isn't what brings about emotional resonance. It may win some points in our analysis by interesting us for a moment, but the music that ends up being what we revisit past initial listens are the songs that give us a feeling we want to experience again. If we judged songs on originality, then Can, Afrika Bambaata and This Heat would be far more revered than Led Zeppelin, Slipknot or Nas. Even when songs sound somewhat similar, if they're emotionally resonant, you still enjoy them.

Excluding the music that music theory majors make, which only other music theory majors appreciate, the rest of the world is looking for music that moves them emotionally. While there are a few nerds who have ingested so much music that they believe they need originality to cure their jaded musical tastes, what they're really looking for is someone who brings a new resonance to an emotion they've come to crave that they mistake for originality.

Familiarity Is Necessary For Resonance
Our brains are wired to respond to repetition and familiarity, which actually gives originality a disadvantage. When songs employ samples, this is usually a hack to give familiarity to a listener, since an audience is more likely to enjoy what's already familiar with a small, new twist. When teen heartthrobs 5 Seconds Of Summer took Duran Duran's "Hungry Like The Wolf" vocal melody and put new words to it, most music nerds' first reaction is to yell "rip-off." But in the demanding world

of major label record sales, they see this as a hack to getting a hit that's worth paying a royalty for (especially since it comes at the expense of the songwriter's royalties instead of the record label's bottom line). Since most of 5SOS fans have probably heard their parents playing the Duran Duran classic in the car, this allows the hook to seep into their brains faster. Originality doesn't pay when it comes to hooks as long they're done with authenticity.

We actually deride music that's too original. If a song sounds too unfamiliar, containing little cues for emotions we've grown to understand, it's hard for us to have an emotional reaction to it. Listeners are often unable to feel the emotions attached to the sounds we hear in the genres of world or experimental music. They give listeners little to no familiar emotional guides, so the music doesn't resonate within us. Music is often only resonant to us when we understand the emotional cues that are communicated, so if the only emotion expressed is sound manipulation or from a culture that we don't have commonality with, it will sound foreign and unrelatable to us. For evidence of this, look to the countless artists who were too ahead of their time or who make music we perceive as original, yet we have no urge to hear their work again.

In psychology, there's a concept called schema, which are mental structures of preconceived ideas or a framework representing some aspect of the world or a system of organizing and perceiving new information. It's difficult to find resonance unless a work has familiar schemas but has small deviations that exceed our expectations. Record producer turned neuroscientist Daniel Levitin did a study that showed our brains respond to a sweet spot of musical familiarity and complexity. To make music resonant within ourselves as well as others, we have to follow what's expected and deviate in small ways that increase the resonance. **Musically, to feel resonance with a song, we must hear emotional cues we're familiar with, along with a few new cues that up the emotional ante to give us more resonance**. Note that for these new cues to be effective, they must augment the resonance of the song since new for new's sake doesn't hold emotional value.

The End Justifies The Means

One of the most interesting aspects about music is no one cares how it happened (outside of those who want to imitate it), they just care that it feels good. While the first Rage Against The Machine record had a disclaimer that read "no samples, keyboards or synthesizers used in the making of this record," it didn't take knowing that to have an emotional impact, but for those who cared it developed a great admiration for the players. Many musicians will want to give every listener a caveat before someone listens to their music, like "it was all done live," " we only had one week to make the record," "this is just the demo," "we didn't use any pitch correction" or countless other qualifications that don't ever make a listener enjoy a song.

Listeners cannot be bribed by context into liking a song, but it can make them respect the artist more and get more deeply involved in their appreciation of their music. Making music that takes context to appreciate it ignores that we want to hear music that inspires an emotional reaction. If you have to make caveats and qualifications to anyone who hears your music for them to appreciate it, odds are nobody will appreciate it since it lacks emotional resonance. It needs to be good enough that they enjoy it from emotionally reacting to it.

Music Is An Emotional Conversation

Linguist Noam Chomsky says that all humans are biologically programmed to gain knowledge. This programming leads us to exhaustively continue conversations until we thoroughly understand the subjects that interest us. Brian Eno once said, "what's exciting about art is you're hearing the latest sentence in a conversation you've been having all your life." This is a great way of looking at why music is more or less resonant to us. When we think of musicians as emotional communicators that inspire conversations about an emotion within our minds, you can gain a deeper understanding of why you enjoy music.

To explore this idea, let's think of genres of music as broad emotional categories where each type of emotion is a genre of music. I think of the musicians we love as teachers of a certain subject that are conversing with your emotions. If you change out the word "conversation" for "music" in this analogy, it probably reflects the music listening experience you've had throughout your life.

When you're young, you're thrilled with most conversations that talk about a subject you're interested in that you can comprehend, whether it's the best explanation of the subject or not. The first time you have a conversation that's emotionally resonant, the person explaining the idea doesn't need to be the person who first thought of the idea as long as they communicate it in a way that's stimulating to you. It's so exciting; you're thrilled by those who communicate this emotion, even if they don't do it best. Later on, you may find those who do it better and think less of who first communicated this emotion. Similarly, the innovators of a genre of music aren't necessarily the ones you enjoy the most; someone may come along and communicate the emotion of the genre in a way that's more resonant to you than others. They just seem to speak your language better. The originators of this emotion didn't find the way to make it most resonant to your emotions, so we may enjoy those who explored the emotion after the originator. This can stem from sharing a common region, age or emotional disposition that's more akin to you than those who are widely celebrated in the genre.

When you have a conversation, it may touch on other subjects and defy easy categorization, just as our emotions are nuanced and cannot be simply described with a single word. There are parts of songs that resonate with us and others that fall flat since they're not emotions we connect with, just as you won't identify with every song on an album. If an emotion is expressed that you don't feel resonance with, it can leave you feeling apathetic, just as when someone talks about how they feel and you've never experienced that emotion.

Occasionally, you'll have a conversation that changes the way you think. You'll hear such a great expression of what you feel, it inspires epiphanies for years to come. Other times, you'll be having a conversation just to pass the time. You may have had this conversation many times and know every source of it and find it to be boring, since you prefer those you've originally had this conversation with.

There are countless reasons a conversation may not be resonant with you. As we have this conversation with different communicators, again and again, we'll grow bored if it doesn't bring forth new ways of talking about the subject and will crave new ways of discussing it. If you have a conversation too many times, it becomes less resonant and you no longer wish to have it, just as a song can be highly resonant at first and then become annoying after repeated listens. If it's done in too complex a way that you can't understand it won't be resonant. Some musicians may only be good at certain conversations. You may only enjoy their ballads or their bangers since, when they communicate those emotions, they align with what's resonant within you.

The Maturation Of Your Emotions In Music

As our emotions change from the angst and immaturity of our teenage years, we gain the experience of having heard different resonances of emotion throughout the songs we've heard in our lives. We also build a tolerance to inauthentic, less resonant acts. When we're teenagers, we don't care that songs are similar, shallow and less authentic since the bar to emotionally resonate within us is so low that we can enjoy the same emotional note hit over and over again. Our brains are continuously growing callous to the emotions we hear in music. We want to hear new ways for music to be expressed. While older fans may grow to only enjoy familiar emotions, commonly the older you get, the less time you devote to being open to hearing new music you enjoy. As the common saying goes, "the music you love at eighteen stays with you for your whole life."

As a listener, we may be stimulated by the first song we hear that has a small amount of emotional resonance, but in time as we hear other groups we grow less impressed by them. These acts hit an emotional resonance for us that we're desperate to comfort as the pains of overly wrought emotion from puberty need to be constantly comforted. We then get past this and mature in our emotional needs, and we come to a place where we need more refined emotional stimulation.

Just as a dollhouse or a toy train is interesting to us as a kid, we grow to become more interested in complex interests to hold our attention. Our emotions mature, so we need to express ourselves in more mature ways. This is one of the hardest parts of making music because your fans turn to you to make a certain emotional lexicon as well, but as you age and mature these emotions change and they grow as much as you do. For your career's sake this hopefully happens together, otherwise they abandon you for those expressing emotions more resonant to them.

Sadly, when it comes to record sales, the majority of music is bought by 15- to 24-year-olds. This isn't to say you need to make generic music to appeal to them but more to say that there's a reason you don't see IDM and prog rock on the pop charts. Most listeners never evolve to the level of musical maturity it takes to understand the emotions expressed in these genres. This is also not to say that complex and interesting music isn't always rewarded with record sales — look to recent hits by Diplo & Skrillex or Queen and Radiohead's success. Even a song like *NSYNC's "Pop" has an extremely complex production, as do countless Timbaland tracks from the aughts.

Even if a song is resonant with you at one time, that doesn't mean you won't change emotionally and forget it. With that said, our nostalgia for who we used to be allows us to appreciate that music we loved back then. But those who communicate this emotion once we've moved past it won't resonate with us, since we're no longer open to hearing their expression.

Chapter 3: The Balance Of The Head And The Heart

"Rational thoughts never drive people's creativity the way emotions do."
— **Neil deGrasse Tyson**

Unfortunately, it's not only financial gains or the expectations of others that get in the way of actualizing the music you love. The way debates play out in your head is often the cause of the greatest failures in making music. There's a constant war between the head and the heart being waged inside every musician, the head being the application of organizational ideas and concepts to music while the heart is what guides you to craft a song emotionally.

To understand this war, we should understand what causes strife between the two. The head often tries to steer a song away from its emotional resonance. Many musicians think about playing a cool chord or an overly complex drum pattern instead of the one that feels good in the song. Thinking about what's impressive to a bunch of music nerds or more fun to play instead of what feels good is a fast way to a song no one wants to hear. The crazy riff you're playing or falsetto note you're hitting needs to work in an emotional context in your song or else your song loses resonance.

The Balance Of What's Fun To Play And What's Emotionally Resonant

One of the biggest struggles between the head and the heart is to gain a perspective on what's fun to play isn't always emotionally resonant. Anyone who's made a rock record has probably struggled with a guitarist wanting to show how fast they can play a scale, a singer who wants to show off their range or a drummer trying to play a fill that stops the song in its tracks. Just as the ridiculous scales you hear in American Idol auditions or rappers who do twenty voice imitations per song rarely make their way to the masses, recognizing that showing off the coolest part you can play is often the opposite of what's emotionally resonant.

To me, this is an easily defined choice since the head is what enjoys the challenge of playing a difficult scale, by craving an ego gratification when others see a "difficult part" played in a song. But what stops the part from being worthy of inclusion in the song is when others give you the reaction that it detracts from the emotion of the song. While I don't believe every time someone says that a part is being played for the musician's own enjoyment is always true, numerous collaborators agree that it's important to take that statement as a huge warning. Some of the best music made is what's both fun and challenging as a musician yet still emotionally resonant. Figuring out the alignment between the two is the key to satisfying the head and the heart. Editing out parts that don't enhance a song's emotion or that favor egotistical showing off is crucial to making resonant music.

The Emotional Check

I'm not saying that every song that's musically complex or fun to play is detrimental to its emotional resonance. If anything, I feel the opposite, which is reflected in my record collection of nerdy, progressive music. The chord voicings or odd time signature mathletics can still have an emotional impact, but emotional content needs to come first. Prioritizing emotion before complex composition is what separates Dillinger Escape Plan, Aphex Twin, Animal Collective, Kanye West, Yes, Battles, Cashmere Cat, Dalek, Radiohead and countless other successful musicians who push the envelope from every other progressive musician stuck in their hometown with no fans. They've learned how to take their massive understanding of composition to reinforce an emotional sentiment they're trying to convey. With every weird chord or strange treatment they come up with for their music, they make sure it's reinforcing the emotion they're trying to convey within a song.

What we're calling the heart is much more subjective. The heart is where your passions are; it's where you hold what you love the most. The heart is also how you emotionally feel when you hear a song. **The single most important skill in actualizing your music is to trust how you react so you can alter your songs to be aligned with the emotion your heart's trying to convey**. This is also the most primitive skill you have as a musician that everyone is born with but at some point messes up as their head gets in the way.

When listeners hear highly resonant songs, they don't know how a musician was guided to get there. They're unaware that a musician has an emotional target in mind, a feeling they're trying to convey that's easy for them to make decisions based on when an element feels either more or less similar to this emotion. This practice is what allows musicians to make decisions that make songs more resonant.

The common confusion for those who understand the head and heart dichotomy is that the head is the enemy. The head has a place in music, so it shouldn't be seen as evil. It can figure out the concepts and the traits we find interesting in music. It gives us some of our best ideas along with organizing them. But we need to use our heart to check the head's contributions. This is a constant balance in creating, so the path you take is a large part of who you are. The head comes up with fantastic ideas, but without the heart there to check that these ideas have an emotional resonance, your songs will suffer from working well on paper but falling flat emotionally.

This is the most evident in those who know music theory and every rule not to break who then make music that's as boring as can be to every listener who encounters it. Odds are you've encountered the musician who can tell you how amazing their music is because "they use all organic instruments" or "compose on sheet paper." Despite their breadth of knowledge, their music is uninspiring of any emotion that yields a song you never want to hear again. It has no feeling and sounds exactly like what it is: someone showing off their musical ideas and not their emotions. They're too obsessed with the methods used instead of the way it feels when hearing it back. When reviewing the sheet music of their work, the chords all work in a genius concept, but even to their ear it doesn't work as well as it should when played aloud. They ignore the heart, so their music falls on ears that wish they were deaf when they hear it.

When a musician learns too much theory, they often turn off their heart's instincts. They assume what they're doing is correct since it's abiding by the rules, like a coloring book. This unchecked imitation turns off the emotional reaction within a musician. If a person they admire sings like this, uses that amp or recorded a certain way, they believe they should do the same. Instead of experimenting to find an emotional texture, they use preconceived ideas or rules instead of checking to make sure it reinforces an emotion they wish to convey. Ideas, concepts, treatments and theory are necessary to figure out how to further an emotion but need an emotional check to see that they further the resonance of a song.

It's important to understand that music focused on the head isn't even resonant to the creators themselves. They're proud they made a work that makes sense on paper or is impressive to other musicians or is fun to play to challenge their physical abilities instead of what's right for the song giving it maximum resonance. They don't even consider a song should have an emotion since they think of music in terms of acrobatic ability or an achievement in impressing other musicians.

Every experienced producer has the story of the chord that shouldn't work "in theory" but sounds amazing in context or a song that breaks all the rules of music theory but is the best one in the artist's catalog. There's also the common scenario of a song that no matter how hard you try to produce, it never has the emotional impact of the demo. Musicians self-sabotage their songs by allowing the head to run wild with ideas they believe add depth but when unchecked by emotion destroy their song's resonance. These decisions must be made by letting the heart choose what's emotionally resonant, not just interesting in theory. **Letting your emotions tell you if concepts, ideas, theory and rules are working in your song is the practice of putting the heart first.**

Early on in my life, I didn't understand this emotional resonance concept at all. I was constantly confused why some songs sounded so powerful while others didn't. When I heard my favorite artists talk about "their heart" or "music that speaks to their soul" I rolled my eyes and thought they should stop talking artsy gibberish garbage. It took me years of rebelling against any saying that sounded new age or hippie to get that there was a real, tangible concept here that has nothing to do with souls or crystals, but instead the practice of finding what you're passionate about by turning that into a song. Once I understood this concept, it became obvious which songs are made from emotional inspiration versus those made to impress others.

The Difference Between The Head And The Heart
To further understand this separation, these are the common roles for the head and the heart:

The Heart
- Tells you a part feels melancholic, happy, exciting, heavy, dirty, etc.
- Inspires emotions to draw from to turn into songs.
- Warns you when a part doesn't feel right in a song.
- Checks your ideas to see if they inspire an emotional reaction such as goosebumps, dancing, head banging or whatever other reaction you'd like to elicit.

The Head:
- Thinks about rules, theory, concepts and other constructs.
- Figures out ways to elaborate on your ideas.
- Checks your emotional response to see if it can be optimized by using some logic, such as speeding up a song for intensity or simplifying a melody so it breathes more.

Separating Thinking About Music From Reacting To Music

There's commonly two very separate trajectories in musicians' growth as they become proficient in their musicianship. A classically trained student learns every rule but ignores the emotional part of performance. As they get older, they learn to play with an emotion that gives their performance a feeling that becomes more appealing to listen to instead of sounding like a quantized MIDI performance. The opposite end of the spectrum is the punk kid who wants to express their anger by figuring out three chords on a guitar while screaming out of key with a ton of passion but little musicality or technical accuracy. As years go on, they learn music theory, honing this anger into a melding of the two into music that has both intense emotion and refined songwriting.

Musicians who don't know music theory are convinced they're better for it, just as those who do are convinced they're in a superior camp. There's an argument to be made for both sides using the example of the thousands of great musicians on both sides of the aisle. What I'd argue is that this is a false dichotomy. Instead, what they have in common is they're both proficient in two different but essential parts of music.

The musicians who don't know music theory are listening to their heart, but at times they don't know a solution to why an element isn't working that someone who knows theory can easily spot. They get plagued by frustrating bouts of not being able to fix small problems, such as rhythms not locking up or an out of key harmony in their music that seems daunting to fix. Their heart allows them to make emotionally resonant music, but their lack of knowledge prevents them from fixing glaring flaws that would be easily spotted by a more educated musician.

But those who know theory get caught in doing "what's right in theory" while being unaware that they're following musical rules that are boring and not at all emotionally resonant. Many classical musicians such as Yo-Yo Ma first learned to be technically proficient at an instrument, later learning to play it emotionally as they progressed as a musician. They learn strict rules they're afraid to break since they're constantly reciting instead of feeling, using far too much head and not enough heart. Amazingly enough, many of the top music schools in America spend little to no time teaching emotional expression.

The artist who doesn't know theory eventually figures it out, even if they don't know the proper terms or how to write it on paper. The theory-trained musician usually has to train themselves to turn off their head to listen to their heart. When both sides come to this stage, they're able to make emotionally resonant work. Part of making great music is evaluating where you are on this spectrum of theory (head) and emotion (heart), to make sure you compensate for the other side. Learning to balance the head and heart by not letting either overtake the process is one of the most crucial skills of creativity. Letting your emotions guide you by allowing your head to sort these emotions into a tangible work can come naturally to some and take years of work for others. Regardless of where you fall on this spectrum, it's important to consider how you can improve this relationship in your work.

Believing Stories Instead Of Reacting To What You Hear
Sadly, the "facts" of how records get made are filled with inaccurate half-truths. Look no further than the widespread acceptance of producer Joe Barresi <u>punking listeners into believing he recorded Tool's</u>

drums in a helium-filled room or a whole Queens Of The Stone Age
record with a single microphone. If that weren't enough, there's a long
line of musicians assuming what someone uses live is what they use in
the studio despite the two rarely being the same. Today musicians see a
synth in a producer's rack and assume that's the reason a song sounds
great, when it's actually been broken for five years but looks great sitting
there. Musicians fall into the trap of trying to emulate inaccurate accounts
instead of trusting their instincts by reacting to what they hear when trying
to find the sounds that'll give them the emotional response they're looking
for. They neglect that the way their idols find the gear they use is utilizing
the same imitation, with an added check to make sure the tool can get
them sounds that will paint the emotional picture they want to make.

There's nothing wrong with reading interviews, but far too many
musicians follow myths they hear about their music instead of analyzing
the techniques they hear about and seeing if they help further their
emotional intent. **The head tries to solve problems to save us the
process of reacting, but the reaction is the most essential part of
making emotionally resonant music.** When it does this, it turns off our
reactions, causing us to forgo checking to make sure we're getting the
result we think we're getting.

Chapter 4: Finding Your Voice And Intent

If all you want to do is sound like someone else, playing in local cover bands is often more lucrative than performing original music. Most of us grow up trying to sound like our favorite musicians but with age, we gain emotions we want to express in our songs, just like those we admire. If you're interested in expressing your emotions, you need to figure out who you are to express yourself. Knowing this enables you to make an authentic expression of yourself. To do that, some exploration of who you are can help you gain an understanding of your character and can make what you should express easy to decipher.

Finding Your Unique Voice

For some, finding their voice isn't a hard process, but for others, it takes some digging inside for what's compelling to you. New age gurus call this "finding yourself" or talk about "self-exploration." Instead, I think of finding your voice as a process where you try to find what's emotionally resonant to you and how it gets expressed so others understand it. When you speak, you use a certain vocabulary along with speed, accent and dynamic that make up the sound of your voice. Your voice contains parts that are naturally a part of who you are as well as part of others who you've picked up details from. When you express yourself musically you do the same thing, forming a collage of who you naturally are that also picks up small qualities from others that you use to convey what you think about each day.

Voice Is A Larger Metaphor

An overlooked aspect of singing is we're all commonly doing an imitation of someone else's singing style. The sounds we make when we sing usually come in the form of an affected accent or pronunciation of words that's far from the way we actually talk. A singer's voice isn't one absolute sound; in fact, many singers are capable of doing various inflections with their voice. These inflections can make them sound English when they're from the Bay Area (Green Day); loud, confident and audacious when they sing, yet their speaking voice sounds nothing like that (Michael Jackson); an alien with an odd accent (Kendrick Lamar) and the list goes on. It's a rare occurrence when a singer sings or raps the same way they talk.

Each singer is picking up accents, turns of phrase, inflections, melodies and vocabulary from those they admire and blending it into a performance that hopefully sounds unique to themselves as well as furthering an emotion they're exuding. By forming a collage of what they've enjoyed that furthers their expression, they build a signature of their own. While there are some parts of your voice that are naturally embedded in who you are physically and genetically, we have countless ways to change that timbre.

This isn't to say that their most authentic voice is singing exactly how their talking voice sounds – in fact, it can be highly creative to affect a voice that gives your performance even more emotional resonance. All these affections, when employed to give more resonance, can be the best way to enhance an emotion in a vocal performance. Tom Waits' application of treating his voice with so many different affectations the same way he treats the manipulation of the instrumentation in his music is part of what makes it so unique and resonant. The Clash's masterful use of different voices traded off between the three singers of the group furthers the storytelling quality of their songs.

Most vocalists are singing with an inflection that they've found naturally from singing along to their favorite music. When we talk about finding your creative voice, this concept isn't ironically named. Finding your voice is how you incorporate your influences into your vocals and bring them into the sound of your voice. This voice is both figuratively and metaphorically one of the biggest factors that defines your sound. This same voice goes for nearly every choice you make in the instrumentation of your music or the production. Choosing to figure out how to find a palette that accentuates your emotional resonance instead of imitating gives you a unique voice instead of an imitation.

Finding What's In Your Heart

"Select only things to steal from that speak directly to your soul. If you do this, your work (and theft) will be authentic. Authenticity is invaluable; originality is non-existent. And don't bother concealing your thievery - celebrate it if you feel like it. In any case, always remember what Jean-Luc Godard said: 'It's not where you take things from - it's where you take them to.'" — **Jim Jarmusch**

Writing that above title is hard for me, since talking about the heart doesn't come easily as I'm the classic stereotype of a man who has difficulty expressing his emotions in words. We call our emotional expression "the heart," since the phrase has become synonymous with saying passion. Passion is what tells us what we're supposed to write about as well as what emotions to evoke in music. Figuring out the emotions you're feeling and how to express them is the most determinative way to figure out what you should be writing, since what you're experiencing is inherently one of your passions.

Expressing what's emotionally resonant in you is not only one of the best ways to help heal emotional faults, but it's also a tool to help understand why you are feeling this way. Feeling an emotion that's overwhelming is commonly cured with the catharsis of writing music that shifts the mood into a better place. Sigmund Freud theorized that we're all emotionally repressed, so the only way to get us to a better place mentally is to express these emotions. This expression is what's at the heart of most of the emotionally powerful songs you've enjoyed. This expression is also what's missing when you hear songs that have no emotional resonance despite doing similar things to other songs you love. The players made a sound that was probably an imitation of other music they heard that sounds like a song that was emotionally resonant to them, but they miss the detail that an imitation has so emotional power.

Who You Are Individually Will Shape Your Perspiration

Making music that's emotionally resonant to you by using your feelings as a compass alleviates the job of trying to be original by allowing it to be a natural occurrence. When you're fluent in expressing yourself by combining your inspiration with who you are, you're bound to do work that's unique to yourself. Every bit of inspiration you've ever taken in is unique to you and is impossible to replicate. Following these emotions leads to new and individual pictures as they get developed instead of impotent imitations. Many musicians make the mistake of imitating others, expecting their results to be as good as those they imitate, instead of tinkering around until they find music that embodies the emotion they want to express. This isn't to say every piece of music you produce will come to you in an emotional epiphany. It can take hearing a song that's similar to the emotion you want to make and tweaking it until you get the emotional resonance you're looking for.

Your expression of your emotions as they've been shaped by those you've learned from is what sets you apart from everyone imitating obvious influences. Frank Turner told me, "Everyone starts out as an imitation of someone else, and it's by getting it wrong that you come up with your own voice." This quote was paraphrased from Elvis Costello, whose quote had a slightly different message, which illustrates this point even further.

You'll also have a different creative output than others from what is encoded in you genetically. Oscar Peterson can reach 18 keys with one hand on the piano, so what he's physically able to do on the piano is more adventurous than others with a smaller keyspan. A person who's constantly feeling anger is going to have a far harder time playing gentle music. When your individual emotional makeup is expressed, it will sound like you as long as you genuinely express it instead of imitating.

It's More Than Jamming Two Ideas Together

Talk of creativity usually says it's all about blending two ideas together by having "idea sex" to make a new creation. While this may work for making Reese's Peanut Butter Cups, what's needed to make emotionally resonant music is to let an emotional expression come first by figuring out how to elaborate upon this emotion using musical instruments. Unlike many other forms of creativity, music that's emotionally resonant needs to be more than smashing two ideas together.

Let's go back to this Reese's example. Someone like myself who hates sugary foods (*I know, I know*) would never know that this combination tastes good since chocolate doesn't taste good to them. To make Reese's taste good, you need to enjoy these flavors and experiment on how to make this combination taste its best. You can combine the two elements, but you'll never be able to figure it out if it tastes good without releasing it to the public to get feedback. Since we don't get feedback on our music until we present it to others, we must use what we're passionate about to understand how to make the best decisions for it. If you're not passionate about continually tasting chocolate and peanut butter, the experimenting won't come easy since you're guessing at it. Good music is made by musicians trusting their tastes and emotional makeup.

What You Enjoy In Others Can Guide You

One of the head's greatest assets is to advise you on interesting treatments to apply into to your music. Figuring out approaches to filter your ideas through is part of the mastery of songcraft. By writing down what you love about your favorite creators, you can start to understand how to achieve the greatness you admire in them instead of playing songs that sound like theirs. Take notes on what you love about each one, then think of how you can apply the aspects you love about these musicians to what you do musically. The cover of this book was an exercise in figuring out those who had the greatest impact on my creativity and making a visual representation of it.

As an example, here's what my list looks like as I write this book:

The Clash
- Their vocals sound like different characters in a movie singing a part but coming from one singer.
- Their grooves are either consistently rushing or dragging making for intense musical emotion.

Sophie
- Vocals are sung as if they were written to a different groove yet still have strong hooks.
- The vocals are pitched to sound like an unidentifiable singer yet still have a character of their own.

Health
- The vocals are always breathy and keep a calm and peppiness. that make the intense and abrasive instruments listenable.
- Interesting envelopes on familiar sounding instruments.

The 1975
- The ability to use unique sounds that don't distract from the vocals.
- Masterfully calls back classic 80's melody themes and tones while making them sound fresh.

White Lung
- Uses lots of notes that still work well together.
- Drums are very stiff yet still feel intense.
- Huge dynamics from part to part.

You can also use this to get you out of decisions where you feel stuck. I'll think about what my heroes would do in a situation that's confusing me. Remembering who I love while finding correlations in their decisions leads me the way I want to go. You can apply this exercise to songs, albums, images, etc.

One of the best modern tools for figuring out who you are is to make a playlist of your favorite songs. This allows you to return to what continually moves you to find correlations of what you enjoy from musician to musician and song to song. I keep a playlist called Great Songs that I add to whenever I find a song I never get tired of. Whenever I have a problem with a production, such as having to reconsider the bass lines for a record, I can sit down for an hour or two and get inspired by all of my favorite works to find an inspired solution unique to my tastes.

What You Don't Want To Do
Your not-to-do list is just as important as your to-do list. Director David Fincher (*Fight Club, Gone Girl*) has said it's much more important to know what he doesn't want to do as opposed to what he does want to do. Knowing what you never want to do can be less restricting, allowing you to be open to finding new inspirations and what you want to do. This allows the heart to do what it wants emotionally. I've done this for my productions and keep it in a Google Doc to revisit from time to time. Here're some of my "don't do" rules for record production:

- Don't make decisions out of expediency; trace the route of the problem and give consideration.

- Too much bass or treble is unacceptable; a balance needs to occur.
- Words should be pronounced so a listener without a lyric sheet can understand them, even in the fastest punk song sung with the worst Boston accent.
- No vocal should stick out as being more tuned than others. There should be a consistency to the pitch intonation through a song.
- Bass should not be an afterthought. It should always be what expands or retracts the emotion of a song while working off the vocal as much as possible. Bass that's not optimized or gets buried in a mix is a lost opportunity.
- Every song should have one tone that's distinct to that song so when listeners hear it, they feel like that's the only time they've heard that tone.

Having both a to-do and a not-to-do list is a common practice for many musicians, even if they keep them private. Coldplay exposed their list on an episode of 60 Minutes, where they showed off a list they had on their practice room wall. David Byrne said The Talking Heads made restrictions on what they would do, like not to imitating black singers (*not out of racism, he found it inauthentic*), no light shows and no saying "Oh baby'" or other rock clichés. One of The Ramones' rules was no guitar solos, which was ironically broken on their biggest hit "I Wanna Be Sedated." This also teaches a great lesson that you can always reconsider these rules later if you evolve, but they're important to have in the moment as you feel passionate about what you never want to do.

What Makes You Unique?

If you're still curious how to develop your voice after you've gained a working knowledge of what you want to do, a healthy exercise can be to figure out how you draw inspiration from what makes you unique:

- What's something you love no one else loves? How can you incorporate that into your music?
- What's something everyone loves that you hate? How do you develop a character from it?
- What's missing in music and can you take it to a new level?

Try not to barf as I quote Ayn Rand's shortsighted worldview in The Fountainhead: "We create because we're dissatisfied with what already exists." One of the greatest indicators that you should pursue an artistic impulse is when you want to hear a sound you've yet to hear someone else make. This means you're craving an emotion that's not being expressed. Finding concepts that you haven't seen before that you blend with emotional intent has made some of the best art throughout time. Pick a fight with an ethic; voice your disdain for a trend you have an authentic bad reaction to by letting your own work show why this trend is wrong. Taking the time to explore your likes and dislikes to find what you think should exist is one of the most effective ways of finding who you are creatively to develop a unique voice.

One of the traits of a great artist is to notice when you don't like a trend and develop a rebellion against it. If I had my way, I'd never put a ballad on a punk record, and if there were ballads I wanted to release, I'd do a record of only ballads. I love records that have a single mood across the whole record. The inclusion of ballads amongst more happy sounding songs takes me out of the mood of a record, which bothers me. On my own records, I rebel against this by keeping a consistent emotion throughout the record. As long as it's authentic and not done out of opportunism, it often leads to some of the best art in the world.

Intent Is King And Rules All

Intent is the practice of using your heart's feelings to make sure an emotional idea or the way a piece of music makes you feel is continuously reinforced, not contradicted. Since a song's objective is to evoke an emotional reaction, intent is the guide we follow to shape it to be as resonant as possible. While this is often called vision, I think of vision as the ability to see intent, but intent is what we see within that vision. It's identifying the emotion you're trying to convey and letting it guide you. While some musicians intend to mimic the excitement they've felt in other songs on a dance floor, others feel a certain emotion they want to translate to music that evokes that intent as strongly as possible. Often it's a feeling inside the writer that's difficult to describe that's expressed by the pursuing sounds that get closer and closer to the sound of that emotion.

Processing Creativity

When you understand your intent, it can guide the entire creative process whenever there's a decision to be made. If your intent is to evoke a sad song with a happy ending, it's easy to elaborate upon this concept by trying to develop the saddest lyrics and chords that match what you feel. You may then figure out how to segue into a key change that eventually brings a happy ending. Intent ensures your options are focused, giving you a clear way of deciding if a part helps a song get closer to its maximum resonance.

Intent allows an emotion, idea, color or feeling to guide you by letting it make the decisions for you. Musicians commonly make the mistake of writing a set of lyrics to then match it to their most recent beat instead of using a process of emotional elaboration where they write either a beat or vocal and then react to the emotion it makes them feel to make both work together. This elaboration is figuring out the emotion of what you're trying to convey by working until the music matches the emotion you're trying to communicate. When fans hear a song where the music seems to match the lyrics in perfect symbiosis, they may assume this was the luck of mashing two ideas together. But far more often it's figuring out how to make each part of the music sound like the emotion the songwriter is feeling.

One of the first questions most songwriters get asked is "Music or lyrics first?" While this is a great question, it isn't the least bit determinative of whether they'll make music that's resonant. Instead, it's what they do next. If you choose to mash whatever riff you like the best with the lyrics you last wrote, odds are your song will be less resonant since the lyrics and music won't be working together to elicit maximum resonance. Make sure that each decision you make works with the original intent by continuing to react to the music, lyrics or song title you wrote first and then through each step of the process. This will result in a song that's as potent as possible.

A common practice for songwriters is to start with a riff or a certain turn of phrase in the lyrics. From there, pursuing more parts that further the emotion this starting place conveys is how a song gets shaped for maximum emotional resonance. While the song may take more shape and alter its feel along the way, having this emotional anchor there to guide you to make sure you're adding constructively, not superfluously, allows a song to reach its potential. It's often said the song tells you what it wants to become and in practice, this is from following the emotion you feel from a riff or lyric by continuing to build off that emotion.

When you're not guided by intent, the creative process is chaotic, lacking a purpose to aim towards. I regularly see musicians trying to craft a song by playing riffs until two seem to go together well enough to move on instead of thinking how the second riff will further the emotion they're trying to craft. Far too many poorly written songs are made by throwing ideas at the wall and seeing what sticks until a song is completed or putting your latest set of lyrics with the song your bandmate brought to practice by happenstance, never considering an emotion that's trying to be reinforced.

Many artists don't even realize they're following intent since it's not a conscious practice. They think the ideas they accept and deny are random, but they possess strong intuition that judges the ideas they hear by whether or not they further help reinforce the emotion they're trying to convey. Even if a song flows out of you in an instant without much resistance, taking the time to consider if it can be improved by aligning it more with an intent allows emotional elaboration to guide you instead of poking around in the dark.

Intent In Your Music

Intent can also be an overarching theme of what you want to create as a band or under a musical alias. Many gaze upon good-looking, poorly spoken musicians and assume their greatness is an accident. Growing up, my first musical impressions were hair metal and Sid Vicious, so I felt the same. But after spending time with many great musicians in my adult life, I began to realize this assumption was wrong. Mötley Crüe and The Sex Pistols might appear as shallow at first glance, although what truly lies beneath is two artists with strong intent. They may have celebrated the shallow side of their endeavors outwardly in music videos and behind the scenes documentaries, but there was consideration of the intent they would evoke in each song as well as their image that can be found in any biography on both groups.

When intent is highly considered, it can drive great artistic heights. Producer Pharrell Williams said this of working with Daft Punk: "Everything is so concise, there's a reason behind everything, nothing is done by coincidence, accident or mistake. There's always a real intention meant to serve a purpose." That quote is the best summation of what it's like to work with a creator with well-developed intent. Every decision is guided by judgments on how they get to their goal. They let their head consider ways of furthering their intent while their heart checks if it's in line with their emotions. They don't record parts for the hell of it; they consider each part as to how it'll assist or deter their intent. Daft Punk themselves say: "We thought about our music before we ever made it." They had intent that they needed to express.

The Seemingly Superfluous Use Of The Word Superfluous Throughout This Book

Now's about the time to discuss a word I use a lot in this book since it's a very important term to agree on the definition of, so let's turn to Google.

Superfluous - adjective
1.   unnecessary, especially through being more than enough.
2.   "the purchaser should avoid asking for superfluous information"
 3. Synonyms - surplus (to requirements), non-essential, redundant, unneeded, excess, extra, (to) spare, remaining, unused, left over, in excess, waste, more.

Any detail to a production that's not adding to the emotion of a song is superfluous. Understanding superfluousness is important since it's one of the most common creative pitfalls. Superfluous contributions are commonly justified since they'll "add more thought" to the production. Whether this thought helps further the emotion of a song or not isn't considered, since it's falsely assumed that more will strengthen the song. Musicians commonly add more parts for the sake of adding more parts. They ride the volume fader on every track since surely this helps make a better song. They add harmonies to a vocal since "that's what you do." Superfluousness adds to a song by doing more for more's sake instead of emotionally reacting to a deficiency in a song and choosing to act upon it.

When you begin to see music through the lens of creating music with the intent to evoke an emotion, you start to notice the flaws in other works as well as understand why you don't enjoy certain songs: you hear superfluous parts added that don't help a song's intent. You notice tones that detract from the intent. You begin to understand why a part doesn't work in a song.

Adding parts to a song without thought as to how they further the emotional intent of the song doesn't add to it – it detracts by taking away attention to other more emotionally resonant moments. If an addition doesn't help further add to the emotion you're trying to convey, it's superfluous. If you can't hear the difference an idea makes or it adds no emotional content, it's superfluous, unnecessary and more than enough.

Intent Gives You The Backbone To Create

One of the saddest behaviors of musicians is allowing their artistic esteem to be controlled by whoever criticized them last. Intent allows you to take criticism and learn from it instead of having it be a detraction from what you create. When artists with no intent receive negative criticism, they don't know how to react, no matter what the criticism is. They then become reactive and guess at solutions to please an audience before themselves. With a positive comment they're elated, but anytime someone doesn't like their music, they sink into self-doubt. They're like a boat thrown around the waters in every direction since without intent, there's no anchor. With the anchor of knowing who you are and the traits you want to embody, you're able to see many criticisms are actually compliments.

A lack of a compass means when someone criticizes an artist for the qualities in their music, they lose their backbone by trying to please their critics. I cannot tell you how many times I've seen a band get offended when someone says their music is "too spacey," yet they deliberately decided to write the spaciest songs possible. This is actually an affirmation. While it's not meant as a compliment from the person leveling the criticism, no good art is universal. There will always be those who find certain traits undesirable, but if they describe a trait you want to embody as problematic, I'd chalk that up to a score for your team. It's commonly said that the best art inspires strong reactions of both love and hate since it's emotionally resonant instead of being unremarkable.

I'm not saying to ignore all feedback on your music, since feedback is essential to actualizing your vision. If your intent was to write dance jams but you're hearing that the abrasive parts of your sound are distracting from your hooks, it can be worth considering if you're optimizing your mixes as best as possible. Intent allows you to consider this criticism since without it, you can never tell if both criticisms and compliments are good or bad. One of the toughest balances is to figure out what gives you character and what can be improved on. Intent allows you to have a compass to judge whether each piece of criticism is worth considering towards how you get there.

It's crucial to develop intent to avoid being what I call a "ping pong ball" that's swayed by whoever's opinion they heard last. If the criticism is positive, everything is great, but if someone puts them down — even about an intentional choice — they react by pleasing the critic. This ping-pong ball bounces around from side to side because since without intent, it's beholden to the last criticism they received.

With intent, you're able to take criticism by judging whether it's complimenting your intent, even when it's meant to be derogatory, and grow from it. When you consider your intent for a song, album or as a musician, you have a value system to judge if you should consider a criticism or dismiss it. If you know who you are along with what you're trying to say, it gets far easier to maintain your mental health in a world where everyone can give their opinion about your art in an instant. Pleasing others when you're making the music you want to hear leads to a guessing game that creates music no one else wants to hear, including your critics.

When It Helps To Have No Intent

Having an intent that guides you through a career can give you purpose. While I emphasize intent throughout this book, there are times where you want to see how a project will develop. While I think emotional intent is imperative to shape a song, having intent in a project can sometimes ground it too early. There are times it can be helpful to explore with no intent in order to discover intent that will guide you later. When starting a new project, it can help to be free of this grounding to see where things go. You can freely explore where a song or a project can go, but when it comes time to draft, edit and elaborate on your ideas, intent not only makes the work easier, but it allows your song to be guided to its maximum resonance. **The key is to consider your intent when it becomes time to make a decision where you need a guidance.**

Chapter 5: Standards, Taste And What Is Perfect?

One of the most overlooked aspects of creating is standards. Standards are the line you draw on whether you find an element acceptable to pass your evaluation. A common place you'll hear about standards is in a cheesy rom-com where a character says, "I can't date him, I have standards," meaning that they won't accept some unattractive feature in a mate. This applies all throughout your life in that standards are what you won't accept below during any critical choice, whether it's not eating at fast food restaurants, how many days you go without a shower or how far you'll walk to a destination.

Standards are the most crucial barometer you use to make judgments. Standards can be the degree you've memorized a song before you're confident enough to play it live or how regularly you mess up a rap before you think you're capable of recording it. It can be whether you'll allow yourself to have a song with only two instruments in it or if you need it to be a large arrangement or even how much work you've put into your vocal melody before you can call it done. It can be the quality of sound that you need to hear to be worthy of releasing. Standards can be found in countless aspects of music, so where you draw the line on each of them makes up much of who you are.

Nearly every choice we make while creating music is affected by standards. If you have low standards for how tight your music should sound, you'll never sound as good as someone with a high standard of precision in their performances. If you hold low standards for song form, you'll be excited that you wrote two verses, three choruses and a bridge and call it a day. Sadly, this means your songs will get repetitive over the course of an album. You may think you can perform a song on a guitar when you bend strings and rub up against other strings in a chord while picking at inconsistent volumes, but a pro guitarist never stops rehearsing until all of these flaws are absent from their performances.

Standards aren't a metric as much as a judgment of your reaction to listening to a part of a song. There's no line in the sand as strong as a decision in your mind. Over time you develop a median of what you feel is up to your standards or not. While you can begin to hear how out of pocket a part is and measure it in milliseconds or the decibel reading of how loud an instrument is, these aspects need to be judged, like anything else, by your emotional reaction. They're a judgment of what's appropriate in the context you're presently working in. Each judgment is contextual, since how loose a dirty hip-hop groove is compared to the pulse of a 909 in a techno song can be wildly different when measured in metrics.

Developing Standards

Developing standards comes from analyzing both your own music as well as others. By taking in inspiration to decide what's acceptable in each of these recordings, you form standards over time as you draw correlations in what sounds right to your ear. In time, you begin to have a barometer of how songs should sound so when it comes time to craft your music you can make decisions on how close your own work will get to the sounds you love.

No one starts out with high standards. You aren't born knowing when a note is off key, just that they sound less pleasant than other note choices. In time, you hear how in key most singers you enjoy are and decide whether to hold yourself to the standards you've observed in others. If you take the time to analyze music, you'll notice that you're playing out of tempo, you're flamming chords, etc. Soon after, you start to know when you can play a song based on how sloppy it sounds to you or how regularly you make mistakes.

When I started working as a producer, my ability to get good performances was stifled by growing up listening to the loose, incompetent performances of punk records from the 80s and 90s. I'd accept horrible performances in my productions since most of what I grew up hearing was sloppy, out of tune but highly emotional. My peers who grew up on perfected hair metal and Steely Dan were getting way better performances than me since I was playing catch-up on hearing the intricacies of performance. I had to raise my standards of what a good performance is by intentionally listening to music with tighter musicianship to gain this heightened awareness. I now listen to the perfected performances on dance and pop records to remind me of the precision that can exist so I can judge how far I should go in perfecting parts in a recording.

Now I've come up with many innovative techniques to get even the worst performer to sound good without editing. This can be punching in every single word of a vocal to coaching a drummer about their flams by punching in two bars at a time while recording. There's a certain level of performance I won't accept below by not calling a song done unless it's up to my standards. Achieving high standards for musicians while not exceeding their budget is what keeps me getting hired as a record producer.

Trusting Your Gut

One of the ways following your heart shows itself is a naturally occurring lack of comfort during the process that tells us a part can be better. We've all heard the saying "trust your gut" being thrown around in all sorts of real-life scenarios where an instinct tells someone to pause to give more consideration before moving forward. Those same rom-coms we discussed before are riddled with instances where someone had a "bad gut feeling" and then regrets ignoring it when that bad feeling turns out to have been a warning of bad things to come. They may convince themselves not to listen to their gut after they find out their love interest was really an escaped convict or whatever cliché these movies are playing out currently, only to regret not trusting their intuition.

Within the anatomy of the human body, right next to the heart is the gut and they have a close relationship. Just like our gut feels bad when we eat bad food, it can tell us with a similar feeling when an element is in bad taste musically. When you eat food that's flawed, your gut warns you before you experience heartburn. It sounds this same alarm when your heart isn't feeling right about an element of your music. For example, your gut may tell you that the melody going into the verse can be better or that a melody can be repeated another time. Learning how to trust this instinct is one of most essential parts of actualizing great music. Sadly, many artists second-guess it or allow environments where the gut's instincts are shut down by trying to avoid conflict.

Listening to your gut and not lowering your standards is how great music gets made. When your gut feels uncomfortable about a part of a song, this is an immediate tip that your standards aren't being met, so you must experiment with other options. When you choose to use the head to convince yourself it knows better than the warning the heart is sending instead of reacting to what you hear, you defeat your strongest instinct you have for crafting a song. Knowledge of music, whether it's theory, an emotional feeling or a standard for how good music should feel, allows your gut to know your song isn't quite right yet. Jon Stewart of *The Daily Show* was known for always telling his staff to "trust your lack of comfort." If you feel uncomfortable about something, your lack of comfort is an alert that it needs more evaluation. If it doesn't feel up to your standards, you need to keep working until it does.

My Heart Is A Compass

One of the other ways "trusting your gut" is described is "your heart is a compass," meaning that you can let it guide you through the decisions you need to make. These internal warning signs aren't always about standards. They can also indicate when you're applying an idea from the head that's diminishing what makes the song emotionally resonant. Whether you're choosing a synth patch or which chord to play, your heart tells you which one feels closer to the emotion you're trying to convey. Using your heart as a compass for the choices you make throughout the process is far more effective than "searching for ear candy" or a "cool part." Your heart keeps a standard of the emotion it feels from your intent, using it to judge every choice you make when composing or sonically treating your song.

A Russian proverb I'm particularly fond of is "trust but verify," meaning trust in the artists to make the right decision, but it's OK to question to make sure you're coming up with the best ideas. While superfluous questioning can slow down momentum, when your bassist's affinity for prog rock creeps into your Americana songs, questioning can help you rethink things and find out you could have thought about a part a bit more.

Technically Perfect Isn't Emotionally Perfect

Developing standards can go too far when they're judged by technical achievement instead of emotional resonance. When you let the head develop a standard without letting the heart check that the head isn't sucking the emotion from it, a lot can go wrong. Musicians will let metrics or exact specifications dictate their decisions instead of what's most emotionally resonant. A ballad that tears at you emotionally but is sung with too much perfection feels soulless. However, with a few expressive breaks in the voice and a gritty push to the vocal's tone, it can feel as though a singer's heart is being ripped out. **Perfection shouldn't be judged like the answers on a test or a gymnastics performance, since the goal of a musical performance is to enhance the emotion of a song, not to be judged by form.**

Bikini Kill's "R.I.P." isn't improved by punching in the vocal until it's perfectly in key. Nirvana's "Something In The Way" isn't improved by enunciating the lyrics more clearly. The Beatles' "Twist and Shout" isn't improved when John Lennon's voice is less raspy when it hasn't been singing for 17 hours that day. Public Enemy's "Welcome To The Terrordome" groove isn't improved by the samples being more on time. Skrillex's *Bangarang* EP isn't improved by taking out the distortion. Ghost B.C. don't become a sicker metal band by making every drum hit exactly on the click track and Johnny Cash's cover of Nine Inch Nails' "Hurt" isn't better without the breaths between words.

If you read interviews with musicians where they discuss perfection, you'll see two extreme sides. On one side, they'll talk about crafting a song until it's perfect; on the other, they talk about leaving in flaws because that's what makes music great. The flaws left in songs by many amateur musicians are left since they don't want to play a part again, instead of for qualities that reinforce the song's resonance. In the studio, if an amateur musician doesn't want to redo a take they'll call upon a quote about how "the flaws make the take," but if they want to keep doing more takes they "must not stop when striving for greatness." Musicians constantly use philosophies to convince the head a musical decision works, but the only way to judge it is if the decision reinforces resonance is checking with the heart.

Perfection isn't a metric – it's a balance of having a standard high enough that flaws don't ruin the emotion you're trying to convey while maximizing the elements that make this emotion most potent. If you're Kraftwerk, your music needs to sound as robotic as possible, and if you're The White Stripes, you're trying to sound as raw and loose as you can while not being so sloppy it's intolerable. Perfection is measured in finding what works best with your intent by achieving the perfect balance of where each part of your sound should fall so it's most emotionally resonant. It's making music that feels great and embodies as much of the emotion you're trying to convey as possible without sucking the energy out of it by being concerned about imperfections. Perfection is a careful consideration of the emotion you're trying to convey while executing decisions that embody this emotion to its most resonant possible result. It isn't laboring over every detail so it's metrically correct or perfectly enunciated.

In practice, this is judging with the heart about whether a "flaw" emotionally diminishes or enhances a song. On Manchester Orchestra's "Shake It Out," there's a kick drum and bass hit that flams and it takes me out of the emotion of the song for me every single time I hear it. On Elvis Costello's "I Don't Want To Go To Chelsea," the misfrets on the guitars drive me mad. The creators of these songs choose to leave these details in the song since they enhance the emotion of the song through a lack of sterilizing the emotion of the music.

While I may be driven crazy by these flaws, I also love the looseness in the vocal performance on each song. The way both songs have vocal doubles that don't always align when the voice adds certain inflections that a more polished singer wouldn't allow is resonant to me since the performances make the song highly resonant. Every one of these judgments is easily judged by the heart by hearing a more polished version and deciding whether "perfecting" them is most resonant. Both of these songs are some of my favorite songs, yet I appreciate some "flaws" and don't appreciate others. Your standards make up much of who you are and how your music sounds, and when you trust your gut on them, you make music unique to you, even if others may not interpret those flaws to increase a song's resonance.

Twenty Pounds Of Crap In A Ten-Pound Bag

Just as you can perfect a performance too much, you can also jam it full of too many great parts to the point where it distracts the listener from being able to focus. Music is a balance of how to work within a constraint, whether that constraint is how many melodies can be played at a time or how long a song is before it's exhausting. Figuring out how to maximize your resonance within these constraints is essential to crafting a great song.

One of the most under-discussed parts of music is there can be too many great parts in a song. If you study your favorite songs, you'll find a balance where one or two of the instruments play parts that are playing a supporting role that doesn't call for the listener's attention. A mistake musicians make when trying to "perfect" a song is to try to make every part catch your ear at the same time. There's only so much a listener can pay attention to and there's only so much space in a mix before emotion is diluted by a lack of focus. This thought can also go for arrangements. There's a reason that the past few centuries of music still only have rhythm (drums), bass, accompaniment (commonly guitar or keyboard) and melody (usually a vocal or a monophonic lead instrument). There's not room for much more without it being distracting.

I point to the Smashing Pumpkins record *Siamese Dream*, which is praised for its huge sound. When you inspect this record, you find a buried bass track along with tiny cymbals that contrast to bombastic drums and extremely loud guitars with a vocal as tucked in the mix as possible. Whether you take that to the hip EDM song of the day or the latest prog rock song, there's a tightrope act where one or two of the parts keep it simple while someone else has attention drawn to them. You can find this balance of give and take in nearly every classic record.

Meters And Grids Are References

One of the most common ways a music fan judges a song is whether it gives them goose bumps or it makes them dance, bang their head or go into a trance. These metrics are all heart-based reactions to music. One of the biggest mistakes made in music — especially in the early days of Pro Tools — is to put every note on the grid to make them "perfect." Whether this grid is a level meter, click track or auto-tuned note read out, these tools are used for you to help gain information about what you're hearing. Music on the grid, whether they're pitch, timing or distortion, doesn't always feel as good for the intended reaction (dancing, head banging) as music that's not directly "on the grid."

The tendency to quantize or do other automated functions can work well for certain results, but A/B testing to consider whether these processes enhance or diminish the intent of a song is overlooked. **Meters and grids are meant to be references to confirm or dispute what you're hearing, not as guidelines that every element must line up with.** You need to trust your ears, not your eyes to judge what feels good, not what looks good since you're the only person who will ever stare at these "correct" readouts on a screen. A good performance is a balance of imperfections that make it an emotion, not an expressionless computer code. Scientific <u>experiments on quantizing performances to grids and other metrics</u> show that when music is too perfected, it becomes less enjoyable to listeners.

Furthermore, these grids lie. There are countless times a note is dead on the grid, but it sounds off time due to inconsistencies within the software as well as MIDI delays. A sound can be off the grid but sound great, in many genres of music, clipping tracks on both tape and digital is a preferred sound. Every experienced engineer has learned that sometimes the computer lies. Which also leads me to remind you that when listening back to your music, don't look at the computer screen. Until the late 90's there was no computer screens to look at, so looking into this screen can cause us to be fooled by auditory hallucinations where our eyes are telling our ears what to hear. Take the time to give listens where you look away from your screen to perceive your music the way everyone else will hear it, with no visual representation aside from an album cover.

Listening Not Looking To Become A Better Creator
There's a great story of a tabla player whose instructor wouldn't allow the student to watch him play. Instead, he'd sit back to back with him during lessons, having the student explore the tabla until he found the proper technique to emulate the tone the teacher had played. This led the student to find the many nuances of the instrument, allowing a greater understanding of the instrument instead of an imitation. This also allows the player to develop their own techniques instead of imitating and conforming.

Ignoring what your eyes see in order to hear the nuances of a performance strengthens your standards as well as proficiency to diagnose flaws and to fix them. Getting to know what you're hearing and then using meters or grids to confirm what you hear is the only way to become proficient in zooming in on the nuances of a musical performance. The reverse order leads to poor decisions that perfect music for the sake of perfecting it superfluously.

When Metric-Based Standards Ruin Music

There are musicians whose standards are too concerned with the head that neglect checking with the heart for emotional resonance by solely concerning themselves with accomplishments of proficiency. The most common flaw in a guitar solo is to focus on heady accomplishments of technical proficiency instead of serving a function of the heart like taking the melodies of the song to a new place. Synth programmers will automate envelopes to show they understand synthesis. Singers want to incorporate the most challenging scale they can sing to show off their chops. All of these practices can work if they are combined with an emotional intent, but far too often they neglect to do so.

The ego can be part of what takes standards in a heady direction. Often a musician asks to play a part without doing punches or employing editing strictly to prove they can do it. Even if no one else can hear the punches or editing, they'll insist on doing this to satisfy their ego. Standards that concern process instead of enhancing emotional resonance are entirely superfluous. While having a good work ethic and striving for proficiency in your work helps to improve your craft, if you concern yourself with accomplishments more than emotional resonance, you're sacrificing the most meaningful part of music. Instead, this becomes a standard that's only for the ego boost of getting past an obstacle.

If a standard is judged by technical means instead of what's emotionally resonant, it's bound to become superfluous. Reigning in collaborators' standards to make sure they're checked for the objective of emotional resonance is a saving grace for musicians who commonly refer to technical standards.

Taste Is A Misnomer

You may have noticed, I've avoided the word taste throughout this book, despite it being a word that's thrown around in creative circles abundantly. I avoid it since taste is mostly contextual. I regularly joke that I don't enjoy ska music yet my favorite record of all time, The Clash's *London Calling,* has ska on it. While discussions of taste are important, I think the term is commonly misallocated. What's often called distasteful is when someone chooses to paint with a color that conflicts with the way they feel an emotion. A common case of this can be one's enjoyment of both rap and rock. While a listener can enjoy both genres separately, when combined, they find the emotional combination repulsive. Many attribute this to taste, but this is actually an adverse emotional reaction to a combination that emotionally conflicts within them.

Taste is commonly talked about like a border that can't be crossed, yet we see time and time again that someone can bridge that border once the right balance of emotional palates is achieved. While many listeners frown on rap-rock, when Jay Z's "99 Problems" comes on, the combination compels them to bop their head in unconstrained enjoyment. The same can go for huge compressed drums that make songs sound aggressive; if they're in a folk song, that's judged as bad taste. Usually, people who don't enjoy these qualities call it taste, but really the emotion of aggression is one the listener doesn't empathize with. **What's considered taste is most often an emotional choice that diminishes the listener's resonance with a song.** The different attributes we find tasteful are forever malleable and dependent on the emotional reactions we have when we hear music. This is why I avoid talking about them as much as possible and instead focus on what we feel is emotionally resonant.

In my own "tastes," I love twangy guitars in country music, yet when I hear them in heavy rock songs or dance music, I hit stop as fast as possible. The misnomer of taste is that we feel a certain emotional attachment to a sound. A twangy guitar to my ear makes me feel a shade of emotions that when put in contexts outside of those emotions, it declines the resonance of a song to me. I can't stand gospel music, yet when their style of vocals are in the background on The 1975's "The Sound," my taste's context changes as I listen to the song repeatedly. **Taste cannot be assigned to specific attributes in music; it will always be contextual depending on how an element is used emotionally. Tastes change when they are emotionally mixed in a way a listener finds pleasing and those borders are ever changing for most open-minded people.**

We need to remember that most innovations in music come from adding an element that was thought to be tasteless by the masses, which then becomes highly resonant when used in the right context. Whether this is Dave Davies distorting a guitar for the first time, John Bonham adding room ambience to drum recordings, Justice bringing metal riffs to dance music or whatever evolution of music you can think of, all of these innovations were tried by others and deemed tasteless until they were presented in the proper emotional context.

Chapter 6: The Race Against A Loss Of Objectivity

Once you've written a great song, the most treacherous part of creating is maintaining objectivity. If you lose objectivity, the ability to judge options is compromised, resulting in poor decision making since you can only guess what's right. When discussing music among those who work at perfecting songs, the most commonly cited problem is a loss of objectivity. What makes crafting music so difficult is that even if you have intent and know exactly what you want, you can lose perspective along the way. If you hear a song the same way too many times, you get used to the element's relationship with one another. You subsequently lose the ability to objectively hear changes to decipher whether they improve or detract from your intent.

Just as treacherous is you can make poor decisions if you don't listen to a mix properly. If you're too focused on the details, you can lose track of the big picture. All of these choices are crucial to consider, yet there's rarely any good insight into how to properly use the tools at hand to stay as objective as possible. Before we go deeper, there are two plagues that kill musicians' objectivity constantly that we should define:

Demoitis - While the CDC has never studied it, the most common affliction among musicians is Demoitis. This affliction occurs when someone has heard a mix of a song for so long that any change to it sounds wrong. The only way the song sounds right is the way it was in the mix the afflicted person is used to. Demoitis is contracted by overly listening to a mix of a song. It's inevitable to contract it after prolonged listening of a single mix of a song. A rare breed of musicians are immune to it, but for most of us, the more we listen to a version of a song, the more we get used to it in that form and the harder it is to be open to changing it.

Analysis Paralysis - Anyone that's ever tried their hand at perfecting a song has probably experienced what's known as Analysis Paralysis. Barry Schwartz explains the term in his book, *The Paradox of Choice*, as the phenomenon when we become paralyzed by the different options in front of us. In music, this is most experienced when we've heard so many options, we can no longer make a good decision. This regularly happens when surfing through plug-in presets or drum samples.

This affliction can cripple us creatively. The loss of perspective from working too long on a song or hearing too many alternative ideas is debilitating for artists. The song sounds different, but all emotional resonance to judge an option is depleted, leading to confusion about what the best option is. This usually causes the creative process to cease, as the song becomes abandoned or is completed as is since the artist can no longer tell which choice to make.

The Ticking Clock Of Objectivity

Producer Greg Wells (Katy Perry, Adele) has said: "The hardest part of making music is you can never hear it the way a listener does the first time." Now, before you crucify me about how much I've written about making the music you want to hear and not concerning yourself with the listener, take in the concept. As you craft your music, it gets harder and harder to tell if you're doing the right thing since your excitement for a song declines in time as you get used to it. Just like the songs of others you enjoy, resonance dies with repeated listens. To make matters worse, while you work on a song, your objectivity gets more and more skewed as you get used to the way parts sound. Elements you find emotionally resonant on a first listen compared to elements you find interesting after hearing the song for the hundredth time are often quite different.

To make good decisions for our music, we need to acknowledge this is a race we're running whenever we develop a new song. At some point, your objectivity gets depleted and your ability to make good decisions will be reduced. You must always be conscious of the balance between under developing a song and developing it for so long that you **lose** objectivity.

Effectively Listening To Maintain Objectivity

Whenever you're creating a song, there's a race to keep the momentum and excitement of the song going. While you want to give enough consideration to the composition, you must execute it fast enough to not lose your perspective. This struggle is one of the hardest balances to strike in the creative process. If you flog a song to death scrutinizing every detail, it can suck the life out of it. With that said, focusing on details can also bring out the magic in it. Finding that balance is crucial to the execution of making a great song.

In order to maintain my objectivity as a producer, I abstain from writing songs with a band from day one. After I initially hear what they've written, I may send a band back to the drawing board and say, "The verse works but scrap the rest of the song," but I won't be there while they rewrite it. If I have to be in the room as a band tries out 400 variations, I have then lost the same level of objectivity as them, which defeats my purpose as a producer. To do my job effectively, I can't sit through the infinite possibilities of songwriting, since I need to maintain an objective, quality control role. I must still have objectivity after a song is as fleshed out as a band can make it on their own, so I need to minimize micromanagement throughout the process. While this doesn't sound very efficient, it keeps me with an objective mind to evaluate what they write. This is much more valuable than any time saved.

To maintain this objectivity, I outsource the tedious tracking of guitars and synthesizers to my co-producer. I leave the room while they get a tone to return with fresh ears once it's dialed in. When it comes time to track guitars for 6-8 hours of tedious tuning and punch-ins, I have to leave since my perspective gets lost if I sit through that. If an extensive development of harmonies is needed to make a song work, I'll also leave the room for that so I don't get tainted by the options and tedium of tracking them. This allows me not to be biased in my judgment of a performance by the effort expended to record it or how long it would take to redo it if it doesn't feel right. If I don't have to punch in the guitars for three hours to fix them, then I can make my decision based solely on making the song great, not my annoyance with the process. I should say I'm not the only producer who employs this method – both Rick Rubin and Howard Benson are famous for this technique.

Demoitis: The Struggle Is Real

If you sit a bunch of musicians and producers down in a room, you'll get an earful of stories on the woes of the creative process. Inevitably, there'll be stories of the big studio budget that couldn't outdo the demos recorded at home. The next story will be how a band constantly compared studio recordings to their demos, leading to the downfall of their record since they weren't open to developing their demo ideas to their full potential. The funny thing is they both may be right or completely wrong in their assessment. Whether or not they were right is obviously subjective, but they may have made a different decision if their objectivity wasn't tainted by getting too attached to their demos.

One of the most difficult balances to strike is doing enough drafts in your demos to get a full picture so that you can make a great song while not drafting them to the point that you're so attached to the demo's sound that you can't hear the song another way. You must give thorough consideration to your demos but not at the sacrifice of your objectivity; you need some to spare when recording the songs your audience will hear. This same idea goes for band rehearsal. While everyone wants to be well rehearsed when going into the studio, there's a point where you're so used to the way a song sounds in rehearsal that any tweaks for the better sound unnatural. This leaves little possibility of objectivity when production decisions are made in the studio crippling the development of a song.

First Version, Best Version

To make the struggle worse, the first version of a song that someone hears and wants to listen to again and again is usually the one they'll like best. Test yourself on this: the next time you hear more than one version of a song from a musician you love, see if you consistently enjoy the first version you hear of the song more. As someone that's polled their friends on this for the years I've been writing this book, the resounding answer is the first version you listen to continuously is hard to get over. This means all of your teammates who listen to your demos numerous times are on team "demo" whenever making a choice as to whether a part of the demo is better since they heard it that way first.

However, there's an exception that shouldn't be overlooked. About 25% of the time, the demo can be beaten, even for those who loved it. But this is so hard to measure that it's almost irrelevant. On projects with a decent budget, you'll regularly see bands who have lost perspective take their record to a mixer or a different producer at the end to help make better decisions. Today in pop music, we see countless producers on a pop song, since suits commonly think a song hasn't reached its potential after a producer completes their work, so they employ another producer to further explore what can be done. The fresh perspective they have can clearly see the dilemmas that have left the musician in paralysis. This objectivity goes for every mastering engineer's job, which is mostly about objectivity in that they're to be fresh ears that put some final touches on what perspective you may have lost in the mixing process.

Avoiding The Loss Of Objectivity From Demos And Scratch Tracks

Since we're trying to avoid getting too used to the way the demo sounds, what can we do to avoid this plague? While you must make the music you want to hear, you need to exercise restraint in your consumption of this music. **The more you listen to a specific recording of your song, the more objectivity you lose.** Conversely, abstaining from listening to your demos won't allow you to gain perspective on what you've recorded. What's so tragic about this is listening to the same mix repeatedly can impair you from making a good decision, yet you'll feel confident that this is what your heart feels is right. Unfortunately, many musicians decide to go with a demo element when evaluating a song only to return to it a year later to discover there was room for improvement that they had been blind to due to a loss of objectivity.

Demos are one of the most useful tools at our disposal, but to make them effective, you must exercise restrained listening with concentrated note taking. Even if that note taking is as informal as cranking down the windows on your car to listen as you would any other song, this is some of the most important time you can spend as long as it's rationed. Excessive listens with half-minded attention only further cement the way a demo sounds, hindering your objectivity to future development.

Scratch tracks can poison objectivity as well. If you've been hearing a scratch vocal while you work on a song for three weeks, inferior vocal inflections can skew your objectivity away from those that further the emotional resonance of a song, as you've become used to how the scratch track sounds. The nuances of the performance become so ingrained that any alterations that stray from the demo seem wrong. To alleviate this, I'll have a singer sing a scratch vocal a handful of times at the start of each day before we start to work on the song. I'll then change the take we hear throughout the day. This way the performance is always different so I can hear the best of their inflections as we record the song. This technique can help preserve objectivity immensely as well as help find a clear picture of what the vocal should be doing when it comes time to track it.

When producing records, I severely ration my influence from demos to maintain a higher level of objectivity than musicians. In the best-case scenario, I won't have heard any demos for weeks before we start pre-production or the recording process. When a band sends me a demo, I try to take it in as fast as I can so I never get used to it. This usually means listening to each song 1-5 times while taking notes. After this initial listen along with one session of reevaluation, I never listen to the demo until we're done recording the song. While the self-produced home studio trend continues to grow, this objectivity is usually what makes a producer worth their paycheck on a project.

While I've talked a lot about the demo being detrimental to your objectivity, it can also be the greatest savior at the end of recording a song. If I've done a good job of forgetting the demo, putting it on once we think the recording of a song is done can be a life-saving safety net to make sure we've exceeded everything good about the demo. I can't count how many times I've revisited a demo after tracking a song to find two or three cool elements to bring back that adds so much resonance to a song.

Preventing Demoitis In Mixes

The other common culprit of Demoitis is how the interaction of levels in demos and rough mixes influence how those afflicted judge a mix of a song. When tracking songs, the vocals and drums are turned up excessively loud to help performers get a good performance. Once a song is mixed, these levels are placed in a more realistic balance, so those who have been hearing a tracking mix feel a loss of excitement when they're mixed. I've found a few practices helpful to prevent Demoitis caused by mixes:

- Don't set levels of any instrument excessively loud compared to the others in a mix. During tracking it can be helpful to have drums turned up loud to perform tight to the groove. Take these down when making rough mixes; otherwise, it can be hard to get used to more reasonable balances when mixing a song later.

- Make different mixes each day. One of the benefits of mixing consoles compared to DAWs was they wouldn't allow mixes to be the same each day. The variance of different fader levels didn't allow your mind to get used to exact balances, allowing you to hear different perspectives on the levels of a song to judge against later.
- Make a change or stop dwelling on the demo. Unless you're adding or subtracting from your demo, don't give superfluous listens without making new versions; come back to it with fresh ears.

Immunity To Demoitis - There are some experienced artists who are immune to Demoitis and they've never even experienced it. This rare percentage can always discern the good ideas from the bad. Many of my producer friends find that as years go on, they get better and better at trusting their gut to discern what's good and bad, as opposed to being biased to the familiar. This also tends to come with those who learn how to judge every choice emotionally instead of with concepts that stem from the head.

How to Regain Your Perspective

It's pretty much inevitable that at some point you'll lose your perspective. Thankfully you can find it again by employing a few tricks.

Revisit The Greats - Your "Great Songs" playlist can be the ticket to regaining perspective. In my experience, losses of perspective commonly stem from making judgments against previous drafts you've made without outside perspective of other music you enjoy. Your head is so inside your own work, you're not regularly gaining feedback from what has been resonant to you in the past to gain objectivity. Revisiting your favorite music to judge how tight grooves are, the levels of certain elements in a mix or the overall timbre of a song can be a reference to help steer you in the right direction. I find if I revisit my favorite songs for an hour and revisit the song I's having trouble with, my perspective has a true north that's easy to see again.

Muting Or Soloing - When mixing, employing the mute button or solo instruments to analyze songs is a basic practice that's commonly dismissed as being too critical. While soloing a track can make a track that's with too strong a groove sound totally wrong, it could also unveil a perspective that shows a flaw. There are plenty of instruments that may sound odd when soloed, especially if they're played to a rhythm track with a less conventional groove, but soloing a track can help give further perspective. Muting various elements of a song is equally helpful in finding perspective on what could be flawed or superfluous within it.

Time - Time away from a song is a commodity many musicians don't have during the song development process. Sadly, it's the best cure for lost perspective. Anyone experienced in making music that's revisited a past recording in hindsight can hear clear flaws or better decisions they could have made. While there's no definite prescription for how much time it takes to regain objectivity, breaks from hearing a song regularly leads to huge epiphanies as well as regained perspective. In fact, time away from a song may be the single greatest way to regain objectivity.

Curing Analysis Paralysis

Analysis paralysis is a particularly tricky affliction to navigate. If it's a regular occurrence, you're probably suffering from self-doubt and need to do some research or gut analysis of what feels right in your heart. The most common cases stem from having to make a big decision coupled with a lack of confidence in knowledge on how to make that decision. On a macro level, when coaching musicians through it in the past, I talk to them about who they'd like to be as an artist and what type of decision that artist would make. Reverse engineering how you can be confident in your decision is crucial since deciphering what would be beneficial about each path makes you more prepared when a choice must be made. This results in solidifying your intent since it's the best guide to avoid this troublesome paralysis. You then need to start creating again; the only way this affliction subsides is by committing to a decision.

Phased Decision Making - On a more micro level, options need to be whittled down over time by doing some batch decision-making. If there are five directions for a vocal you can't decide between, get it down to three and the next week get it down to one. If there's an unclear decision between two key elements, make a decision and if it still annoys you weeks later, revisiting with a different mind will usually give your thoughts clarity.

Giving Up - Analysis paralysis commonly occurs at the end of a project where uncompleted songs are left hanging to avoid making a crucial but confusing decision. Further consideration of what best reinforces intent and resonance is the only way to consider this. Time away can help regain objectivity to make that decision, but don't give up during a tight deadline; employ outside ears to consider the decision after hearing your intent.

Your Lifeline

Just as the show *Who Wants To Be A Millionaire* has illustrated for years, occasionally we hit a point where we've either lost perspective or don't know what to do. Perhaps democracy has broken down or you've lost perspective and the only way to regain it is from trusted ears. You need an outside opinion whose thoughts may help us come to a decision. The "lifeline" on the show is a person you can call who's not on the stage that can help you get through a tough, paralyzing choice. Once you hear from this trusted person, you usually regain objectivity by knowing whether to trust your instincts or not.

Throughout my life, I've collected friends I can turn to for various dilemmas. Producer friends constantly shoot mixes back and forth when we've been working on a song for too long or received feedback on a song that's perplexing us. You should find someone outside of who you regularly make music with who can help give you perspective. Keeping these lifelines in mind can save your songs. Throughout post-mortem album interviews, you hear that musicians let their friends listen to songs to set them back on course. Sadly, they probably won't make you a millionaire by answering a question.

Putting Together A Record And What's Presently Resonant

One of the toughest parts of putting together which songs go on a record, as well as their order, is judging them by their quality versus which ones you're currently excited about. The songs that are oldest in the process can often be strong, but since they're old, they feel less resonant than they used to. In my last book, I argued that it helps to have outsiders give an objective perspective on choosing singles as well as an album's order. Since the artist, producer and other team members have heard so many iterations of a song by the end of the album, perspectives can be skewed, favoring the most recent material since it's more resonant.

Processing Creativity

Musicians often employ outside ears due to loss of perspective from constantly feeling their latest material is their greatest. Producer Bob Ezrin has done this for both Pink Floyd and Nine Inch Nails. Rick Rubin is famous for helping prolific artists like Kanye West with this qualm. More often than not, musician's reach out to trusted ears to get outside feedback for confirmation on whether the material they favor is truly their best.

Zooming From Macro To Micro

Little consideration is given to developing the skill to zoom the view you're looking at a song in when analyzing music. What I mean by zooming is usually talked about in the classic saying, "seeing the forest for the trees." In music this commonly refers to listening to a single instrument instead of the whole song (or vice versa). Learning to do this type of zooming is how you consider both the details of the song you're making as well as the overall picture. If you only focus on the larger forest picture, you'll miss crucial flaws and the opportunity to accumulate subtleties in your music. If you only focus on small tree details, you'll make decisions that may hinder the overall resonance of your song by neglecting the bigger picture.

This problem is musically illustrated in the classic story of the mixer who spends eight hours EQing a kick drum instead of listening to the interaction the kick drum is having with a song; they spend so long zoomed in on this small element that they fail to see obvious flaws and never get a proper perspective. This common beginner problem also plagues those well into their career since they forget to change their perspective by zooming in and out regularly while evaluating their music.

When I hear a new part of a song, I commonly give it two listens. One to analyze the performance considering a micro view of the pitch, timing and inflection and again to consider the part's place in the song overall. Each of these listens requires a concentrated focus on their specific function. When evaluating a record as a producer, I make these evaluations in various zooms:

Long Zoom
- Does this fit with the sound of the record?

- Are there too many parts like this on the record?
- Is this adding to the diversity of the record or making it too diverse?

Medium Zoom
- Is the song too long?
- Does the chorus repeat enough?
- Is there enough tension built before the release?
- Is the bridge the right one for the song?

Micro Zoom
- Is the drum fill going into the chorus right?
- Is the vocal melody too cluttered?
- Are there too many different parts in the accompaniment?
- Does this part rush too much?

Obstruct Your View To Change Focus

While there are micro and macro zooms, unlike in photography, a blurred picture often shows us a valuable perspective. When developing a song, you can be zoomed too hard or soft and get stuck in that zoom. When I have a song on playback while checking email or reading Twitter, I'll notice very obvious things that were oblivious to me in a focused state where I zoomed in too far. This semi-distracted state isn't one to strive for continuously, but it can be helpful to take us out of the zoom we're presently in. When I'm on a particularly involved mix that's been thoroughly labored over, I find it helpful to take a break but keep it playing while I sit in the other room doing email. The flaws in the mix usually jump right out when I can't hear subtle EQ balances or a stereo image. This technique is used by countless engineers making music in every genre.

This is similar to why you'll see multiple speakers in a recording studio. The big monitors in the wall are there to give you a detailed and loud picture. The medium sized ones on the console are there to give a medium view that's optimized for critical decisions in the studio. The small speakers give a less detailed, more real-world vision of how a mix translates to the general public. Headphones give a hypercritical listen to tiny details that zooms in further than most speakers, which some feel is too tight of a zoom to make good choices.

Best Practices

Inspiration As The Picture Gets Clearer

Demos are like fuzzy, out of focus pictures; you can hear the broad strokes and big ideas, but the details are usually clouded in the lack of clarity, tightness and refinement of a demo. After all, that's what makes it a demo and not a final recording. As we begin to see this picture more clearly, it becomes more obvious what we should be doing to make a song reach its potential. It's inevitable as the picture becomes clearer that you'll begin to see mistakes, timing inconsistencies, clashing notes and other flaws in your song.

One of the hardest parts of recording music is it doesn't sound mixed and mastered while it's being recorded. Garageband demos can sound unbearably harsh and cloudy, making it difficult to know if you need to work harder to achieve that feeling you get from your favorite records. Even in an expensive studio with a great producer/engineer, the rough mix doesn't quite sound like a finished record, so it can be confusing whether to critically judge what's being heard or if it'll sound better as the process goes on. To make matters worse, our brains have a tendency to see new flaws once we're able to concentrate on other details. I find singers get tunnel vision in their consideration of a song until their vocal is done, then suddenly they can see parts of a song they never noticed once their tight focus on the vocal is completed. Since commitment and solving problems give you clarity to focus elsewhere, it's only natural to gain the ability to notice new elements in a song.

When you've been working on a record for a while, it can be a tense moment when someone points out a flaw that should've been caught a few weeks ago. Just as despised is when someone realizes during the mix another melody or harmony is needed to complete the song. While we can wish this epiphany came weeks earlier, until a song is heard in it's in near completed form it's often hard for musicians to know how a song sounds. The reaction of those paying for the session or trying to get home at a reasonable hour can be harsh when a drum track recorded a month ago all of a sudden has a newfound flaw.

Experimentation - One of the biggest fights in the studio is when someone decides to start "experimenting" when another member of the team is concerned there's not enough time to accomplish everything that's needed to make the song actualized. When this experimenting is being done "on the clock," it can start to become detrimental to the recording coming out optimally. While this doesn't need to be a fight, the anger is not without justification in many cases. If studio time is limited so that you can only record the ideas you had before entering, taking precious time to experiment can be detrimental to the overall project.

Before entering the studio, it should be considered that even the least inspired musicians gain some inspiration in the studio as they hear what's possible. If time isn't allocated for reconsideration, you won't be able to bring your songs to fruition as you see where new parts should be added. This means if you want a song to reach its full potential, you need to consider experimenting with solutions as the picture becomes clearer.

Developing Performances With Increased Perspective

This inspiration also goes for the development of nuance in performances. I recall the first time I got to record one of my favorite singers. I wasn't as nervous as I was when working with some of my favorite musicians in the past. Instead, I felt ready for this moment of working with a peer. He got on the mic, asking me to give him three takes on each part of the song. After each take that was up to his standards, he'd say, "Keep that one." When he got to the end of the song, he said: "OK, burn me that as an MP3!" I was horrified since these takes were way below my standards based on what I'd heard him do before. I then figured that some magical editor fairies must be making him sound great in the post-production process, so I better brush up on my skills, since what I had to work with was far below my expectations. Thoughts started going through my head of how embarrassing it would be to have my name on this track, but I kept my cool.

As I tried to figure out what to say, he urged me to track keyboards for a bit. I saw him listen to his iPod with a piece of paper in the live room, taking notes with headphones on for a while. Upon completion of the keyboard track he informed me, "I'm ready to do this vocal for real." We then went line by line working to get great takes where we both challenged him to get the best of the vocal. By the time we reached the end, I heard the incredible vocals I was used to hearing from him. But to get to that level of performance, he needed to take the time to consider the nuances of his performance with as clear a vision as possible.

This taught me a valuable lesson: performers need time to contemplate their compositions by hearing them back. Often times when a musician completes a performance they exclaim they can do it better, but a producer is hesitant to devote more time to the performance. When a musician performs a part they are gaining a deeper consideration of the nuance they can bring to the performance after hearing it clearly. It's hard to have clear perspective to think about tone and inflection, along with all the other aspects of a performance until you have the chance to hear it back to react to what can be done with it. Once they gain a clear perspective, allowing someone to develop their performances is usually some of the best time spent.

I regularly employ this method when I get a lackluster performance from a musician. I make them a mix and say "tomorrow you'll have listened to this and thought about how to bring this song to a more emotional place." I tell them to take detailed notes and listen to some of their favorite artists to get ideas on how to emotionally elaborate on their performance. This is one of the best tools in my production toolbox.

Working With A Clear Picture

One of the quickest ways to lose perspective is to build a song on unedited tracks, thus laying an unsteady ground for other decisions. When you lay down your rhythm tracks, be sure they're tracked tightly as they will determine the feel of every track put on top of it. If you don't deal with quantization or any other editing you need to do immediately, these timing or pitch inconsistencies can blur the overall picture and cause bad judgments. This rule also goes for fixing flaws. Hearing an unedited track for too long commonly skews your perspective on editing decisions. If you hear an out of tune vocal for thirty straight listens, a tuned vocal can sound odd. But if you tune the vocal after a few critical listens, it's easy to make judgments on whether the tuning has sucked the life out of it. All editing in my productions happens immediately after a track is done so that I lose the minimum amount of objectivity.

The looser a track is, the more small inaccuracies in the groove of a track become blurred. This is why many classic rock recordings were able to be so loose yet still feel good. Whereas once you start playing to quantized drum machines, the timing inconsistencies in each track become more apparent. The same goes for pitch; once a digital synthesizer applies its perfect pitch to a song, the intonation of a guitar or vocal becomes glaring. This is why dance music vocals are commonly tuned more heavily than rock songs. Whereas in a 70s rock song when a vocal used to be coupled with poorly fretted guitars and bass, mild intonation was easily covered up by the already "loose" overall inconsistencies in the track.

Fixing It In the Mix - Not only is "fixing it in the mix" one of the laziest, most destructive habits in music, it leaves flaws that blur the picture in your view. To make good decisions, you need to track with as good a mix as possible to get the best possible tones to build upon. This also goes for spending the time to work with a clear rough mix. Experienced producers work with a mix that's as close to a finished product as possible without slowing the momentum of a session.

One of the most notable improvements in the quality of the vocal performances I get from singers is to mix the instrumental of a song before I do vocals. Not only do musicians perform better to a good mix, but the judgments made are enhanced by hearing a more clear vision of how the song will sound later. Most musicians aren't trained in hearing what a rough mix should sound like, so by telling them "everything will be fine when it gets fixed in the mix," their concerns during the process are silenced, making for diminished participation and doubting of their instincts. This closing down of a conversation hinders creativity immensely. To alleviate this, I give playbacks of a vocal performance with a typical mixing and mastering chain on so that musicians with untrained ears can judge what we've done without having to qualify it with "it's not mixed."

Commitment
Many beginners feel empowered by never having to commit to a sound when they start recording on DAWs. They let virtual instruments stay live to be tweaked until the final mixdown or guitars that can be reamped along with five mics on a snare drum which can give you all the options in the world to get the exact sound you're looking for. Yet, nearly

everyone who makes influential records does the exact opposite by committing to sounds to narrow their options throughout the creative process. They develop techniques to commit to decisions made as they go. This comes with a variety of benefits:

Freeing Your Mind - Commitment allows you to free your mind to concentrate elsewhere. To make good decisions, we need to know commitments have been made in order to focus laser-like on the next concern. Psychological studies show that once we feel a decision is made, our focus can shift. If we have too many decisions to make, we're more likely to fall into option paralysis.

Narrowing Your Attention - Commitment allows your attention to be put in other places. Similar to freeing your mind, if you don't have five tracks of snare options to tweak, you have a finite amount of tools to make it work such as compression, distortion, EQ, etc.

Reacting - When you commit, you're reacting to a less varied sound, which can determine the groove, pitch or other parameters in your song. If you don't commit to MIDI Instruments in your song while constantly tweaking them, it can be hard to focus on the tones and mix. You should commit in stages of your song so you can enhance your focus to different elements of the song.

COYA - The contrarian's argument against commitment is: what happens when it hinders your creativity since you're stuck with a less optimal outcome? When we talk about commitment, we're not talking about it in the sense of the Catholic church's "'till death do us part" marriage stance; we're talking about making some decisions, which if you need to go back to once in a while, you can always divorce what you choose. This isn't some game you're playing with yourself where you need to pretend a technology no longer exists where you can't easily replace a snare sound once you've realized it isn't working. Many musicians commit by simply making certain options inactive or leaving their options in previous versions which can be revisited. If you don't yet feel confident enough to commit to guitar sounds, commit to one and save your DI track so if you need to bail yourself out later, you're all set.

Separating Out Demoing From Recording In Your Home Studio For Commitment

There's a lot of talk of the writing and demoing process in this book, but with each year that passes, more and more musicians are writing and recording their music all within their own studio. This process takes away the traditional separation of writing and recording as two separate modes that have existed for nearly a century. I've always welcomed this change since musicians having more control over their vision gives us more interesting creative flavors. With that said, it's worth analyzing what this lack of separation can bring to your process or possibly detract from it.

The best part of the traditional divide of writing and recording was commitment. In the 1930-60s, the way a song sounded in rehearsal was a commitment since little would be able to be done to enhance it past what you had come up with in the studio since overdubbing and effects were so limited. After this period, the advent of producers who helped shape, polish and eventually co-write them led to a commitment that an artist needed to craft a song as good as they could get it on their own, but a producer would patch up any flaws. The producer, mixer or in some cases outside writers would then help shape the songs into a better work.

Many producers and A&R bemoan this erosion of standards for being a degradation of the craft of songwriting since musicians aren't working tirelessly to a song's ultimate actualization. Instead, when songs are brought into the studio they're "good enough to record," and that standard seemed to slip lower and lower with the advent of Pro Tools and musicians believing that anything can be fixed by a computer wizard. This "fix it in the mix" philosophy is the Achilles' heel of countless productions.

This border line of commitment became a zigzagged scribble by the time home recording became what it is today, which is a part of nearly every great record's process to some extent. While many musicians may only use home recording as demoing and drafting, the line has been blurred for almost every musician making music today. With that established, is there still a benefit to separating writing from recording when you record your own music? I think the answer lies in the commitment it brings.

What many home recordists do is have a demo time where their soft synths and other sounds can still be tweaked and arrangements are malleable, but if you watch interviews with most of the top "bedroom producers," they all say that they eventually begin a commitment process. They print down or freeze the synths to begin to work on perfecting a song that's essentially the recording process. They then start a mixing process and commit the way traditional recordings have. This practice is commonly lost on novice home recordists. Having a controlled process gives many musicians a focus that benefits from the past but has the flexibility of the future. While it's beneficial to not have a ticking clock on the mixing process at home, the distinctions between the parts of the process are often able to bring a project a separation that benefits an artist's focus.

In pop productions, the process most often has the initial writer demo a song and it goes through various stages as a beat writer will hand it off to a producer who polishes the song and the vocals. Then there's a later commitment as it goes to mixing that all tracking and editing are completed. Seeing your production in stages can help you gain focus by committing along the way while gaining objectivity.

Chapter 7: Inspiration, Research And Fluency

"True inspiration is impossible to fake."
— **Arthur (Joseph Gordon-Levitt) in the movie *Inception***

Inspiration is to creativity what food is to energy. Without inspiration, there's nothing to draw from creatively. Even if there's a limited amount of inspiration, the perspiration is weak like an athlete trying to compete without proper nutrition. What we take in as inspiration leads to how open or closed our mind is to possibility, which forms how we express our intent. If your mind hasn't been opened to the possibility of certain options, it's far more difficult to understand they're available to use in your expression.

"Inspiration is for amateurs — the rest of us just show up and get to work." — **Chuck Close**

Some of the most generalized advice about creating is to sit down and force it out, whether or not it's good. The above quote is used by inspiration deniers that think you sit down at a desk and start plunking away until a song comes out, with no concern for the potency of what's created since content must be made. This thought neglects that you need to have inspiration to express emotionally to make good music. While you can always produce some bland content, great music needs inspiration to fuel a potent expression of what you want to say. The boneheads who push this argument value content generation, not the potent expression of new truths that music can bring us.

Inspiration is often compared metaphorically to fishing, but I find a better comparison in farming. Your inspiration is the seed of what you can perspire. If you're keeping the soil healthy by regularly watering your inspiration seeds, they can grow into perspiration. While not every seed of inspiration grows into a healthy crop, you need to take in enough inspiration that you have crops to choose from when others don't fully grow. Time needs to be spent nurturing these seeds by nurturing the proper nutrition for them to grow, along with perspiring enough of it that you have sufficient choices to harvest.

One of the reasons there's so much bad advice about inspiration is the huge spectrum of where artists fall in how inspired they are presently. On one side, there's someone who's extremely inspired with ideas oozing out of them who doesn't need to ingest anything else since the last thing they need is even more ideas. On the opposite side is a more experienced artist who's empty from creating so much that they no longer have enough inspiration to make anything that lives up to their standards. Also on this side of the spectrum are those who are new to creating in a format that don't have enough inspiration to make resonant work. They've yet to take in enough nutrition to perspire a new expression they find emotionally resonant. Most artists are in need of some inspiration in the many different facets of creation, so the idea of just getting to work ignores the fact that much of the work is getting inspired.

To muddy the waters even more, some songs come right out of us in a seamless flow whereas others are struggles to find what we're trying to express. This can be confusing, to say the least, but the most common reason a song isn't meeting our standards is the inspiration hasn't come to us on how to express ourselves to paint the emotional picture we're trying to convey. To realize it, there's a variety of practices needed to get it out into the world if we want to continually sustain the ability to easily express the inspiration within us.

Research Is Part Of The Process

"Waiting for the muse is a bunch of bullshit – you need to go out there and find it." — **Molly Crabapple**

No one would ever tell you to write a book or a movie without doing research. But in music for some reason, the word research is bad. There's an idea in musicians' circles that if you're listening to anything but your favorite song, you're committing a mortal sin against art. **Inspiration is research, only in a much more fun and interesting way.** In fact, the two terms are laughably similar in definition with practices that are nearly identical. The difference is when we say inspiration, it seems so much more fun since getting inspired is a largely enjoyable process. But research – as someone who just finished reading 450 pages of scientific studies on creativity, I can tell you it's one of the most boring things you can do.

If you read articles on how a musician made a record, you'll hear them talking about "crate diving" or having intense listening sessions. Nile Rodgers talked about doing research for David Bowie's record *Let's Dance* in his memorial to Bowie: "For the next few weeks, we went on an art search. We were looking for inspiration: what would this album, which would end up being called *Let's Dance*, sound like? We didn't know. So we just went out and started researching. This being way before the internet, we actually went to the New York Public Library and to people's houses who had large record collections. We also went to record stores to go bin-diving."

Along the way, this research won't be all fun, as Albert Einstein said, "If we knew what we were doing, we wouldn't call it research." I joke that no one listens to more music than me to not enjoy 99% of what I hear. Every week I'll listen to a dozen or so records while I work that I greatly dislike. This isn't out of some sort of musical masochism. Instead, I listen to a lot of music to find inspiring thoughts to apply to my work. Part of my job as a producer is to understand the inspiration my collaborators are taking in so I can make them happy with what we create. I need to have an inordinately large musical vocabulary to understand how I can help express their vision.

The ride of research is about discovering what you don't like just as much as it is about what you do like. Just as you wouldn't expect everything you read when researching a term paper for school to be worth putting in your paper, this process also explores what not to do. Part of research is taking in some inspiration you dismiss as well as ideas you feel passionate towards that you investigate further. Just as we talked about when finding your voice, figuring out what you don't want to do by finding why music isn't emotionally resonant to you can be more helpful than knowing what you want to do.

Steal From Your Favorite Thieves

One of the worst fictions of being creative is that to make good music, you must never steal, otherwise you're not creative or original (which are somehow synonymous). If you hear someone else's idea and apply it yours — no matter how creative the recontextualization — you must be a hack. The first mistake of this thought is a concern with how your music is received instead of making the music you want to hear. The second mistake is that there's never been a song where an educated ear can't spot an inspiration point.

Anyone who's made "original" music that's a breath of fresh air knows where their influences come from. They view their own work as being quite derivative, since they know exactly how those influences shaped their creation. These influences are either not the common influences everyone is used to or they possess diverse enough influences that it doesn't sound derivative of one single artist. They've learned a vast vocabulary of inspiration to draw from so that it doesn't sound like an imitation. A common creative quote attributed to a handful of people is: "Steal from one author, it's plagiarism; steal from a hundred, it's inspiration."

A perfect example of how inspiration can be both veiled and obvious at once is the classic Beastie Boys' song "Girls." While the lyrics are excessively sexist (*to put it kindly*), there's no doubt this song was solidified as a classic a long time ago. But until producer Rick Rubin revealed it, you'd never know that the song form is stolen from The Isley Brothers' ubiquitous song "Shout." While the song doesn't share the same chord structure, emotional intent, tempo or lyrical content, it imitates the form by saying "girls" instead of "shout" in between every phrase. Had Rubin gone to his grave with that, few listeners would have ever noticed. Whether or not you know the inspiration, the song is still thoroughly enjoyable.

The takeaway from this example is the use of one small element from an influence applied perfectly to a very well researched sound. Since they draw far more from hip-hop influences and, in this song's case, childhood nursery rhymes and frat boy clichés, the influence of The Isley Brothers song is hidden in this recontextualization until the inspiration is exposed. The inspiration helped further the song's intent while being thoroughly disguised among a collage of influences.

Expanding Upon Great Ideas

"Amateur artists imitate; great artists steal" is a famous quote that sounds great but neglects the way great artists interact with their influences. For example, take the influence The Beach Boys and The Beatles had on each other. Brian Wilson was famously blown away by The Beatles' *Rubber Soul*, specifically that it contained no "filler tracks" or covers. The Beach Boys were still filling albums with padding for singles and cover songs, so *Rubber Soul's* elevated creative height struck Wilson as a new mark he had to hit. The innovation in *Rubber Soul* was groundbreaking at the time, so Wilson responded by crafting *Pet Sounds*. The Beatles then heard *Pet Sounds* and responded with *Sgt. Peppers*. Paul McCartney would later say, "Without *Pet Sounds*, *Sgt. Pepper* wouldn't have happened ... *Pepper* was an attempt to equal *Pet Sounds*."

When gaining inspiration, a musician will ask, "How can I do something just like this?" What they should be asking is how can they do work that improves upon this with their own strengths, tastes and emotional intent? As a creator, learning to hear the ideas an artist is expressing by elaborating on them with other influences is the key to making worthwhile work. Instead of imitating, try to gain a vision on how this can be improved upon within your voice by drawing from what's emotionally resonant to you.

Research Helps You Obtain Vision
Musicians are often unaware that playing a part softer in a vulnerable soft song will help elaborate on the emotion they're trying to convey or composing large dynamics in their song will help reinforce a dichotomy evident in their lyrics. They can't even hear the little inflections in their favorite music since they haven't studied it sufficiently. They've never heard the difference between a soft drum hit to start a song and a big one that determines emotion. They don't know the nuance of a dark cymbal making the mood of a song darker than a bright one. Too many musicians have never put the time in to hear what emotions they can convey by playing a different gauge of string, using less treble on their tone, or putting a quiver or more breath on their vocal. They simply hope it works out instead of choosing intentionally.

Research allows you to obtain this vision. As you research, you can begin to find the subtle shades in sound that can help your vision of how to express yourself emotionally. If you know the tools at your disposal, you can expand on performances to reinforce your emotional intent.

Being Fluent Gives You The Ability To Express Your Authentic Emotions

As we do research, we learn the tools available to express our emotions; the more tools you understand how to use, the easier it is to find the right one to express yourself with. Since we respond to the authentic expression of emotions, it's crucial to understand how you develop the ability to express yourself. Fluency is the ability to draw from inspiration by turning it into the expression of our emotions. This skill is important to express yourself authentically since you need a wide vocabulary to express your emotions. If you're trying to tell someone how you feel yet you only know a hundred words, it can be hard to describe the complicated nuance of emotion you feel. Fluency allows us to express the emotion we're trying to convey as authentically as possible since we have more tools to describe this emotion.

The greatest creators are always fluent in what they make. It isn't a passing interest they're lightly interested in. When a musician has a limited amount of fluency, it's obvious to everyone listening. They have a limited palette to express themselves with and it shows by making a less potent expression. This is what regularly leads to being perceived as derivative or imitating since the tools being used aren't diverse enough, therefore the origin is easy to see. When they're well researched, there's a huge lexicon of inspiration to draw from. The embodiment of fluency is the ability to draw from hundreds of sources instead of a few. If they have a limited lexicon of research, the expression is less potent since they can't find the most effective devices to express their emotions with.

Chance Favors The Connected Mind

"Talent hits a target no one else can hit. Genius hits a target no one else can see." — **Arthur Schopenhauer**

When we see someone create something amazing, we often have no idea how anyone could even come up with it. The first time you hear "Master Of Puppets," "Bombs Over Baghdad" or "Come To Daddy," it's easy to ask yourself how anyone could even craft a song like that. But there's usually an explanation for it; the artist is fluent in their craft, so they're able to make connections which they can then express in ways those who aren't as fluent can't understand. It's said that Einstein wasn't the best physicist of his time, but he saw everything instead of knowing everything. He had a great oversight of knowledge that was able to connect things others couldn't understand from being fluent in many aspects of science.

One of the common assumptions made of successful musicians is they lucked into it. While they may be lucky, more often than not luck is mistaken for knowing how to make the best of life's circumstances by seeing what others don't see. While you'll occasionally see a musician succeed as a one-hit wonder or have a short career, the musicians who continually make great music are more fluent than others. They know when to take the right chance, connect it with something else and turn it into opportunity, which is commonly mistaken for luck.

"Chance favors the connected mind." — **Steven Berlin Johnson**

This quote gave me one of my biggest epiphanies in all of my research for this book. The more you do research, the more you see how each piece of the puzzle connects together. When your mind can visualize how the pieces fit together, it can see a small piece of inspiration to take advantage of as "luck" happens to come your way. This is why luck is rarely actually luck. Instead, those who are well researched are constantly making connections others can't see that can maximize what's given to them in life to make the most of this inspiration. When you happen to be in the right place at the right time, you're able to see what's available by making something great from it by exploiting chance. This happens every time a lyricist hears a great turn of phrase that would fit perfectly in the subject of a song they're working on.

But it's not just luck. One of the reasons research is so important is it helps us develop an expertise of our creative medium. Once we gain this expertise, we can achieve more than stringing two ideas or a mosaic of a few elements together. We can piece together a vastly complicated collage of our emotions that's inspired by the makeup of our research to express what's emotionally resonant to us. **When we're fluent, we understand countless tools that we can utilize to express an emotion that enables our expression to be more resonant since we can choose the most potent tools to express ourselves with.**

Processing Creativity

Anyone who's being creative is stealing from their favorite thieves, whether or not they know it. It's not that we enjoy the most original music – we enjoy the music where creators have made enough connections to know the right ways to elaborate authentically on their emotions for the maximum amount of resonance. They have a large lexicon to draw upon when they need to make their intent as resonant as possible and are proficient in the skills to correct flaws and mistakes. When you have a limited lexicon, you draw from a limited pool of resources that aren't always the right elaboration on your intent.

Those with a vast vocabulary can find the most effective emotional tools to elicit the most potent expression of what's inside them, which is commonly perceived as "originality." Since our emotions and vocabulary are unique to ourselves, the more fluency you have in expressing yourself the less it sounds derivative. The works of those with a limited vocabulary are inherently derivative since they only have a few tools to draw from. However, for this music to be emotionally resonant, this vocabulary needs to be an expression that's elaborating upon the intent, but because there's more to draw from this also results in the sound being perceived as fresh or original.

When you only know Tiesto and Galantis' tools, you won't be able to draw upon a wide enough set of options to express yourself. Your language is so limited that to articulate yourself you'll never be able to express the nuance and detail needed to give a listener a proper understanding of an emotion. But once you learn the words and their many uses, you can begin to express how you feel even when it's complex.

This musical vocabulary can be expressed in many different palettes. Those using a traditional rock band instrumentation or the standard dance synth set need to employ different rhythms and sonic trickery to express their emotions more potently, whereas those who use different ethnic influences are incorporating other musical languages to communicate with.

Fluency In Emotional Expression Is Constantly Evolving

In James Flynn's TED Talk on IQ, he talks about how the average IQ of each generation is about 30 points higher than their grandparent's generation. Despite the internet being full of articles on how each generation is getting dumber from various ailments – video games, iPhones, Snapchat or whatever advancement conservatives who wish it was 1950 are pretending poisoned our society – *the science doesn't agree*. What Flynn describes is our grandparents never talked in hypotheticals. Instead, the most common expression was plain language and the occasional light metaphor thrown in for relation. The way we're able to convey emotions to relate the human condition is constantly evolving, and we're becoming more fluent in how to relate it to one another.

Everyone has had thoughts they can't figure out how to express. As we're able to build on the vocabulary of others who learn how to express a thought we've been trying to say, it becomes easier to express new ideas as we learn to talk about them fluently. As we begin to understand the world better by figuring out a more macro understanding of emotions, we develop new ways to express how we feel. A decade ago the fear of missing out (FOMO) was rarely discussed or expressed concisely, now it's one of the most common emotions expressed by artists today (take a look at this Google trend chart to watch it continually grow and inevitably decline as the concept becomes obvious). As we figure out emotional shorthand, we learn to elaborate on thoughts that bear greater resonance to our present experiences.

Our musical instruments also evolve to create new envelopes and tones, which can express emotion in new ways as these new sounds sound closer to what our emotions feel like. The sound of distorted guitar opened up the doors to express more aggressive sounds in music, and the invention of the sampler allowed all sorts of lyrical narratives to be painted in hip-hop. As instruments evolve, we can make new sounds that express emotions in greater resonances. The way we express ourselves is constantly evolving through lineages of inspiration. For example, you can't have a Daft Punk record without Kraftwerk coming first and Detroit techno after them, since it would seem too weird and noisy. Without Daft Punk, you skip the inspiration for Justice and then Skrillex. With each subsequent year, the way we're expressing ourselves becomes more and more complex. By hearing possibility, we're influenced by it and continue to build off the new possibilities shown to us by those we're inspired by.

Just as The Beatles went from love songs to talking about spiritual enlightenment in less than a decade, we're forever evolving the complexity of discussing the human condition. We're furthering our discussion of the nuances of life. Every year our language evolves to talk about more complex feelings in more detailed ways. It's commonly said that lyrics are emotional shortcuts and as we begin to understand what they hold, clichéd shortcuts lose their resonance. To express new emotional territory, you have to devote yourself to become fluent. There's a reason there's rarely a moderate-selling record that employs only a single instrument and voice. Our need for more complex emotional elaboration deepens as we get used to artists finding ways to further the emotions we want to be comforted with using more narrative tools, so we continuously crave new ways to express emotions. While there are classics that never die as well as those who appreciate this simplicity, the vast majority of us are looking for new heights to be hit in emotional power.

The Low Hanging Fruit Is Gone

It can seem pretty ridiculous how little creative output musicians release today. Releasing a dozen songs every two or three years is a pretty common occurrence for established artists. Looking back on artists of the past, this is at an all time low (let's remember The Beatles' entire catalog occurred in nearly seven years and they recorded about 275 songs). Once the Ramones and The Clash had their intent down, it was easy to crank out four classic records in about three years. With classical composers, you'd have Beethoven — who's not even in the top five in this measure — churning out 110 minutes of music every single year. This is not to say that an artist that's turning out a large quantity always results in high quality work, but with these outliers that was the case.

One of the reasons we see this slowdown in output is the immense amount of time it takes many artists to contemplate an expression that isn't overly derivative. Most of the low hanging fruit in creativity is gone today, so artists now need more time to develop a large understanding of music since the most simple emotions of the past have already been expressed. Today, if you wrote a song with an emotional expression at the level of The Beatles' "She Loves You" you'd be laughed right out of existence even at a fifth-grade recital since that expression is taken for granted as being a given. While "In My Life" is one of the most thoughtful and beautiful expressions of love ever written, it has been expressed countless times and anyone looking to do this sentiment needs to find a new way to do it since that ground has already been tread heavily.

The common complaint in classical music today is that every new work ends up being avant-garde since there's no new emotional ground to express in "classical classical" music's multi-century existence (*this is also caused by most would-be classical composers creating IDM and other forms of electronic music, but that's another story for another time*). To make music resonant, we must dig deeper than some of the more obvious themes made in the music of yesterday. We need to find new ways to express ourselves, since hearing the same musical conversation over and over again gets boring.

You'll see this evidenced in pop records that regularly employ 50+ producers and songwriters. While internet memes will mock this throughout your Facebook feed, there's a reason for this that has a parallel in science. Before 1975 there were plenty of lone wolf inventors who made great strides innovating scientific breakthroughs, but now that we've discovered most of the low hanging fruit of innovation, we need contributors who are experts in multiple disciplines to make innovative creations. The same has happened with music today. To make music that's resonant to the masses, a few heads are usually needed. The pop groups of yesteryear wrote amazing songs, but we're tired of those songs. We crave new emotions and, since the bar for emotional communication has been raised, it becomes more difficult for a single creator to have all of the skills to evoke a new emotional expression. The cumulative skills of these collaborators may not always be necessary but are a faster route to an inspired output that achieves the results record companies want, which is sales.

The innovators of every genre never had it easy. To express an emotion within them, they had to become fluent in their expression to give us new heights of resonance. You can trace this back to their pedigrees. The Beatles played covers for thousands of hours in Hamburg, learning every tool of emotional expression in the book available for rock instruments. Mozart's most famous work was #25; becoming fluent in his expression took many lackluster works. The Ramones changed the sound of music despite many cynics equating it to an accident from a bunch of dumb guys from Queens. It was no accident. While their songs seem simple to play, the true intensity of the Ramones was derived from Johnny Ramone's innovation of doing all down strokes that brought a new aggression to music. He developed this sound by disciplining himself to play only down strokes; after being a bass player in the past, it was easier for him to deal with the smaller gauge of strings to handle this expression most musicians shied away from.

Just as the simple one-word band names are all gone, so are many of the simple ways of expressing an idea. As time goes on you need greater fluency to make emotionally resonant work since we crave new ways to comfort our emotions. Barely a decade ago, artists rarely had access to good quality reverb. Now, every computer can include it for a few hundred dollars. As we get access to a larger palette, we find more ways to express our emotions. To hit new heights, we need to form ways of expressing ourselves that are more complex than those of the past.

Those developing new emotional resonances in electronic music are spending hundreds of hours in front of a computer composing a track. In rock music, they have to gain such a large fluency of a genre to evoke new emotions that it becomes more rare each year. This is why the artists who win the Grammy for rock these days are rarely expressing themselves with traditional rock instruments. The low hanging fruit is gone, so for there to be any resonance among the masses, they need to discover a whole new way of communicating with different tools.

Since the low hanging fruit has already been plucked, we need to gain more fluency than previous generations of musicians to express ourselves. We, as listeners, want to hear more resonant expressions of an emotion. To do so today, you can't just come up with three chords on a guitar in a simple strumming pattern like The Rolling Stones used to. We've heard people express themselves with tools that elaborate upon emotion further than this can convey. This is why music is ever evolving. You need to become familiar with the vast amount of tools available to find how to reach higher levels of resonance.

Finding Inspiration

The Possibility Of Possibility

Science has observed that creativity is inspired by "the possibility of possibility." When you see others coming up with creative ideas you'd never think of, you're suddenly inspired by what's possible for you to do. Take, for example, a study showing that people are more creative if they listen to standup comedy before doing a creative endeavor. Standup comedy is one of the ultimate forms of creativity since it commonly strings together connections that others haven't thought of to make us laugh through a fast-paced exposure of the possibility of connecting thoughts to form a new work. For artists and directors working in visual mediums, music is often the catalyst for a vision of what's possible, just as musicians often take inspiration from visual works.

The same goes for why taking a walk helps us be more creative. Seeing all the different stimuli in the world makes your brain aware of the possibility of possibility. This exposure allows your brain to free associate to make new connections. Our brains are given a constant dose of possibility when we observe the various wonders of the world and see the many ways someone has been creative. I find that if I watch an experimental movie or see an inspiring piece of art, I'll have a much easier time creating. Getting your creative juices flowing is about giving it the nutrient of what's possible. If you feed yourself with a nutritious bit of small inspiration beforehand, the ideas will come to you more easily.

The possibility of possibility gets even bigger. Whenever a new genre or movement happens in music, you'll see numerous musicians come to it at the same time. The same goes for technology, which is why we see clusters of inventors doing the same innovations at the same time. As we see what's possible from one creator, a handful of others get inspired by the same creator and expand upon their idea. In music we hear new heights emotions can be taken to and figure out how to expand upon them with our own emotional tools.

Reverse Engineering (Also Known As Learning Cover Songs)

In hardware or software development, it's illegal to reverse engineer another person's work. For the Luddites out there, if you open up computer code to learn how an engineer made a piece of technology and then do a few tweaks to it, you're breaking the law. Designers are taught in school that they can grab the color scheme from another work in Photoshop and tons of other tools to reverse engineer the way a design was put together. Everyone with even a cursory knowledge of music is always happy to point out that The Beatles started as a cover band.

The way we figure out how to express ourselves emotionally is examining other songs that have given us a similar emotion, then figuring out what can be applied to the new song we're going to make. Covering songs can be fun, but deconstructing and observing what makes them tick is some of the best research you can do.

This also works for the songs you don't like. Whenever you hear a song that doesn't sound right to you, you should figure out how you'd fix it. This can help inspire you on the tools that'll develop your own songs. Inspiration is learning tools that allow you to be fluent in expression, and this technique is one of the fastest ways to gain fluency in these tools. While this is cursory knowledge for most artists, it can be overlooked that you should continually reverse engineer what makes your favorite songs tick so you can figure out how to express your intent with the tools your favorite artists use.

Creative Fan Fiction

One of my favorite exercises is to get an album by a band I love and open a blank session on my computer. I listen to a verse and then write what I imagine the chorus might be before hearing theirs. I may listen to one song and then mess around to figure out what I'd do for the next song on the album. Hearing the difference between theirs and mine usually inspires a totally different idea that I can later apply elsewhere.

The group Spoon says after singer Britt Daniel makes a demo, they'll think about what filter they can apply to the idea. They may consider what Dr. Dre or Elvis Costello would do with a song to parse how to apply that influence to a song that isn't a direction that the inspirational artist would normally do. Inspiration is commonly finding an influence you admire to figure out how to apply what you enjoy about them to your own compositions. While this practice is mistaken as imitation, if you pull from a wide variety of influences in all of your songs you end up with a collage that resembles who you are. If you're choosing properly, it'll be choices that augment your emotional intent.

Inspiration From Collaboration

When you hear stories of the most classic rock bands, <u>pop stars</u> or even <u>Daft Punk</u>, you'll hear talk of how important it was to listen to music with their collaborators. The discussion of what they find inspiring and how it can be brought into their intent is one of the best ways to do resonant work. This collaborative research is now often pushed to the wayside with tight budgets and limited time. Today, artists don't schedule the time to communally listen to the records they love to bring the parts of music they enjoy from others into their own music.

This research not only gets everyone on the same page, but hearing the different ideas collaborators extract from the music you're using for inspiration leads to great epiphanies. Finding collaborators to discuss mutual inspiration points with can reward you with insight that leads to huge artistic breakthroughs. In my time producing records, collaborative research and the discussion of what each person hears can exponentially increase the resonance as each collaborator brings different observations and expertise.

Find Inspiration Inside Your Own Work

Inspiration can even come from what's already in your song. Rick Rubin <u>says</u> Eminem often finds his cadences from rhythms already in the song, "He hears internal rhythms in tracks ... his phrasing is glued to the music that if small details are changed, it ruins the interaction." Listening to what's already in a song to find ways to change up existing melodies and rhythms can help reinforce hooks inherent in the song. This goes for listening to your past work as well. Hearing how you didn't do something right and figuring out how to improve upon it in the future is often the genesis of ideas that are in line with our intent.

Inspiration On Display

"Collect books, even if you don't plan on reading them right away. Nothing is more important than an unread library."
— John Waters

A common trait among creators is to have some of your favorite creations on display to be reminded of them. It's common to keep books on a bookshelf where you most often look to be reminded of the ideas inside them. The same can go for posters, vinyl and other physical media for music. Maintaining playlists of the music you've enjoyed can be employed to remind yourself of where you've found inspiration. Having a reminder of those you respect in sight keeps them on your mind to remember what you should consider in your work.

Shaking Up Inspiration

A lot of the research I talk about here is very deliberate and nerdy, but there are far more fun ways to gain inspiration. Brian Eno's Oblique Strategies cards allow you to draw a card that you agree to pursue the intent of in advance. These cards contain instructions like, "don't be afraid of clichés," "simple subtraction" and "abandon normal instruments." These cards are meant to give you a random way to leave your comfort zone with imaginative prompts to find new inspiration.

There are tons of ways to shake up inspiration outside the normal methods we are commonly told. David Bowie would write chords on a chalkboard and point to them at odd times for musicians to change chords. He'd later take the best bits to work into songs. You can devise all sorts of games and exercises to get odd outcomes and find how to build them into your songs where they're emotionally appropriate.

Your Inspiration Diet

Just as you'll only be as healthy as what you eat and your exercise regimen, your creative output is dependent on the inspiration you take in and how regularly you perspire (just as you perspire during your workout). Since inspiration is akin to nutrition in this analogy, your music will be the product of what you listen to the most. If it's what everyone else is listening to, you're more likely to make music that doesn't find new resonances. If you're taking in new inspiration from uncommon places in music, it'll bring on inspired work.

Right about now you're probably thinking "but what if I only like rock or pop that's on the radio?" Well, that may be resonant to you, but to make music that has new heights of resonance you'll need to dig deeper. To find new ways to express the emotions in you, you need to find new ways to explain how you feel. The palette of only understanding what's currently popular won't allow you to discover the most resonant expression of your emotions. Most musicians who only enjoy what's on the radio are that way because they've yet to do the research to find more tools that could be emotionally resonant to them. Instead, they settle on what's easiest to consume by flicking on their car stereo rather than taking the time to get to know the many other influences their favorite artists have consumed.

I'm not saying to make good Afro-beat music you should superfluously listen to classical music and EDM on a regular basis. This research doesn't need to be diverse in genres, but if you're going to stick to one or two genres, make sure you know those genres exhaustively. This can take effort for some and isn't always easy. Simply turning to the classics or what's popular won't be enough. You need to search until you find influences that are resonant to you and explore them to become fluent with all the tools at your disposal to express yourself with.

There's a balance to strike between being authentic and doing this superfluously. Forcing repeated listens to Mahavishnu Orchestra to get better musical ideas can be good for some musicians, but forcing that influence into your music when it has no resonance with you leads to making inauthentic drivel. Being weird for weird's sake or "inspired" for inspired's sake won't lead to resonant music. We won't love everything we ingest, but we need to continually find what we can take from what we find resonant. It's healthy to try new inspirations in an exploration to find who we are, but forcing yourself to get inspired by music you think will give your music a great depth doesn't make it emotionally resonant.

Making Sure Your Inspiration Is Properly Nourished

There's a famous saying that gets tossed around stating that you're the product of the five friends you hang out with the most. In finance, there's a similar adage that you're as rich as the five people you talk to the most. This also goes for musical influence. What you listen to the most largely shapes the songs you write. With years of music listening, this can be diminished down to what you listened to over the course of your life, but for beginners, this is especially crucial since you don't have years of accumulating influence, standards and palette to draw from.

After establishing that inspiration is research, we need to recognize that you should be conscious of the inspiration you're taking in as if it were a diet. When I'm trying to get inspired for a record, I try to consider my inspiration diet to nurture myself so I'm sufficiently ready to perspire. This is what I consider so I'm on the best possible diet for a project:

Favorites vs. Fresh - It's easy to get lost in your favorite records since getting to know them is some of the most important listening you can do to figure out what you love about them. Plus, it feels great to listen to them. But you also need to be taking in new records to gain fresh ideas. Even if these records weren't recorded in recent years, you need to continue to get inspired by new source material. The inverse can be true by focusing on new records versus exploring your favorites to figure out what makes them tick. If I give a concentrated listen to many of my favorite records, even after listening to them for decades, I can still find new details from them to get inspired by – but there's nothing like fresh, new ideas to get you inspired.

The Greats vs. The Local Trash - For every one of your favorite local groups doing amazing music that the world may never hear, there are ten other bands in the scene who aren't that special but get listened to far too much. I've seen many musicians get lost in listening to their friend's music that's just poorly done versions of great bands. This particular affliction goes especially for bands who only listen to the other bands they tour with. It drives their standards down, which makes them think subpar ideas are great, instead of getting used to the high standards, they need to achieve what the best musicians have.

Bells and Whistles vs. Solid Songs - On some records, an artist can be filled with inspiration for song structures and hooks but lacking in how to do the moody soundscapes they hope to explore. I'll often go on an inspiration diet depending on what a band needs from me. If a band needs help coming up with soundscapes, I may end up listening to Mars Volta, Clinic, The Talking Heads and Chrome to get ideas of what we could do. If they need help with song structures, I'll listen to artists with inventive structures. If the band has a mind for those bells and whistles, I may try to get into the mind of their favorite songwriters to make sure we stay focused on solid songs. Consider where you feel deficient inspiration-wise and consciously take in inspiration that'll help nurture what you need on a project.

Intentionally Take In Inspiration

"If you stuff yourself full of poems, essays, plays, short stories, novels, films, comic strips, magazines and music, you'll automatically explode every morning like Old Faithful. I've never had a dry period in my life because I feed myself well." — **Ray Bradbury**

If you're feeling drastically uninspired, it's time to go down the inspiration family tree of reading interviews with your favorite creators to see what inspired them. Perhaps click on the Related Artists section of your favorite group's Spotify or see who MetaCritic says they're similar to. Observe this family tree to see who your favorite acts are influenced by, check out who they're compared to on review sites or research the acts they wear shirts from. Make a playlist and give each song a few listens to try to find their merits.

Fasting To Get Inspired

"Removing all stimulation around you is a really positive thing in terms of stimulating your creativity." — **Grimes**

Just as we talked about inspiration being a diet that requires nutrition, you can also do a cleanse or a fast to get creative results. While you need inspirational nutrition to get inspired, there can also be a time in the process where you need to abstain from inspiration so you're not influenced by others. Many songwriters become thoroughly inspired and then isolate themselves in an intense famine when they start writing. By keeping a distance from their influences, nothing comes out that's too derivative. This regularly occurs after an inspiration period during the early shaping of their songs and ends when they need to get inspired on how to complete a few final details.

This famine can even go for expressing yourself as well. Robert Smith told me during the making of The Cure's classic record *Disintegration* that he wouldn't speak to anyone all day. He could ask someone to pass the salt, but he wouldn't fulfill his need to get feedback from other humans on his emotions. Without his ability to communicate, when he wrote his lyrics, he'd have an extreme thirst to communicate how he felt. This technique was also applied when he did his vocals for the record. It would leave him dying to express himself by the time he hit the mic each day to sing. It goes without saying that the desperation to connect resonates through the recording of an album known for being one of the saddest records ever made.

For all three books I've written, I've written down as many thoughts I can think of on the subject as I can get out before I start my research to not have the established books in the genre cloud my judgment and own unique voice. I then begin to read other books on the subject to get new inspiration and figure out how to reconsider what I've come up with after the main form is shaped.

I also employ this famine when I mix records for artists where I wasn't involved in the recording process. I'll mix the song the way I hear it and then listen to the rough mix the band had as well as the reference mixes they give me of other artists after I try out my natural instinct. If the rough mix or references make me think my mix can get better, I bring in all those elements. I trust my gut along the way to decide what influences I should take in but don't allow my objectivity to get influenced by others, so I can form what's emotionally resonant to myself first. This allows me to give a fresh perspective to the project but then blend it with whatever other influences they may have had to get the best of both worlds.

Inspiration From Other Disciplines

One of the most overlooked ways to get inspired is from other disciplines. In practice, this is architects learning from filmmakers who talk about how much improvisation they do on the set or about how they re-think form in their discipline, evolving it by picking up useful techniques from other creative disciplines. This is why you see Kanye West talking about being inspired by Steve Jobs, Steve McQueen and Stanley Kubrick. Much of this book I drew from the ideas of business bloggers, photographers and directors as much as I drew from musicians. If you work in other creative outlets, you can apply these processes to whatever field you create in.

Every skill I've learned in record production makes writing a book easier. I've learned I should capture my ideas while I'm in a flow state and then edit and draft later, just as I do when writing music. If you're fluent in creating in another craft, it can often help your expression skills manifest in unique ways that allow you to add resonance others aren't fluent in. In every book on the subject of creativity, this is a skill noted in every creator who has gone on to do work that changes the way we see a discipline.

Metaphor Quotient

In science, there's a concept called field theory where you take a theory or technique that works in one field of science and apply it to another. To apply field theory to your work, you need to develop the ability to observe how you can apply what you see in one field to another field. The ability is measured by Metaphor Quotient (MQ). Just like IQ (Intelligence Quotient), MQ is the ability to apply metaphors into your art, whereas IQ is the measure of intelligence. MQ is the measurement of how well you can apply metaphors to your art. MQ manifests itself in countless ways. Here are a few examples:

- Honing in on your ability to see the creative process of someone in a different field and apply it your own.
- Seeing how one lyricist applies a metaphor and figuring out how to do that yourself in a different way.
- Hearing a rhythm in your radiator and applying it to a song.
- Finding the roots of a word or a concept and finding other ways to recontextualize it in your lyrics.
- Finding metaphorical sound effects to help emphasize your lyrical narrative.

In her book *The Creative Habit*, Twyla Tharp talks about the importance of Metaphor Quotient as it inspires new ideas that aren't obvious. She even argues that MQ is as valuable as IQ in the creative process. The best songwriters and producers commonly cite movie director advice (this is a recurring theme on my podcast where I interview record producers) as being inspirational to the way they work. You can always catch an insightful mind knowing many great quotes as compared to those who can't see past their nose thinking the world "is what it is" or whatever reductive statement of the moment idiots use. Artists who purposefully seek out metaphors and then apply them to their work can fluently express their intent.

One of the reasons this concept isn't discussed is because there's no real way to measure it on a scale since it's too wild, so any measure is purely observational. Since our fluency varies so much from medium to medium, MQ is hard to pinpoint on a simple test. For example, my brain can take business practices and see how they work in music or film in an instant, yet the second you talk to me about how a painting's color subtly express an emotion, the whole idea is lost upon me. I've never taken the time to learn the intricacies of expression in visual form so my MQ is very low in fine arts. While I'm fluent in one field, I'm nearly blind in another.

Many great creators consider the field they're known for to be their second discipline. Kurt Cobain, Lars Von Trier and David Lynch all consider themselves to be artists more than musicians or filmmakers despite being renowned as some of the most innovative people in their fields. Outsider art is cited as being the example of inexperienced creators being able to make great creations, but the key to outsider art is that those who do it well have a high MQ and are applying field theory to a new field. High proficiency in one field can be applied to others.

Improving Your MQ

MQ is one of those few skills no one is born with. It's instead learned and can be developed with practice. In Daniel Pink's *A Whole New Mind* he suggests "Improve your MQ by writing down compelling and surprising metaphors you encounter." Watch movies to find subtle hints like film noir showing characters that are conflicted or lying are lit with their face in both the light and dark. Reading interviews with artists who are highly metaphoric or take the time to observe details in great artists' work can bring out your metaphor quotient.

A habit that helps me develop my metaphor quotient along with an understanding of artistic growth is to take in my favorite artists' work in series. I'll watch all of my favorite director's movies in a row (even the movies I don't enjoy) or listen to my favorite musician's records in chronological order (including the B-sides). This practice allows me to take in their tools and details to understand the correlations in the metaphorical tools they use. I watch a few of their movies in a day or one every few days, but I do it in as short a period as I can to keep the correlations fresh in my mind. If I understand their earlier work, it helps me understand the greater depths of expression they achieve later.

Most importantly, when I do this, I concentrate. I don't look at my phone unless the work is on pause. I don't do bills while they're on as I try to see the details in what I may have missed before when taking them in casually. When I do this with music, I make sure to have headphones on so I can take in as much of the details as possible, so I'm influenced by as little outside sound as possible. I try to ingest as many metaphors and hidden subtleties in their work as I possibly can.

While my approach to this is a bit academic for some of my friends, it can be applied to some of the most annoying moments in life. When you're dragged to see a movie, hear a song from a genre you don't appreciate or have to go to a museum you have no interest in, make the most of it to find what you can learn from the metaphors in use throughout these works. Not only will it make the time less miserable, but you may even get inspired.

Inspiration Shapes Your Palette

Your palette is one of the most determinative factors in what your music sounds like. One of the main ways inspiration affects creators is learning both what they do and don't want in their palette. Hearing others' music to decide what tools to use is one of the most defining aspects of what your music sounds like. Think back to the most basic example of palette, in the 1950s recording studios didn't have instruments on hand for musicians to explore their every indulgence. Unless you knew someone who played an instrument, you couldn't use that instrument as part of your palette for a recording. Since the 80s, as sampling technology became prominent, musicians have been able to employ any sound they can think of. Most sounds now come stock within a Mac laptop that costs $900.

Not everyone wants to be The Flaming Lips, Beck or The Polyphonic Spree, who will use any instrument in the world to create with. Instead, most artists paint with a smaller palette of instruments. EDM artists mostly use synthesizers while punk bands rarely dare to exceed the guitar, bass, drums and vocal format. Hip-hop producers who largely sample will keep their palette limited to sampling specific genres and instruments to keep their palette within their tastes and certain flavors.

Being conscious of your palette can have many benefits for your music. Many studies on the subject show those who impose limitations on themselves end up with a more creative result. To some artists, knowing every instrument is an option can create an eye-opening world of experimentation. Others experience option paralysis and benefit from the focus of limitations. If you're Jack White, you see the challenge of not using the editing tools inside a computer program and a 16-24 track tape machine's limits as being what excites you. He knows he has to make the most of the limitations he's imposed on himself using a finite amount of tools to accomplish his intent.

There's an artistic cliché that goes, "Don't be held down by the palette everyone else paints with." While this saying encourages some artists to superfluously use different instruments, it's really trying to tell you not to feel bound to the same old tools as everyone else. Figuring out the instruments and tonalities that help express your emotional intent is a large part of what makes you unique. Figure out who you are and what parts of palettes you like to employ for research into your music.

Palette can be taken to many other examples than just tone and instrumental use. The arrangement, syncopation, harmonization and production tricks in your lexicon give you a greater vocabulary to use to express your intent. This is an essential reason research is crucial to your work.

Chapter 8: Incubation, Flow States And Retention

After we're inspired, our ideas aren't always ready to perspire. Our minds usually need a bit of time to do further development so that when we're ready to perspire, it can pour out of us effectively.

Where "Random" Ideas And Sudden Epiphanies Really Come From
"Creativity is the residue of wasted time" — **Albert Einstein**

One of the worst parts of short articles, memes and the rest of today's internet culture is that we rarely hear all of the amazing details within these stories. The part of the story left on the cutting room floor is usually an idea that was being tinkered with in the creator's head, both consciously and subconsciously, since it's pretty boring to show a person thinking in a movie.

A great idea never comes to anyone that hasn't been doing some research. It's not possible to understand how to execute an idea unless you've been tinkering with related concepts. Even though we can't always trace where ideas come from, we know they don't come from the ether or the blessing of a muse. Ideas go through an incubation period where your mind isn't thinking about the idea you had in a way that's evident to you. Instead, your mind is toying with this idea in the background to make connections that can later lead to an epiphany. This semi-distracted state where you're partaking in menial tasks allows your mind to nurture your hunches into epiphanies.

The apple falling on Newton's head when he discovered gravity was not some divine epiphany; it is a myth. Instead, he was tinkering with an insane breadth of work in physics and this was the chance encounter that stimulated his connected mind. A famous case of this is Charles Darwin talking as if he thought of his theory of evolution in a sudden epiphany. Historians studying Darwin later went through his journals to find he was slowly coming to this "epiphany" <u>over months and months of research</u>. The same went for Tim Berners-Lee when he invented what would become the world wide web. For ten years he was making concepts that were close to the hyperlinks and connectivity the web is built on.

Most great ideas get developed over time. The idea for a great song may not be so great when you first build the skeleton. But, with a few more great ideas, this could be a song that becomes your best work. Great work won't fall on top of your head just by chance - it involves development.

How To Get Your Brain Into An Incubation Mode

Graham Wallas' _The Art of Thought_ made one of the first attempts to define how the creative process works. One point he made in the book is that usually, a great idea has a lead-up to it. Then, after the initial idea is formed, there's a subconscious period where the idea incubates and you finally see how to put it into practice. You shouldn't expect that once you get a great idea it will be fully formed or immediately executable. Continuing to take in inspiration while tinkering with your ideas helps your mind develop these hunches into more realized ideas. You can even nurture the incubation of ideas by using a variety of techniques.

Musicians are regularly accused of being lazy (_my last book may have done it a dozen times_), but what looks like laziness is often incubation. To incubate ideas, the brain needs to be in a state that's not fully engaged while paying slight attention to another task. This is evidenced in University of California research, which found that "engaging in simple external tasks that allow the mind to wander may facilitate creative problem solving."

Many scientists believe the brain in an unconscious incubation mode can actually do more complex work than when you're consciously thinking about a creative work. This means taking a break when you get frustrated can give you the time you need to further develop an idea. Taking walks, exercising, commuting and that odd state you're in when half awake in the morning or at night is when so many of the best ideas come out, since your brain is in a state where it can subconsciously nurture your ideas. This semi-distracted mindset allows us to be engaged in enough thought to give our brain the resources to figure out the problems going on in our minds and later form an epiphany.

A University of Central Lancashire study found doing boring activities such as attending meetings, commuting or tedious writing exercises nurture divergent thinking. The bad news is video games and TV are too engaging for the brain to incubate. You can't force your brain to incubate a thought – all you can do is devote time to activities that encourage incubation while seeking out more inspiration that may nourish an epiphany.

Conscious Incubation

Incubation can also come in the form of consciously tinkering with ideas. A University of California study found that daydreaming allows your mind to go into incubation, which may give a clue as to why you may see your favorite musician staring into space all the time. It's said that Mozart was judged to be quiet and aloof since he never had his attention in the room he was in. When reviewing Mozart's notebooks for his scores, he had dramatically fewer cross-outs than the majority of composers, since he was constantly developing ideas in his head.

In this day and age where we're constantly looking at our phones for entertainment, we should remember that the time we spend in a state of low attentiveness is the time where our minds can play with the ideas we've been accumulating to develop them into bigger ideas. In the age of constant distraction, it becomes less common to sit alone with your thoughts, trying to connect things. Breaking the habit of looking at your phone any time something isn't holding your attention can be crucial to the nurturing of good ideas since this practice can be effective for many artists.

Flow States

An idea can be perspired once it has been inspired and incubated, and the most effective way to perspire is to enter a flow state. Ever since Mihaly Csikszentmihalyi wrote the book *Flow*, we've begun to understand this part of the creative process that's crucial to our own enjoyment as well as crafting great work. Flow is the state we get into where time seems to pass us by, as suddenly our inspiration seamlessly turns to perspiration and by the time we realize what's going on, we have a portion of our work completed. It can often be known by other names like "in the zone," "losing yourself" or "in another world."

When we talk about playing music as an escape, flow is the ultimate escape. There's a hidden gem in one of the most overly quoted parts of Steve Jobs' thought on creativity where he says, "they feel a little guilty because they didn't really do it." One of the strangest parts of flow is it runs right through us and we often can't figure out the details of how it happened. We lose track of time once we're in this state. We get inspired and take action, losing self-consciousness. Any concern for aches in our bodies, identity, problems, bills or conflict in our life disappears as we create with minimal friction.

This is also what's so addicting about flow since it can make us leave all our troubles behind as we evoke something new. What makes flow so special is we get our mind out of its own way and push out amazing ideas or performances. Without these mental blocks, we can perspire and have epiphanies that help us hit creative heights. We're at our happiest in a flow state; neurologists have seen it's a happier place than playing with kids or on vacation. They see it as a "theta state" that's akin to monks meditating.

Flow is a naturally occurring state for musicians during the creative process. The experience of flow comes in many forms. It can be writing lyrics onto a page where they seem to pour out or jamming with your band to realize it's been twenty minutes when it felt like two. Sitting in front of your computer experimenting with how to best tweak a song. Improvising lyrics for a song while on loop. If you've ever fallen in love, you've probably experienced a flow state. It's that special feeling where all of a sudden perspiration pours out of you where you can't stop expelling brilliant ideas, thoughts or a great performance that you've never said before. You don't think about your next move, it simply comes out of you in a burst of perspiration.

While flow isn't necessary to create, it allows us to do our best work. Sadly, in this day of flipping from app to app, where attention deficit disorder is seen as a given by many, flow isn't as easy to achieve when you're constantly distracted or never able to sustain a thought for more than a few minutes. Even stranger is some musicians can easily achieve flow on stage but can rarely achieve it in the studio or vice versa.

Understanding what goes into flow can help us get to these states of higher creativity.

The Ingredients To Achieving Flow

While flow is a natural occurring state for our minds, you'll need to have a few boxes checked to achieve it. The more you're able to increase the amount of these elements at your disposal, the more flow will help you to create:

Inspiration - Just as we've discussed before, perspiration cannot happen without inspiration. Flow isn't a hack that gets you around this rule. Flow allows inspiration to perspire from you effectively and without resistance.

Proficiency - To be able to get into a flow state, you can't get obstructed by your inability to carry out what your mind is trying to perspire. If you lack proficiency on the instrument or tool you're using to create with, flow will cease as you struggle and become self-conscious. The struggle to get out what you're trying to do can halt flow as you try to figure out what you're trying to communicate. This is why flow comes easier with the more proficiency you gain on an instrument or tool. With that said scientists have found flow often when works best when you are taking slight risks to exceed your abilities by challenging yourself to perform at a slightly higher level than normal.

Limitation - While flow can go far beyond what we were initially inspired by, it can help to have focus. In music, having key and tempo restrictions along with making the choice of which instrument you'll be using allows flow to be more effective.

Lack Of Distraction - When trying to get into these states, it's important to get in a distraction-free environment. The greatest killer to a flow state is a text message, knock on the door from a housemate or social media notification. Designating a time where you won't be taken out of these states is imperative for getting to this state and can help sustain creative bursts. While distractions and breaks have their purpose in creativity, you should be as free of interruption as possible when trying to perspire.

Collaborative Flow

Flow can also be collaborative. If you've ever had a conversation where ideas perspire from you that you've never put into words but you all of a sudden become funny or insightful, that's collaborative flow. Jam sessions regularly give us our best flow states. We're inspired by others to get into a flow state where we're able to feed off one another to create a new expression. In music, this collaborative flow is often in the form of improvisation. What we hear others doing is an immediate inspiration that can put us into a flow state.

One of the biggest misconceptions of improvisation is the belief that it's solely made from new thoughts that come from flow and not rehearsed parts that are up our sleeve that we can deviate from and revisit. This also illustrates one of the most important aspects of flow. Usually flow takes a bit of incubation and rehearsal beforehand, just like any other part of good music improvisation needs to achieve an intent. By picturing how your intent would sound and elaborating on past ideas that apply to this emotion, improvisation reaches its greatest heights. It's usually helpful to prepare for flow by doing some rehearsal as well as pre-meditating on your intent.

These pre-rehearsed ideas you've already thought of, but are now being expressed in a flow state of improvisation often takes them to greater heights. When a rapper freestyles, they're drawing from rhymes in their rhyme book while improvising a few aspects about the present location or foe they're up against, fitting these variables into some fixed tropes they've already rehearsed. When a jazz musician does this, they know modes, scales and keys they must stay within, as well as a melodic line that's already been established that they can vary. These ideas are contemplated and practiced for years at a time. Notorious B.I.G. didn't show up to that bodega in Bed-Stuy and freestyle without first becoming proficient in tons of rhymes as well as practicing improvisation before the camera was rolling.

Flow Usually Needs Refinement And Editing

"Dance first. Think later. It's the natural order." — **Samuel Beckett**

There's a great myth in music about how magical the first take in the studio can be. The idea is that a musician sat down and played an amazing song on the first try. Yes, to a fan of the Grateful Dead, the idea of a first take jam sounds great, but there's also a reason their fanbase is known for being stoned out of their minds. All joking aside, even the Grateful Dead would do countless takes of their songs and later edit together the best bits of their recorded material. While flow can give us some of our best ideas, they usually need to be refined once the flow state has ceased. The key is to allow flow to occur for as long as possible and then edit it after it has ended.

Since flow allows us to ignore self-doubt and criticism, it commonly needs further consideration after the state has left us. There were countless failed takes of *Kind Of Blue* before Miles Davis got the right ones to put on the album. Contrary to the belief that editing takes in Pro Tools is cheating, The Beatles were doing the very same technique on their records along with nearly every other group since recording switched from vinyl discs to tape. Harnessing flow and collecting the best bits has been the way to great music for half a century, yet somehow some musicians frown on this as if first takes and a lack of editing are akin to winning some video game instead of viewing it as a tool to get the most emotional resonance.

Making Flow Work Optimally
There are a few best practices for flow that can help you more optimally achieve this state:

Notifications Are Distractions - The iPhone has a Do Not Disturb mode where all notifications cease, allowing only those you put on a list to call you in case of emergency. For those who aren't concerned about contact from the outside world at all, airplane mode or turning your phone off works even better. Turning off wifi on your computer can also keep you from bad habits of switching away from your DAW.

A Cleared Mind - Flow only happens when you can focus and have passion, so it's less likely to occur unless the stress in your life has been dealt with. If you have trouble getting into flow, try clearing your mind by writing down your thoughts to retain whatever keeps popping up.

Guard Your Space - Put a "do not disturb" sign on your door as well as let housemates know you're not to be disturbed until you come out. Too often flow is disturbed since others don't realize it's your priority.

Isolation - Author Jonathan Franzen locks himself in a room with nothing on the walls and noise-blocking headphones. The less distractions you have, the better.

Always Be Recording - If you think you may enter a flow state, be sure to have a way to retain it. Too many musicians forget they should always be recording rehearsals and noting time stamps of parts to revisit.

Meditate - Many people find meditation - more specifically, transcendental meditation - to be helpful in getting deeper and more sustained flow states.

Retaining Inspired Moments

Inspiration is like fresh bread. When straight out of the oven — even if it's not made from the best ingredients — it'll taste pretty amazing. But if left around for a few hours, it'll be a little less flavorful. By the next day it's pretty stale, and after a week it's inedible. The longer you wait to capture your ideas, the more details they lose. For this book, I'd regularly take a note to write about a subject that could yield decent results. But if I wrote the passage the second I had the inspiration, it would flow out of me in full, coherent detail. I've found this to be the case with nearly every song I've ever worked on as well. Learning to capture an idea as it perspires is the most effective way to get the most from your inspiration. Every moment wasted wiring a DAW or preparing a recorder can be small details of what your brain is trying to exude that can be lost forever.

One of the most overlooked skills of creativity is retention. It's assumed that if there's a voice memo app on your phone and you remember to record your song ideas, you're a master of retention. Contrary to that assumption, mastering a few good practices can help make your output more potent and less stressful. When being creative, the most valuable asset is your ideas, but they're worthless if you don't remember them. Getting in good habits of retention not only makes sure you never lose your inspired moments, but it also helps make your creativity more potent. Unless you figure out how to remember the inspiration that's trying to get out of you effectively, that opportunity may never rear its head again so that idea may never come to full fruition.

When you're trying to remember ideas instead of retaining them properly, your mind is always trying to keep track of them. When your mind knows you've outsourced a way to keep track of parts of your life, it's able to focus elsewhere. It's been proven countless times if you're storing ideas effectively, your brain frees up space it uses to remember them, allowing you to focus on new ideas that expedite development of what you're working on. If you feel cluttered in your thoughts, dumping the ideas from your mind can be an extremely effective way to gain clarity on your next move. Much in the way you check off items on your to-do list, putting the thoughts in your mind down on a list allows your mind to get past old ideas and devote brain power to new ones. It's sadly common that unless we experience the benefits of regularly retaining ideas, we don't believe they exist.

Thankfully, since music costs so much to make, most of the ways you get better at retention cost little to no money and take very little time to implement. Along with the benefits being extremely worthwhile, practicing how to retain is time well spent.

Perfection And Perspiring
"Have no fear of perfection, you'll never reach it"
— Salvador Dali

Author Kurt Vonnegut once said he feels like "an armless, legless man with a crayon in his mouth" when he writes. The beginning for any creator is an outline or broad strokes, not the consideration and nuance you'll hopefully apply later on. Skip the thoughts of subtleties like syncopation, whether you should use an upstroke versus a downstroke, an accent or apply vibrato. Instead, focus on an idea when it's flowing and leave the details for less inspired moments.

While rules are meant to be broken, the most effective way to deal with the demoing process is to perspire, then edit. There are very few unanimous truths for creators, but one is that if good ideas are pouring out of your brain, capture them as fast as you can, not stopping until the inspiration well runs dry. Inspiration can come fast, so worrying if an element is perfect or even good enough can kill it fast. When first expelling an idea, we need to rid ourselves of thoughts of perfection or other judgments and only evaluate them after our inspiration has passed. Editing can slow the process by shifting the brain into a whole other headspace that can deplete this inspired perspiration. This is not to discount that if you realize the verse is better at half its length, you shouldn't make that edit in the moment, but make sure it's not at the expense of any inspiration that may be currently in your head that'll be far less obvious at a later date. Don't wonder where the song is going, just feel it and leave the contemplation for later.

Figure Out Where You're Creative To Make It An Environment To Capture Ideas

"I've never been a very prolific person, so when creativity flows, it flows. I find myself scribbling on little notepads and pieces of loose paper, which results in a very small portion of my writings to ever show up in true form." — **Kurt Cobain**

Despite recording studios being the place designed to capture musical ideas, in many of them it takes far too much effort to get those ideas down as they're happening. When I'm working on a song, I always have a live microphone I can put into record at the end of a DAW file if I need to remember ideas or grab a bit of inspiration. If need be, I'll write down anything else I can remember in the notes app on my iPhone. Producer Mutt Lange (AC/DC, Def Leppard, Shania Twain) would keep a cassette voice recorder in the control room so he could retain ideas as fast as he could since the trouble of getting ideas into the tape machine could take far too long. Thankfully, we all now have a voice recorder on our phone that can retain our best ideas easily. Many producers have a "scrap" MIDI track or another recorder always rolling in case someone has a fantastic idea for this same reason.

Many artists have great ideas while going to bed at night, so they employ a way of capturing them. Grimes keeps pen and paper by her bedside, whereas Ezra Kire of Morning Glory takes it a step further by keeping a pen tied to his nightstand along with a notebook under his pillow. Others are flooded with inspiration in the morning, so they do morning journaling each day where they write down stream of consciousness thoughts that they review the next day to see what they can find to apply to their work.

Always Be Rolling

There's a piece of recording engineer wisdom that you never let a performer do a "practice take" that isn't being recorded. Instead, you record them, even if they're warming up, since if they do a great take and you didn't record it, all of a sudden you're the worst person in the world, even if they told you not to record it. As an engineer, you may tell a musician they're practicing, but you're actually recording each take they do in case a great moment happens. This also goes for when you're recording yourself; in an age where storage costs are next to nothing, making sure you're always recording is essential to capturing your most inspired moments.

Good Note Taking

"The faintest ink is better than the best memory" — **Chinese proverb**

Listening back to your songs can be an amazing thrill, but forgetting to write down every tiny little detail you hear that could be accentuated, diminished, changed and so on means these ideas may be forgotten and your song may never reach its peak. Writing illegible notes that are hard to decipher later on can cause you to miss a crucial detail you hear for years to come that you kick yourself over every time you listen.

As a producer, I need to take notes on songs, mixes or other ideas every day of my life. In some weeks I'll take notes on over 40 songs. A lot of this time is spent in inconvenient environments such as hopping subways and buses across New York City. Needless to say, it can be hard to concentrate and even harder to take notes. Because of this, I have strict rules to make sure I never lose any thoughts that come to me while hearing these mixes. Whenever I'm listening to a song I'm working on, I must have a note app open to take clear notes that I'll remember later. If an idea is coming at me fast, I'll open Music Memos or Voice Memos on my phone to record a note, no matter how crazy I look singing a part on the L Train. I know I must never lose inspiration since it may never come back.

Being A Good Librarian

Many songwriters write riffs and melody ideas but never bring them to full demo form. Collecting ideas as you have them is commonly done in iTunes or folders on a computer. Sadly, when I work with songwriters on drafting their songs, their riffs and beats are scattered across numerous devices and labeled horribly, so the songwriter can never seem to find them. There are a few easy practices that can help to sort these ideas:

- Label files with more than just "Voice Memo 19" - instead, put a descriptive name like "Creepy Song for Neon Demon opening scene Key of E, 148 BPM". Tempos or emotions can be great descriptors, as well as the key.
- When you're too tired to create, take time to make folders and organize these demos by tagging them to review so your mind can incubate them.
- Date files if you'll remember a time when you wrote them when trying to find them. If you'll remember the place you wrote them later, tag a file with that as well. I find dates are better since you can often remember what you were doing on a certain date compared to version 7.

Spreadsheets - Rivers Cuomo of Weezer uses spreadsheets to keep track of riffs, lyrics and song title ideas so he can figure out what fits together later. Since titles of songs are limited in information, spreadsheets can allow you to add more information that'll help you sort through your ideas.

Inboxing And Sorting - David Allen's life-changing book *Getting Things Done* says that you should have an inbox that you capture ideas in to later file them in their proper place. When I work with musicians on their record, their iPhones are commonly cluttered messes of hundreds of voice memos with their ideas. This lack of order costs tons of time in lost and unsorted ideas. To make matters worse, they also have Garageband demos as well as more developed Pro Tools demos scattered in different places. Instead of this clutter, I sort all of these files to iTunes with playlists that file ideas by category. Having playlists for each song, final demos, riff ideas, etc. can make your creative time far more effective.

Commonplacing Notebooks
        I'm not one to celebrate the past, but one of the lost traditions of creative minds was to keep a commonplacing notebook. These

notebooks are a place where you retain quotations and other points of inspiration throughout your life. Essentially, anything you feel resonance with that may be worthy of further thought or development should be retained in one of these books. As you add these inspirational thoughts, you review them from time to time to put thoughts together to make epiphanies. John Locke, the economist and political theorist, was one of the first people to push this practice and later had notebooks manufactured to mimic the way he employed them in his creative pursuits.

Composer Aaron Copeland said, "Most composers have a notebook where they put down germinal ideas that occur to them thinking, 'well, we'll work on that later.' You can't pick the moment when you'll have ideas. It picks you, and you might be completely absorbed in another piece of work. You put the ideas down where you can find them later when you need to look for ideas, and they don't come easily." This summation of why this type of retention is important couldn't be summed up better.

In the modern age, this can be a note in your phone, a Google Doc or, for the twee folks, a Moleskine notebook where you keep track of what inspires you creatively. Later reviewing what inspires you is one of the clearest routes possible to inspiration that'll put your mind into an incubation state that can continually reward your music. I think about how much less I'd know about creativity if I hadn't had my mind opened by watching Jodorowsky's Holy Mountain for the first time, which I wrote down in a small memo pad I carried in my pocket.

Checklists Retain What You Don't Want To Forget
Atul Gawande wrote a life-changing book called *The Checklist Manifesto* that talks about saving lives with medical procedures that compensate for our inability to remember crucial systems that insure processes don't fail us. Although this book is written about medicine, its application to the creative process is broad and rewarding. Gawande says Rivers Cuomo of Weezer has developed checklists of considerations of songwriting tools. Many musicians notice they commonly forget details and considerations in the development of their song. In order to make sure they evaluate these considerations each time, they will employ a checklist at the end of their process to make sure

no stone is left unturned. If you find yourself forgetting these details, employing a checklist can ensure they don't get skipped.

I make lists in an app called <u>Checklist+</u> for remembering to listen to my mixes on different devices and with different perspectives, such as being sure I listened on three sets of speakers and listened for various elements. This ensures I don't skip crucial perspectives needed to make my mixes great and eventually become habits I don't forget. If you find yourself forgetting to consider your work in ways that are helpful, consider making a checklist so you can make these reflections.

Chapter 9: Building A Better Album

Building an album is probably the most conformist process that so-called nonconformist musicians blindly follow. They often study a record they love and say, "Well this record I love is a twelve-song record, so we should have twelve songs on ours too." That may diminish down to ten songs if they feel especially unambitious. This is not only lazy, but it hardly considers one of the biggest options in your palette, not to mention it being one of the largest statements in your musical output.

When it's time to consider what I want to do with an album, I take a survey of my favorite albums to figure out what I actually enjoy in an album. The results of this exercise are usually surprising. When I first did it, my collaborators and I found a lot of patterns that didn't line up with what we thought we enjoyed in albums. For example, I thought 35 minutes was a perfect album length, yet most of the albums I loved were between 45 and 50 minutes. Also, who knew I usually enjoyed a band's third album more than their first? With a little bit of thought and planning, you can make a record that represents who you are much better than a blind imitation of everyone else (*I explored this practice thoroughly in both discussion and spreadsheet form on an episode of my podcast Off The Record if you want to go deeper*).

Local Act Album Development

There's a common practice in the world of musicians on how to build a record that goes something like this:

Step 1. Someone writes a song at home.
Step 2. They bring it to their collaborators and finish writing it.
Step 3. They consider the song finished and if it's not already recorded in their DAW, they record it, mixing it down until there's a releasable mix of it.
Step 4. They repeat this until there are enough songs they find worthy of release.
Step 5. They release an album.

REPEAT!

While this cycle is perfectly acceptable to the majority of musicians, there's a method that yields far better results.

The Parts That Make Up An Album
Before we go forward, it's probably best to get a few terms straight:

Bones - Melodies, lyrics, bridges, riffs, verses, choruses. Any part of a song that wouldn't be a complete song if you played it to someone.
Skeleton - The beginning of a song. While this may be missing a bridge, syncopation or well thought-out drum fills, it has enough of a song's development to see the potential in it.
Flesh or **Fleshing Out** - Flesh is the details of the song that make it better but aren't essential parts of it. These are syncopation tricks, production tricks, percussion, little inflections, etc.
Demos - Compositions you've recorded down that you consider compositionally done but haven't recorded in their final form yet.
Beings - Songs that are mixed down.
Album - Whether it's a four-song EP or a 22-song album, whatever you envision as what you'll put out that contains more than two songs.

Quantity vs. Quality Optimization

One of the most common dilemmas you'll encounter is if you write too many songs and your audience hears every idea you have; it inevitably leads to a lower quality musical output. But the idea that with increased quantity you get less quality is also a myth. This may be the case with what you release, but to actualize a great album, you need more material to choose from. In all of our lives, there's a finite amount of time; so if you imagine your time as a pie chart, whenever you devote time to one task, it takes away from the others. For most musicians there's only a certain amount of time you can work on your songs, so spending that time wisely is imperative to birthing the best album possible. Therefore, optimizing this time can give you the chance to make better music.

One of the most interesting processes of recording an LP is to see how much of the material isn't used. Many music fans don't realize that B-sides are commonly the unused songs that were recorded for an LP. No matter how masterful a producer or musician is, some songs don't end up right for the LP they were intended to be a part of. Rick Rubin is famous for asking bands to write 2.5 records worth of material for each record they release. Meaning that if a band wants to make a 12-song record, he wants 30 songs to choose from so that he can trim down the material to the best songs an artist is capable of.

He tells it this way: "I'm very much of the school of recording more than less. And I always request that artists overwrite. Write as much as possible — and then we can narrow down — because you never really know." The output released on a record to the public diminishes if a group is unable to write 30 songs. With Black Sabbath, he had to alter his normally high input to get the best output possible, saying: "They probably wrote more than twenty. We probably recorded sixteen and there are eight on the album."

If you've ever heard the punk group Rancid, you can't imagine that they record 40+ songs for a 20-song record when you hear the gravelly rage in their songs. However, that's a big part of crafting their records. Some groups can get away with just being aggressive, but Rancid knows their records are more about well-written songs, so to ensure they get the best out of them, they have a wide variety of songs to choose from. The same goes for The Cure, Bruce Springsteen or any other classic group you see with an abundance of B-sides left over for box sets.

It's helpful to record a few more songs than you'd want for a record since some don't develop properly in the studio or the direction of the record veers away from a few songs that are best left on the cutting room floor to keep a consistent trait across a record. As a record develops, it becomes clearer that some material isn't appropriate for the intent of the record. This is why a few songs will be recorded and mixed but don't make it to the final record. Even if you plan to release a string of singles, it's best to get a few recorded before you release the first so you can strategically release them.

While budgets don't usually allow for the excess of fully recording two records for every one you release, the idea can be accomplished by anyone. If you're trying to craft a great album, having as many song options is one of the most effective ways to raise your quality. Recording more songs than you'll release to their full fruition allows for better evaluation, and when constraints don't allow this, having skeletons or demos to evaluate and choose from helps to increase the quality of what you release.

How Many Songs Will You Be Trying To Make Great?

Despite having more songs to choose from being a way to increase the quality of your output, we also have to factor in our limited time and attention resources. The most important consideration when planning a release is how many songs you'll release. With each added song you plan to release in a period, you'll need to develop them, which costs you both attention and time. If you have twenty songs to concentrate on making as good as possible, your attention is divided among all twenty of them, allowing less attention to each song's development. A four-song EP can allow extensive attention that's much more manageable.

Developing songs can cost money, but your time and attention are just as important to allocate a budgeting of resources towards. Many groups will decide to jump into making a full length album before they know how much attention and proficiency they'll need to have to make an LP that they'll be happy with. Consider that your attention will be divided with each additional song you will be developing over a period of time and that it reflects your ability not to be overwhelmed by the evaluation needed to make each song as good as possible.

The High Input, Low Output Process

Derek Sivers has a saying that goes, "ideas are a multiplier of execution," meaning that if you have an amazing idea, it has a high value, so its worth depends on how you execute it. If you have a weak idea with a value of 5 and weak execution with a value of 1,000, you end up with 5,000. A strong idea has a value of 20 and strong execution has a value of 20,000, so you end up with 400,000. Once this is recognized, it's obvious you should only execute the best ideas you have. This means only bringing each idea to the optimal place to judge them and then only executing on the best ideas.

To get the results of the records you love on a small budget, we need to hack this process a bit. We first optimize the songwriting process by cutting away with unneeded time spent optimizing subpar material. The problem with the "Local Band Album Development" method is time wasted by developing subpar material. The first step in our quest to make an amazing album is to take your best bones and put them together with the parts that fit together. Bones can be a chord progression or set of lyrics. The start of the process is jamming these together until there are a few skeletons.

What Does A Bone Look Like?
"The first draft of everything is shit" — **Ernest Hemingway**

A bone is the point where you've expressed your inspiration, having run out of any further ideas until a point later where it will be reconsidered. This can be a riff you played in a particularly inspired moment or a fully fleshed out demo or any part of the song from a riff on up to a fully developed verse or chorus. At some point, whether it's blanking or the need to bring in collaborators, we say "this is done – for now." We then choose to take it into another stage of further fleshing out. What a bone looks like in true form is hard to say, but I think of it as the first finished incarnation of an idea whose potential could be understood by others to find other parts to build with.

When capturing ideas, we should always retain every detail we can about it in the spur of the moment but be open to using only the good parts of it later. It doesn't matter whether you start with a title, lyrics, beats or riffs first, what's important is to collect many great parts so there are good options to build off of. As we collect bones, there are more options to emotionally elaborate upon to make a great skeleton.

Skeletons Aren't Songs, They're The Optimal Form A Song Can Be Judged By
As you accumulate bones, you start to tinker with which of your best ideas may fit together in a resonant way. Putting various bones together or taking one to develop further to form song skeletons is how

we get to the point where we can judge if a song is worth further execution. Songwriters use various methods to form a skeleton; whether the inspiration comes in one sitting or takes some tinkering, the possibilities are endless. But once we're satisfied with the main elements of a song, a skeleton is formed.

Lady Gaga has said that she always starts with the chorus since if it isn't great, "you're fucked anyway." Other songwriters write down a turn of phrase they like and try to find what music goes with it. In time, it's easy to find how your mind works to form these skeletons.

One of the common mistakes is to think skeletons are fully developed songs. The whole purpose of calling these parts a skeleton is that they're not yet a fully developed song or demo. The reason we call the forming of the rest of the song "fleshing out" is we're figuring out what the skin and other details of this skeleton will look like. They're the optimal amount of development a song needs so we can judge whether or not it's worthy of further time and attention. The skeleton is the most important part of a song that allows us to judge whether they'll be worthy of the effort to flesh out or be cut up and used for bones in another incarnation later.

For me, this is having a rhythm, bass, accompaniment and melody part for both a verse and a chorus. The main details are in place such as verse and chorus melody. The accompaniment part has a solid chord progression and the groove is well considered. A skeleton is often missing a bridge, syncopation parts, complicated transitions, harmonies, well thought-out fills or bells and whistles. All of that can happen when we feel like a skeleton is strong enough to be developed.

Nearly every song can be stripped down to an accompaniment part and melody at its very core. Most commonly, the verse and chorus are what tell you if a song will amount to your best material. Musicians often get lost in the details and constructed soundscapes that make a song great, but the best songs have a great skeleton that, when stripped down to this bare bones element, still excels at being a great song. If you begin to dissect the most progressive songs from Tame Impala, J Dilla, Aphex Twin or any of your favorite adventurous artists, even if you took them down to just an acoustic guitar or piano and vocal, they would still be great songs. Even EDM floor bangers or the angriest punk songs can be boiled down to these bare elements to judge their potential. The same goes tenfold for songs in a standard pop format.

While bells and whistles can help take songs to new levels, usually the ideas behind them can be applied to a variety of good songs. The interesting sonic landscapes, tricks and details that help enhance the emotion of a song are often applied to subpar material whereas if they were matched with a song with a stronger verse and chorus they'd have reached a greater potential. It's not effective to waste countless hours writing bridges, thinking about percussion parts, ear candy and all sorts of details on skeletons that should never be fleshed out into full functioning beings. **Any experienced producer will tell you great songs are the easiest to build off of. You can waste hours forcing great ideas on mediocre songs. Instead, focus on putting your best ideas with the songs that have a great basis to build off instead of wasting time, money and ideas that could have been used on better songs.**

There are two sides to skeletons; To some extent, we have to be happy with them to move forward instead of pursuing another idea. On the other side, they usually suck. Most ideas need drafting to develop them into their full potential. In her brilliant book _Bird By Bird_, Anne Lamott talks about "shitty first drafts" that don't often give you chills, but you need to get it out to start the consideration and development it takes to make something great.

For each person, the definition of a skeleton differs since it depends on where they can judge a song properly. Figuring out this definition is crucial to optimizing your process. In pop music, there's a distinction between beat producers who write the music of a track and top line producers who work on the lyrics and melody of a song. Both of these parts can be skeletons, since you may deem one part worthy of keeping and another worthy of abandoning. In your process, when you've put together enough parts to judge whether a song is worthy of further development, the skeleton is then done.

Reverse Engineering Down To The Skeleton - One of the best production tricks used by countless producers is to reverse engineer this skeleton process. When a song isn't right, they strip it down to the skeleton to rebuild from there. This practice allows you to focus on the most important parts of the song before getting lost in counter melodies, harmonies or other sonic trickery that can put makeup and good clothes on a skeleton that should've never been fleshed out.

Choosing The Best Skeletons To Flesh Out

Just as Rick Rubin talked about earlier, I advise bands to cut 25% of their material before turning skeletons into demos and then another 25% of their material before entering the studio to turn them into beings. Optimizing these songs leaves you with an excess of material to develop and begin to see what's being shaped before cutting down to only the songs you'll record and potentially release. After collecting a handful of skeletons, it's time to figure out which ones have the best potential to become amazing songs that we turn into beings. If there are 24-36 good skeletons for a 12-song album, you can then choose half of them to devote your precious time to fleshing out to make as good as possible. The skeletons with the best potential to be a great song should be considered by their resonance, actualization as well as any intent you have that would align with the release you have planned.

The fleshing out is when we add bridges, syncopation, sonic trickery and the little details that help make a song exciting. It's devoting your attention to make a song great as a whole and apply every bit of detail you can so you have a clear skeleton to judge if it should be brought to life.

Demos To Beings

After the best skeletons have been fleshed out, it's time to demo them. The purpose of the demo is to not only listen back and react to what you hear, but to also do a demonstration of what the song will become for your own ears to evaluate if it should be brought to full fruition and slaved over in the time-consuming recording process. Even if there's no cost to your demoing process, making mistakes and reacting to what can be better before the commitment of a final recording reaps huge rewards.

Once our demo has been recorded, we evaluate this song and make sure it's worth the labor of recording, mixing and mastering. If this is the case, it's time to do the final part of the process and record final takes and ideas that have been considered and actualized.

Skeletons Aren't Dead Forever

It should also be said that if you choose not to develop a skeleton or a bone further at this time, it doesn't mean they won't one day become a great song. One of the most liberating parts of creating for years is the realization that bones you wrote a decade earlier can be the crucial part that makes a new song come together. A skeleton is often missing one bone that's later the missing piece to one of your best songs. Top songwriters like Stargate say they constantly put these skeletons on the backburner if the top line isn't working. Radiohead's *A Moon Shaped Pool* contains the song "True Love Waits," which they've been playing live regularly for 21 years in drastically different ways before putting it on a record. There's always a chance a song that's not right yet will have its day. This process can be tweaked to death; it's one of the most commonly used by musicians since the 70's to get the best of their material from album to album. Choose your own adventure and figure out what gets you the best result.

Chapter 10: Drafting And Development

There's a disconnect with musicians about what goes into actualizing great music, in that they're often scared to ruin their good ideas by exploring them further. The majority of musicians find the drafting, experimenting and developing of ideas to be the most important part to achieve great work. The Beatles and Weezer are both known for doing fifty takes as well as alternate versions of a single song. Beethoven would write seventy different versions of the same phrase. Porter Robinson took three hundred hours to make "Years Of War." Bjork says she spends 90% of her time editing the good ideas she receives from collaborators. This is not to say every song that takes a long time is great, but to make great music you need to dedicate yourself to an arduous process of experimentation to vet your ideas.

Drafting is the process of gaining further resonance for your initial ideas. Figuring out how to elaborate is a skill that if developed properly leads to the best possible execution of your intent. While it can seem as easy as just working on them, there are countless techniques and lenses to look at each of your ideas through that can help enhance your songs.

Drafting Over And Over Again

Just as research is often a dirty word to musicians, somehow for many songwriters there's an idea that the first lyrics they write down are solid gold, so any refinement will surely mess them up. Writing a different set, Googling, employing a thesaurus or a rhyming dictionary to further their lyrical intent is asking too much of them. Unfortunately, it's much more rare that the first set of lyrics is the best possible choice compared to a bunch of considered revisions. On *Mad Men*, Don Draper would implore Peggy Olson to write 25 different taglines for a product, and if you don't think this same process hasn't been used in every genre of music to make songs you love, you're mistaken. Listening to most of the great lyricists talk about their craft, it's not uncommon to write down twenty different ways of saying the same lyrical turn of phrase before choosing the combination that works best.

In clinical studies on creativity, when you ask people to free-associate the color green, everyone says grass first, but when you get to the bottom 20% of what they come up with, there are much more creative ideas. This is also the case in music, as the first ideas you come up with are usually more obvious than those that come if you keep digging past the low hanging fruit. Continuing to dig for an answer for even a few more minutes than usual can lead to way better results. I regularly see musicians give up on improving their ideas the second the room goes silent and no one has a better idea. You should write excessively and then trim back to get to better ideas since the excess is usually useful for other parts of your music. I tell the lyricists I work with to have more lyrics than the song can hold, in case we need to add, substitute or write a new counter melody.

But what about option paralysis? If you do a lot of brainstorming, you start to learn what works for you as well as shortcuts to get the best ideas. You skip the obvious ideas to get more interesting outcomes faster. Watch David Bowie's _Five Years_ documentary, Jay Z _Fade To Black_ or any of the documentaries on Metallica's recording process to see how they're averse to "stock" or "overdone" ideas. They skip right past the obvious ideas, digging deeper to more advanced treatments like making the chorus quieter than the verse or having an intro hook that never happens again in the song.

When a part of a song feels like it can be improved, challenge yourself to develop ideas that squash your lack of comfort. Try committing to taking an hour for each song with a thesaurus or doing free word associations, figuring out other words and imagery that connote what your heart's trying to convey. Pass your lyrics to someone else to get feedback on what could be done better. Try small variations on your riffs and beats to find what's optimal. These subtle drafting tweaks are how you find the resonance in a song.

Are You Drafting Enough?
On the podcast I host for Noise Creators, the most common complaint of the producers I interview is that when a group begins the recording process, they're on their second or third draft instead of ninth. Sadly, the first draft may not even be done when many bands walk into the studio to lay down a final version. All of these producers agree the

work done before starting the recording process is far more important than any work done during recording.

While many songs can suffer from too many ideas, far too many never even try to excel to find their limits to be edited back to an optimal level. I don't consider a song done until I have to hit mute on a track in the mix since we went too far after having too many ideas on how to add resonance. Without going too far, you'll never know if you could've made a song even better.

First Instinct, Best Instinct

With all this analysis, I'm sure some of you have been wondering what to make of the fact that your first idea is usually your best one. While not everyone feels that their first ideas are their best, it seems to be a common thought in muscianland. There is cause for this; some artists get in an emotionally resonant zone while creating a song, which is why they continue to develop it. Often they were in a specific emotional place, so when they try to elaborate on their demos they don't feel the same, so subsequent drafts are thrown out, making the first idea the one that's kept.

The other common reason for sticking with the original idea is that demoitis has set in, so nothing sounds good but the original idea. If you've listened to your demo too much or played a song for too long before going through the drafting process, you'll be more prone to liking your initial demos. I find it important that once there's a good skeleton for your song, you should get feedback and start drafting as fast as possible.

Blame The Head - One of the strongest culprits for the first idea being the best idea is some musicians can't help but let their head wreck a good idea. They get inspired by an idea and instead of retaining it for the right time, they use it immediately on the song they're presently working on, whether it works with the intent of the song or not. For example, they'll be working on a heartfelt acoustic ballad and the bassist will hear LCD Soundsystem's "Dance Yrself Clean" and decide to force this idea on this tear-jerking sad song. They're convinced an arpeggiated synth bass will enhance the song instead of considering the other 11 songs being worked on to find a more appropriate fit for this idea. When the other collaborators hear this idea it's immediately rejected, so the original demo is kept since this inappropriate inspiration is as far from being emotionally in line with the song as can be. Original ideas are often preferred since later inspiration isn't in line with the song's emotional intent.

Confirmation Bias - The other reason artists trust their first instinct is it's easy to count to one. If your eighth draft is normally the one that's best, you're less likely to count that high, whereas it's very easy to notice when the first idea stands the test of time. You think your first idea is always best, so you notice it constantly, but you don't keep an accurate count when it's a later revision.

Your First Draft Being Daring Enough

BJ Novak, an actor and writer on the show The Office (US), talks about how the show would employ a "blue sky" period in which no one was allowed to criticize one another's ideas no matter how crazy they were. For the first four weeks of writing any season, the writers would be challenged to dream of the craziest scenarios possible to then have them be dialed into a digestible form for a primetime viewing audience. Adam McKay, director of *The Big Short* and *Anchorman*, employs the same technique.

In music it's not often said that you should go too far with your ideas and then take them to a more rational and considered place. You may be wondering, what does too far look like? Perhaps it's making the solo of the song excessive or experimenting with multiple ideas for harmonies to then figure out what's great along with what's too much. It can even be setting the mark to do better than the ideas you're inspired by, not just getting to their level.

Developing Songs Emotionally

The Alignment Of Lyrical Emotion With Music

The decisions made to further a song's emotional resonance can be difficult to match with the emotion you intend to convey. The most common pitfall of this task is that a set of emotional lyrics are poorly matched to music that doesn't convey the same emotion as the lyrics are conveying. When a songwriter is limited in their output, they may only have a few skeletons to match to a set of lyrics. Finding this match is one of the most important considerations in making your music as resonant as possible.

While having a hauntingly dark lyrical premise matched with gleeful music can be good fun, more songs suffer from a bad match of lyrics and music than is often discussed. If you polled ten songwriters on whether they write lyrics first and music second or vice versa you'll usually end up with an even split. You'll then even get a few who come up with a song title and try to make the lyrics or music fit to it next or even do both at once. How you get there's a personal preference, but making sure that the two are acting as one is the most important part of actualizing emotionally resonant music.

In an interview I did with Ezra Kire of Morning Glory, he talked about his inability to "force a song." He talks about how "every lyric set has a perfect match for each song emotionally." He says he has to write music and then finds the lyrics that pair perfectly with it. Finding this pairing and being patient for it is crucial to the process. Some songwriters may find this match instantly; if it doesn't come, settling for a music and lyric pairing that doesn't fit emotionally is the death of a song's potency.

Emotional Elaboration

One of the toughest parts about executing a song properly is figuring out what to add to it. When there's intent behind your music, it actually becomes easier to elaborate upon your skeleton. By narrowing the options of what can be done to specific emotions, you gain an added focus.

When considering options for a song, it can be helpful to consider options that go with the emotional imagery you're trying to convey. If you're trying to convey extreme loneliness in a song, having a doubled vocal or a gang vocal or another person singing can feel less lonely from the imagery it invokes. Conversely, a reverb that mimics being alone in an empty bedroom can take this imagery further. If you want that song to be lonely but comforting at the end of the song, introducing that gang vocal or duet can convey the imagery of no longer being alone.

Delving deeper to find how to elaborate on an emotion is often about how you find the attributes that give your song even more of the emotion you want to convey. If you make a throwback blues music recording in a pristine studio, this is the opposite of this practice. Instead, record in a dusty old shack where you can hear an old and dingy sounding room tone that can help further that image. In dance music, they'll put in the sounds of partying to get more of the party vibe (my favorite use of this is the first Basement Jaxx record).

Justin Meldal Johnson said this of producing M83's highly influential record, *Hurry Up We're Dreaming*.

> *"We were always looking for an emotional reason for doing something, so the production was always informed by an emotional choice ... At one point in the record an example of doing it from an emotional standpoint and having that be the generator of ideas ... When we were overwhelmed by what we had to do, we went down to the craft store and got these huge pieces of paper and on the paper we lay out these inspirational touchstones that relate to the song such as a piece of prose or a picture, the names of movies or records and they would get added to gradually as time goes on. It's this collage of child-like guidance and reference of source material."*

This is a perfect example of emotional elaboration leading to a highly emotional record. Accumulating subtle details that compliment the emotion you are trying to convey like stacking up small pieces of hay that build to a haystack is how a song that's highly resonant is built. With each detail you find that can help paint a clearer picture of the emotion you're trying to convey, the more resonant the song becomes.

One of my favorite ways to get more emotional resonance is to think of ten questions to ask about a song. This helps us develop ideas on what choices we could make in line with the song's emotional content. Recently, when working on a song about losing one's mind, we'd decided to evoke a chaotic sound where sounds sneak up on you, so you feel disorientated. Here's a few questions we asked along with the answers we came up with:

Q: What vocal sounds would be in the background of a crazy person's mind? A: Yelling "Hey" at random times that are very close to the end of verse lines.

Q: How does crazy sound rhythmically? A: Lots of parts with double whole notes and then sudden 32nd notes at times. Random bars that change time.

Q: What does crazy sound like dynamically? A: Loud at very random points with quiet.

Q: What does crazy sound like tonally? A: Big contrasts of bright to dark, so we need to have parts that have a very bright then dark EQ.

Q: Should the song end with a resolution or is it better that you don't know if you're sane again? A: Leave it on a note that it's OK but could always go back.

Emotional Decisions In The Most Technical Aspects Of Music

Many think that the emotional response you get from music ends with the musicians, but emotional choices extend all through the recording. The compression ratio you use determines how hard a sound feels to a listener. If it's set too hard, it can feel emotionally violent in a gentle song, which detracts from its resonance. A microphone with less treble can calm a hard, aggressive sound whereas one with a strong midrange can excite that same sound. An empty room ambiance on a recording sounds more lonely than a tight recording that sounds in a vacuum. These details often get overlooked and kill the potency of a song in the recording process.

Many internet commenters confuse "the loudness war" of mastering for being about volume, but really the pushed level of volume is an emotional choice. As the transients are clipped off a master, more information is pushed to the front of the stereo image. When this level is optimized in a record, it gives an emotion of more intensity to many listeners. If it's overdone, the recording becomes distorted while lacking in dynamics, which makes it unpleasing to listen to and less exciting as the songs sound flat without the dynamic accents that bring excitement to the music. Finding the right balance for this loudness where the frequencies are excited by distortion or left alone to keep the sound pure is an emotional decision for those who understand it, not one of competing to gain more volume.

Being Intentional In Your Creative Choices

There's a moment in every project where a collaborator comes to a sudden realization, "all of our songs ____ the same way." When this happens, it's always a jarring moment where collaborators are eager to fix the problem as fast as possible. The whole room realizes this flaw is undeniably true so a change must be made. The most common instinct is whatever song is newest must change, but most often this is the wrong approach. An important part of drafting is looking at your creative body of work to make the appropriate changes to the right candidate. It's best to figure out which songs of the group fall victim to this similarity and pick out which ones are weakest to see if they can then benefit from some further thought. This is why it's important to draft according to the body of work you'll be releasing.

This is not to say that similarity should always be varied for variety's sake. A formula can be a style that works for a record, whereas other times it sounds monotonous. What would have happened if a producer told Nirvana that "too many songs go from quiet to loud" or if Refused or Beck were told that they were too diverse? A record's focus or wideness can make or break it, depending on intent. What's crucial is the consideration of the similarity or variety to make sure it elaborates upon the intent.

When explaining why The Cure's classic record, *Kiss Me, Kiss Me, Kiss Me* is emotionally all over the place, Robert Smith says he "likes records that take you all over the place just like a horror movie will have comedy and sex in it." While many of my favorite records are diverse like Prince's *Purple Rain*, I tend to find I have the most emotional resonance with a consistent mood like Purity Ring's *Shrines*. Regardless, contemplating your choices with an intent allows you to make decisions that are in line with the emotion you're trying to convey. When you hear that a musician chopped a great song from a release, it's usually because they're trying to conjure a mood that brings an emotion throughout a release. They want this release to reflect an emotion along with an idea inside them. Sometimes a great song may be best to stand alone or see the light of day on a future release instead of having it cloud a coherent emotion on a record.

Do Your Tastes Align With The Record You Want To Make?

An exercise I'll regularly do with artists is to have them make me a Spotify playlist of their twenty favorite songs. It can sometimes be too chaotic to include a whole band, so I'll try to keep it to the leader or two main creative minds in the group. I then ask for the five records they've listened to the most in their life. Often, upon listening to these examples, I'll notice these are nothing like the songs they've chosen to put on their record. There will be three feedback-filled noise tracks of screaming, yet none of their favorite records or songs have that. Even more common is all of their favorite songs have choruses that repeat, but they have countless songs with little repetition.

This part of the process is not as much about making their record be a direct reflection of their tastes as much as it is making sure they're considering their decisions. If the artist's intent is to make a record that sounds like falling in love where it gets pretty and then sounds like a fight by the end, the three feedback noise tracks at the end of the album are very well justified. But if they want a record that's "singles front to back," it's time to consider writing more songs that are more conventional. This process vets that we're making a record that's more than "here are the best 12 songs we wrote," allowing reflection to make a record that they would enjoy.

See It Another Way

Whenever we talk about geniuses, it's said what makes them excel is that they ask better questions than others. While this goes across the board no matter field you talk about, with music you hear great artists have an ability to see things differently than others. Producer Noah Shebib talks about Drake this way: "Drake can barely tap 8th notes of a hi-hat on a pad, yet he can hear when a vocal is ten milliseconds off since Drake says he 'hears the space between the beats, not the beats.'"

Oftentimes finding a different perspective on a song can lead to the biggest breakthroughs. Whether it's questioning sacred cows or asking what influences can you bring out to shake up the norms of the music you make, figuring out how to question what you're doing in different ways can lead to more interesting outcomes. When trying to get inspired, one of the best tricks is to question norms. Does the chorus have to be the biggest part of the song? Is this song better played on an instrument you don't normally use? This re-thinking of the boundaries can help you find the spice you need in a song to make it feel resonant.

Focus And Presence

While we talk about trusting your gut to draft your songs, at times you can't even hear your gut. New age hippies talk all day about "being present" but it's a real thing. If you're distracted, texting on your phone, thinking about adult world responsibilities or anything other than feeling your song, you'll miss the gut alerting you to problems. When I began to produce records, I had a hard time focusing and self-misdiagnosed myself as having ADD. The truth was I had to get used to listening intently by exercising a muscle to get better at evaluating creative judgments. In time, I had no trouble focusing while learning to trust my lack of comfort when an element of a song felt wrong. The more you can focus, the more you'll be able to be alerted by gut impulses that can help actualize your vision of a song.

While many use meditation to allow them to focus, that's not the only way to get there. Closing your eyes and putting the phone out of sight to give a song your full attention while working is enough to get many in an attentive enough state to properly analyze a song. I also find deep attention to be contagious; the effect of having one focused person in the room gets even the least focused members to a more focused state. This is one of the most game-changing practices that allow emotional responses to dictate a record's choices.

Analysis In Drafting

One of the most important parts of drafting is that when you have a part of a song you love, you need to make sure that the other parts of the song live up to it. We've all known that feeling when a song has a great chorus or bridge, but there's a part that ruins the song as a whole. This part kills the emotion of a song, inducing a cringe when we hear it on each listen. Making sure all the other parts rise to the greatness you've achieved elsewhere is a crucial part of drafting a song on the macro level.

Grading As A Means Of Improving A Song

The job of the record producer gets compared to a book editor in that they'll keep the majority of your idea but neaten up parts along the way. I find the best way to fix up a song is to grade it the way my writing teacher did. I'll first break the song form up into sections on a spreadhseet, assigning each section of the song a letter grade. If I have enough time, I'll try to get all the elements of a song up to an A+, but if there's little time, I'll work from the lowest letter grade on up to get to what needs the most work. If a part gets a D or an F, I won't make any more comments on it since it needs to be rewritten. A grade of a D means there's one element left to be spared that we can probably use to build off as we rewrite, but an F means the part needs to be fully rewritten. If a part gets an A, B or C, I'll further deconstruct the section to figure out what needs improvement.

I'll zoom in on this as well; my first listen will grade the intro, verse, chorus, bridge and any other parts as a whole. I'll grade every line of lyrics with an A-F scale. I do this to every beat, drum fill, section of the accompaniment track and bass. I'll then apply constructive criticism to each part, writing what I do or don't like about each part so we can understand how to improve it. Starting on the A's will guide me on what should be applied to the lesser grades, especially the F's, since by recognizing what's good about a song we can clearly show how to improve the bad parts. I do this all inside a spreadsheet that allows me to keep track of the consideration we need to put into a record.

Pick One Thing You Dislike And Voice It

Years ago I was having drinks with a friend who worked at a major label who was being mentored by some of the top minds in A&R history. I asked what advice he'd been given. He told me that when hearing songs back, you should *always* "pick something you don't like about the song and say that needs to get fixed, even if it doesn't bug you too much, it'll improve the song." This advice took my breath away immediately. The idea of forcing yourself to find a flaw in a recording so your job is justified was both horrifying and enlightening as to why I've fielded so many ridiculous requests from A&R over the years. After some reflection, I realized that with some tweaks, this theory could be effective.

It can often be helpful to listen to a song while trying to find the weakest element so you can then work on strengthening that element.

Our brain isn't always in an analytical mode, so if we consciously look for at least one flaw, it can help find an area of weakness. This doesn't necessarily mean it needs to be changed, but instead it will only be changed if you can find an improvement. While it shouldn't be mandatory to find a flaw while using this lens to examine a song, finding the weakest element of a song can confirm what the rest of the collaborators already know to be worthy of improvement. Of course, this practice has to cease at some point for a song to reach completion, but far too often we don't put on our analytical hat to try to find a point of improvement when listening to a song.

There's More Than One Way To Solve A Problem
          With every creative decision, there's usually more than one way to get to an objective. When a musician evaluates the mix of a song and wants to bring more attention to a part, their first instinct is to say "turn that up." While this can be the right road to get what you want, other times this results in a part that's now too loud when turning down another instrument would have gained a mix with greater resonance. After all, if you turn every track up, you end up with a mess of a mix.

          When we analyze problems in our songs, there's usually a handful ways to solve the problem that isn't our first instinct. Most musicians' default is to turn a track up, but turning down another track, EQing it differently, muting another part or changing the octave the part is in all can get a result that'll make the desired part shine. There's usually numerous ways to get the desired outcome, so figure out if going past the obvious answer is the best way to a solution.

Chapter 11: Executing Your Emotional Expression

Inspiration can be pouring out of you, but if you give up too soon or lose it from being unable to effectively express yourself, it's all for naught. To execute your ideas, there's crucial skills and philosophies that enable your songs to come out as great as possible.

The Skills Of Execution

Even when you're authentically fluent in your influences while bearing high standards, that doesn't mean you're equipped with all the skills you need to make the music you want to hear. There are other crucial skills that'll help you execute your intent effectively.

Diligence

When we hear musicians talk about the great songs they've written, they talk of rewriting parts of a song over and over again. This practice comes from having a standard for how good a part should feel and not stopping until it's achieved. Far too often musicians know what they want to hear but give up before ever getting there. The skill to not stop until your vision gets realized goes by a few names like diligence, grit or persistence.

Throughout the creative process, there are times it'll be annoying, hard, expensive, time consuming or even all of the above to achieve what you know can be reached emotionally with a song. The perseverance to keep going when you're not yet feeling emotional resonance is an essential skill of execution. This drive you need to get through annoying hurdles and stubborn collaborators can be daunting, but until you gain the resilience to pursue your vision, your music won't be as resonant as possible.

Every detail you allow to go below your standards is usually one you'll regret for years to come whenever you hear that song. If you've put in countless hours of development into your music, letting all of this vision cease from being too scared or too tired to pursue the execution of it is the epitome of wasted opportunity. The standards and elaborative choices you've developed are the keys to making your song as resonant as possible. The diligent pursuit of getting your vision across is one of the most important skills you can develop.

Diligence is another muscle that needs development. Trusting your instincts and learning to elaborate on your ideas takes practice for everyone. When the going gets hard, you can't give up. Can you imagine how Queen felt halfway through layering the vocals for "Bohemian Rhapsody"? The vocals were recorded for 10-12 hours a day for three weeks straight. But without this exhaustive dedication, we wouldn't have one of the most ambitious songs in music. Now, you'll probably never go through this, but understand that emotional impact is achieved by focusing diligently on the details.

Proficiency

One of the most vastly under-discussed skills of great artists is proficiency. Without it, you're handicapped by difficulty in expressing what you want to express. After your gut sounds an alarm, it's important to understand how to solve the problems that are giving you pause with the right solution. Novices who don't know a lick of music can tell you a part of a song doesn't feel good, but they're clueless to the remedies of what's causing this part to sound bad. Whereas an experienced musician or producer often knows the ailment along with how to cure it immediately. When you first develop these instincts, the solutions can be confusing, but with experience, you know you need to experiment until you find the solution that quiets your gut instinct. In time, you'll know the solutions to the instinctual problems you commonly feel.

Bruce Springsteen puts it this way: "Your artistic instinct is what you're going on, but your artistic intelligence hasn't been developed yet." He goes on to say that in his earlier work he was instinctual by saying "that doesn't feel right, that doesn't feel right" over and over again. But he didn't know how to express more than that. Anyone who's seen the documentaries of him taking six months to a year in the studio to record both *Born to Run* and *Darkness On The Edge of Town* can witness him not knowing how to get the sound in his head but continually saying it's not right yet. Proficiency is knowing what the problem is caused by as well as how to fix it.

Proficiency is important since it allows inspiration to flow through you while it's fresh and potent, instead of struggling to communicate it. By being fluent in how music works down to its smallest constructs, you're able to understand how to solve problems properly as well as communicate your vision.

But what does proficiency look like in music creation?

- The ability to play your instrument well enough to get a good recording in few takes.
- The ability to spot flaws and understand their cure, instead of experimenting or guessing at the solution.
- Knowing your musical instrument and recording equipment well enough to get the sounds you want to hear.
- Being able to focus on the subtle details of performance that enhance a song.

Proficiency Helps Keep Objectivity - We're in a race against the loss of our objectivity, so if you're not proficient at your instrument, it'll require more listens as you punch in a part repeatedly. Proficiency allows us to move faster instead of having to punch in a part 400 times while hearing a song over and over; it allows us to get it in a few takes to maintain objectivity. An even greater time hack is when numerous members of the group can nail live takes from being proficient enough to play well together. This is why you hear of experienced musicians making records in a short period, while their imitators fail when they do the same.

Proficiency Helps You Make Good Decisions - As you write songs, you'll inevitably hit a point where a part doesn't feel right. One of the most common mistakes I see is that someone will think the chorus needs more bass to make it "bigger," so they'll EQ in more bass, when really the problem is the bass isn't playing in the lowest octave possible. Musicians who lack proficiency often blame the wrong problem to get to a solution that ends up crippling their song.

Proficiency Within Your Own Compositions - One of the biggest complaints producers have with musicians is that they don't even understand what's happening within their own songs. Whether it's guitar strumming patterns that aren't consistent between players or a bass riff being off from a kick by a 16th note. Getting to know the innermost mechanics of what makes your songs tick is essential to being able to fulfill your vision. Taking the time to delve into the details of what other instruments are doing along with how they work within a song, even if you'll never play that instrument, allows you to learn how the relationships work to get what you want creatively.

Proficiency In Imagining New Directions - Back in 1970, The Rolling Stones made *Sympathy For The Devil*, <u>a movie directed by the amazing Jon Luc Godard</u>. The movie chronicled the recording process of the song of the same name, along with some artsy short films thrown in for good measure. The movie shows the Stones trying extremely different versions of the song, trying to find the music that would match well with the extremely visual lyrics in the song. You hear countless other ways the song could've been played that don't evoke that same creepy vibe the song evokes in the version we all know today.

Today, we're able to hear countless covers and remixes that show the potential for how different a song can sound by heading to YouTube. When crafting your song, the first idea that comes to you isn't always the match for making the lyrics and music combination its most potent fit for the intent you're trying to convey. Trying whole new versions and imagining other ways a song can be helps you figure out its best form. Learning to vastly reimagine songs is one of the greatest proficiencies you can achieve.

Proficiency And Equipment - If you've ever read interviews with great musicians, you see that they often have very little concern for the equipment they create with. I frequently think of a video where <u>Dave Grohl sits down to play on a toy drum set</u> and, despite it sounding like a toy when others play it, the second he plays the set it sounds like a real drum set. It's easy to drool over analog synths, vintage guitars, tape machines and $4,500 tube compressors. I did it for many years and then, one year, I abstained from buying equipment. I got to know the equipment I had, instead of obsessing over what I could have. In that year I got immensely better at what I do, realizing you can hand a $4,000 Les Paul to an amateur and it sounds terrible, but a $40 guitar in a great guitarist's hands sounds amazing. Getting to know your equipment and its limitations always sounds great. Those who do this get the attention of the public that helps them buy more expensive equipment.

Proficiency In Diagnosing Problems - Even the most successful suits are inexplicably uneducated in what's wrong with a song when it's not right. "The mix" is commonly blamed when the tempo is too slow or there are huge flaws in the vocal performance that can't be fixed by a new mix. Just because a suit is successful doesn't mean they're good at diagnosing what has gone wrong in a recording. I was once part of a large indie record that had ten mixers do mixes before realizing the engineer who tracked it had distorted every instrument so much the only answer was to re-track the whole record. There goes over $10,000 of mixing for a bunch of songs that needed to be re-recorded.

There are times you'll need to call out members of your team. If you don't understand every aspect of the process, you won't be able to communicate with them effectively. If I had a dollar for every person that incorrectly said "the tempos are all the same" when they're actually very diverse, but the songs are similar in feel, I'd be so rich I'd own all that equipment I just talked about lusting after. Being proficient in knowing what each step of the process entails is part of being able to control your creative results.

Musical Proficiency Allows You To Focus On Details
Proficiency allows you to focus on the details that make a song outstanding. If you have to focus on remembering your parts, playing them properly or staying both in time and in tune, inevitably your attention has little room to focus on the subtle inflections that make a performance great. Proficient musicians don't have to worry about these concerns. In time, the details amateurs struggle with begin to be natural and no attention is even given to them. They learn their parts, executing them without considering basic factors like timing and pitch. Instead, they're able to focus on details and expression. They're not struggling to play their parts, so they can think about changing up strumming parts, the subtlety of the velocity of their hits, small fills and tweaks that make up the details we love in a performance.

This proficiency is easily seen in the exceptional singers of any genre. What Hayley Williams, Mike Patton, Kendrick Lamar, Joe Strummer and Michael Jackson all have in common is they're so proficient at enunciation, pitch and rhythm in their singing so they can focus on small details in their performances that make them come alive. You hear this in the details of inflection they all bring to their vocal performance. They're so past thinking about whether they'll hit a note or not, they can think about what a slight hiccup in their voice, putting their hand in front of their mouth, a cool pitch bend or accent does to their performance. These details are what make these singers so enjoyable to listen to. When you're concentrating on even getting to a note you need to hit, your attention cannot be brought to these details since doing the basics of your job takes up all of your attention. When your attention is devoted to struggling to play a part there's no emotion in it, leaving your song devoid of resonance.

Effective Considerations

One of the most important parts of executing your ideas is giving consideration to how you'll execute them. This process is known as pre-production in music and is valued by music producers as some of the most important time to ensure an album reaches its potential. This time is crucial as many of the decisions of this planning will determine whether you're promoting amazing music or songs that fall flat.

Parkinson's Law

When planning how long a project will take to complete, there's a tendency to guess at an amount of time it'll take to accomplish it. This guesstimate is usually coupled with no analysis of whether that time budgeted compensates for human traits to procrastinate and plan properly. You may decide your writing and demoing period will be two months before moving on to the actual recording of songs. These two months commonly include a lot of relaxing at the beginning followed by intense cramming to compensate for procrastination for the last quarter of the allotted time. Parkinson's Law states, "work expands so as to fill the time available for its completion," meaning that if you have a month to record a record, you'll find a way to get it done in a month, but the same goes for any reasonable amount of time. How long you decide it should take to do the various creative phases of your process should be more than a guesstimate.

Many musicians leave themselves less time to do the writing for their record so that they don't slack. This is born out of an observation that they're more creative under deadlines. However, the science shows the opposite. Teresa Amabile did a study on deadlines that found they don't help creativity. To make matters more confusing, creators commonly believe deadlines make them more creative, but when analyzed, it just isn't the case. In fact, creativity can even be suppressed for days after a deadline. Execution can be helped by momentum, but when it comes to getting good ideas, cramming doesn't help. The time to incubate ideas and regain perspective after breaks should be free, whereas execution should hold a deadline.

Others leave excessive time to work at a leisurely pace, even though they'll probably procrastinate, which leads to being stressed by the end of the process when they're inevitably behind. Recognizing Parkinson's Law allows you to consider your past output to improve your use of time budgeting. If your last album suffered from cramming at the end, so you wrote some filler material instead of having sufficient time to incubate it properly, it may be best to explore what went wrong so you can either devote less or more time to getting your writing done. If you know you always cram at the end, it may be time to learn to break that habit or allow less time to procrastinate by committing to a more intense schedule.

Devote Your Resources Properly

One of the most common quips musicians make when they hear how long a musician spent in the studio is "what the hell do they do with all that time?" When a musician gets a decent budget, there are countless ways to allocate this budget to get a better result. If you're the type of musician who thrives on live performance, this allows you to have more time to get takes of a song and decipher the best way to perform it.

A common bit of advice is to decide if your record will be a minimalist or maximalist record. Will you be trying to make great songs with a simple arrangement or a record that has lots of ear candy? The supposed wisdom is if you're making a minimalist record, all your attention should be devoted to the songs and on a maximalist record, you can skip the songs since the bells and whistles will make up for it. This advice misses that all the bells and whistles in the world won't make up for a bad song. Instead, if you're making a maximalist record, you need to devote even more time to making good songs as well as how the ear candy works to reinforce it.

One of the most effective evaluations of executing your music is to figure out how to use your resources. When your song's most exciting feature is the vocals, booking tons of time to play with analog synths to make ear candy when you should be putting thought into vocals is a gross misallocation of your resources. Choosing tones for a full day was a luxury that was mostly left behind in the post Napster-era of the music world. But if your songs are already fully developed and your music will only be exciting if you have the most optimized tones, you should allocate the time to do so.

Will They Hear It? Or Won't They?
You should strive to hear no flaws in your recording that annoy you since they'll annoy you even more as your standards begin to develop over the years. Every musician who's made more than a few developed recordings can tell you about all the mistakes they made on previous recordings. Most often they weren't trusting their instincts to fix or rework parts and settling for what was easy in the moment. The great musicians work tirelessly until their songs reach beyond their expectations, even if that means going to great lengths like re-recording songs.

One of the most common dilemmas in a recording is when someone points out a flaw and another person exclaims "no one will hear that!" This statement is used when a small detail is off in a performance, such as a rattle in a drum, an overtone in a chord or a slight pitch intonation on an instrument. I've been on both sides of that argument, but the truth is someone will always hear it. If the argument is whether someone will be able to hear it or not, you're having the wrong argument. **Since we're making music for ourselves, if it annoys you, you should fix it. That's the answer every single time.** Whether or not fixing it will make a production too slick or lose its character is an entirely different discussion which needs to be dealt with using personal taste.

Perfectionism And Finishing Your Work

When Are You Done?

"The cost of perfection is infinite budget and time" — **Some Debbie Downer**

It's said that no project is ever done, it's abandoned. While abandoned is a strong word for songs you may be playing live for years to come, this saying has truth. Without a deadline, budget or the ability to go back to your recording to tweak, the only limit you have is when you decide to give up on making a song better. Most often this only comes when you become exhausted from experiencing analysis paralysis.

My barometer for when a song is done is it either has to have hit an emotional high point for me where ideas have been thoroughly vetted or we've gone too far with layering, resulting in a more restrained arrangement. I use my heart to tell me when a song is fully developed as well as my head to consider whether each part has been maximized or even overly developed.

Living And Dying By Deadlines

Usually projects end with deadlines, which is crucial for many artists to ensure they don't dwell on their songs forever. Deadlines are another subject where you'll hear advice that neglects the nuances of creative personalities as well as the pitfalls that force artists to release whatever they've come up with whether it's good or bad. Some say deadlines are imperative so artsy types "stay in line," whereas others say that having a deadline poisons a project by restricting its ability to become actualized.

Common knowledge is that time is the best resource to have available for any creative endeavor. Even Rick Rubin, who I praise throughout this book, is on this side. The story goes that the first Beastie Boys record took two years to make. Contrary to what you may assume, this long gestation wasn't caused by them fighting for their rights to party the whole time. Rubin waited until they had a set of songs that sounded like a unique record instead of saying "Well, it's been six weeks and that's it." It was important that the record would be a cohesive work that could bridge the border between rap and rock to change music. Rubin is cited as saying, "the things that can't be a factor are time, chart position, radio success, sales — none of those things can get in the way of something being great. All they do is cloud the picture." Quite contrary to what most suits push on artists.

What both sides of this argument miss is the need to compensate for the different types of artists' personalities and their inherent flaws that commonly ruin records. On one side of the scale is the "obsessive" type of musician who never stops fiddling with a mix. They're happy to change the EQ on the snare daily, even though it makes no real difference to the song's resonance. If left to their own devices with an infinite budget, their inner Axl Rose will take nearly a decade to finish a record. Obsessives' dedication can be rewarded by making a great record, but these personalities usually need a reminder to ensure there aren't excessive tracks that cloud the picture or too many details that suck the life out of a song. Without a foil that keeps them in line, they'll destroy what makes their music great.

The other side of that scale is the underachiever. They hate the process of creating while being only concerned with the macro, not the micro. They want the process to be done so they can move on to the "fun part" where they get attention for their music. They need to get as far away from the scrutiny and ego bruises of the creative process as possible. To these types, however the record sounds at the end of the allocated time to execute is fine by them since they want it done — they don't see the possibility of how to improve upon it. Without someone to push them towards fulfilling a great version of their songs, they'll settle without ever achieving actualization, even if there's great potential there.

Phased Check-Ins

A way to keep both obsessives and underachievers in line is to have check-ins. Instead of saying a record must be done in four weeks, it should be due for a considered check-in then. This way your team can advise you on what they're hearing. If your record lives and dies by its groove and the whole team tells you it feels stiff, you may need to start over from scratch. If the songs and performances are good but the mix isn't there, it may be time to start working with a new mixer. If you're on check in three and the mixes are no better than check in number one, your self-producing obsessive mixer/guitarist may have lost perspective, so it's time for someone to put this obsession in check.

Despite their usual incompetence, major labels frequently employ this phased approach. The first stage is to hear demos from an artist to judge if they've written material that's developed enough to justify the large recording budget it will require to sound worthy of the time and money allocated. If this isn't the case, outside songwriters are usually suggested or the artist is sent back to write more songs. If they have an album's worth of good material, they're allowed to record an album with a producer. Once the producer helps them complete the song, they make some rough mixes of what happened during the recording process.

The label, who are supposed to be experts at how songs should sound at this stage (*this is definitely up for debate*) will then often utter the clichéd "we don't hear a single." The artist is then sent to a producer who's a bit more of a heavy handed writer to get a single out of them and a couple of songs they did with the last producer hit the cutting room floor, being replaced by this "superior" material. Repeat this until a single is heard or the artist is dropped from their contract. If all goes well, they then go on to mixing the best songs to release on a record. A mastering engineer smooths out the differences in the recording and a record is completed. Well, after the mess of artwork, marketing and other considerations are sorted out. If you have a good team along with friends you can trust, this phased approach can be executed without the idiocy that goes on at major labels.

Unfortunately, under tight tour schedules and limited time off, this process has been all but abandoned since managers, booking agents and labels expect artists to churn out gold after a 30-day writing period. While it may be less and less employed, this process has saved more projects than can be counted. Like most decisions made in the music business, the abandonment of this practice is poorly considered. Making sure a band doesn't enter the market with a subpar record that won't make a good impression will save money instead of wasting it. Incremental check-ins optimize budgets instead of wasting them. It's important to have checks along the path of the process to ensure the way your process compensates for any inadequacies in the creator's personalities. Simply making sure a record doesn't enter the recording process without sufficient development of songs and that the songs are fully developed before being mixed can save thousands of faulted records a year.

Measure By Gut Not By Time Spent

Many fools try to measure how to make a great record by the time spent making it. This is always a giant eye roll considering that it's nearly impossible to show a formula where making great music consistently happens with a certain amount of time spent. I often point to two of the best mixers in rock: Nigel Godrich (Beck, Radiohead), who usually takes around five hours to mix complex songs like those on Radiohead's *OK Computer,* and, Dave Fridmann (MGMT, Tame Impala, The Flaming Lips) who often takes a day or two to mix only one song. It could be argued that both of these mixers are putting out some of the more daring and complex mixes each year, yet both take totally different approaches to getting there.

Robert Smith talks about writing The Cure's "Friday I'm In Love," which he said was written in about 30 minutes. As opposed to the months or years it can take him to make a song. When it was time to do the vocals for this timeless song, he couldn't get it, since he was never in the right mood. He kept going back to the microphone experiencing one of the slowest births he's had for a vocal, until one day when he was in the perfect melancholy but happy mood to do the vocal take that emotionally embodied the amazing mood that song evokes. While I've tried to find best practices for parts of the creative process, there's no formula for the length great music will take, it needs to be improvised and felt emotionally.

Chapter 12: Creating A Nurturing Collaboration

When you go to art school, you get critiques of your art every week to gain an objective perspective on your work. In film and TV, if your script gets developed, you'll receive opinions from producers, screenplay writers and actors who will have a say on how to better tell your story. Somehow, with music, there's a stigma attached to hearing feedback more than other creative fields. While I would argue since we're striving for an emotional expression it can be tough to tell someone how to express their emotions better, there's plenty of considerations that can be made to reinforce that emotion in a group setting. Despite whatever animosity is held towards feedback on your work, it can be one of the most rewarding parts of your life.

Collaboration allows us to take others' proficiency and fluency so we can achieve greater creative heights. In a healthy collaboration, we should harness everyone's best qualities to make a stronger work. Sadly, in many settings, it can be a nightmare when collaborators don't behave as they should. As if we didn't have enough problems in our own heads with fear, self-doubt and getting inspired, we have to work with others on our music and deal with their baggage. Navigating how to collaborate properly takes evaluations of others' reactions to your ideas as well as their input. This navigation is especially complicated since, in a way, you're collaborating with everyone who gives you an opinion on your music, which now comes unsolicited via social media everywhere you look if you have any success.

You'll inevitably hear opinions from outside your group (if you even have one), managers, booking agents, A&R, writers and every negative mouth-breather who can comment in a Facebook thread. As the saying goes, "no man's an island," so if others are going to hear your music, you have to get good at them giving you feedback if you don't want to be a nervous wreck all the time. Getting good at hearing this feedback from everyone you encounter is one of the most important parts of who you are as a creator.

Establishing A Nurturing Creative Environment

Failing And Mistakes Are Part Of The Process

"Creativity is allowing yourself to make mistakes; it's a matter of knowing which ones to keep." — **Scott Adams**

Studio budgets are usually below our ideal scenario. Time equals money, so those paying for a project can get pretty antsy about making mistakes and failing at ideas. To make matters worse, impatient musicians who want to get the creative process over with force their will on the process to get it over with as soon as possible. No matter what obstacle your team presents you; know that there needs to be room to make mistakes without punishment. Bad ideas lead to good ideas in time, so knowing what not to do gets you closer to what you should do. Expecting every idea to be a good idea is a ridiculous notion. Pixar's Ed Catmull puts it this way: "Mistakes aren't a necessary evil. They aren't evil at all. They're an inevitable consequence of doing something new."

"The more you fail, the more you learn." — **David Chang**

Skrillex and Diplo decided to work with Justin Bieber when he was at the lowest point in his career. This production duo was at that rare point where they were maintaining cred in hipster circles while being wildly successful. <u>When Skrillex was asked about why he worked with the Bieb, he said</u>, "My fans get what I do and like that I'm not afraid to fail and not afraid to do things people don't like." This attitude netted them not only their biggest hit yet, but also a song regarded as very original by pop music standards that's changed the sound of the genre today. This lack of fear has allowed him to go from being a popular emo singer to unknown EDM producer to having the most streamed record of 2012 and now a successful pop producer. To call this career trajectory rare is a huge understatement. But it's inarguable that this lack of a fear of failing has allowed him to achieve great heights in multiple genres.

"Try again. Fail again. Fail better." — **Samuel Beckett**

Study after study shows that innovators fail constantly, but they persist past these failures until they find what they're looking for. Allowing collaborators to pursue a bad idea is how you get to good ideas, and nothing will hack the need for that experimentation to get to good ideas.

Creating An Open Environment

To get the best ideas for your songs, you must keep an open mind and try any idea given by someone who is passionate. Dismissing others' ideas by saying they won't work before hearing them destroys the passion of the person with the idea as well as makes them less prone to share ideas in the future. This behavior creates a closed-off environment and makes the project suffer when they withhold future contributions. Even the worst contributors to a musical project usually have at least a 10% success rate of contributing worthwhile ideas that help the greater good.

This need to try ideas instead of discussing them is further evidenced when someone describes a part with words instead of playing it; the idea usually sounds terrible. But that same part often sounds amazing when played within the context of the song. Even when these ideas are bad, they usually inspire better ideas by hearing the possibility of possibility. I can't count how many times I've tried a terrible idea that then inspires an epiphany, leading to an idea that makes a song dramatically better.

This openness isn't only there to keep egos happy and passionate towards the project. Trying out others' ideas is what leads to improvements. An environment where everyone is free to share is one that continually improves its output. Even if you're a solo artist with a dictator-like vision over a project, lending the time to hear others' ideas will often inspire better ideas of your own.

Serve The Song

Part of being in a musical project is working within the limits of what the rest of your team agrees on to find the best emotion for a song. These collaborations can be a constant minefield of ego wars and tip-toeing around pressing issues. However, no matter how much you dislike your drummer or his taste in music, once you join a project, you're both on the same team so you should be working toward a common goal *together* — a great song. If you pay attention for long enough, you'll hear interviews with producers or musicians where they describe the best musicians as those who "serve the song." This cliché is a cool sounding way of saying that the musicians who make great songs don't think about what's fun to play or make others who play their instrument respect them. The goal everyone has to work towards is what's best to further the intent of the song.

It's often said that in any song, one instrument will play a part that's pure utility of staying out of the way to let the other parts grab the listener's attention. The key to serving the song is to consider when it's time for an instrument to shine and for another to stay out of its way. It's crucial to recognize these dynamics in collaboration by knowing what role you should be playing at different points in a song, which allows songs to reach their maximum resonance. Knowing this role and that you aren't always the person who should be getting the most attention is crucial to putting the emotion of a song first.

If everyone can agree to put ego aside to do this serving, you'll all be rewarded by the best song you can create. Despite what your recognition-craving ego tries to tell you, what both you and others enjoy are musicians who serve the song. Take the selfless road by considering what you can play that furthers the emotion of a song. Not what's only fun to play or challenging to your chops. Trust me, every musician you want the respect from will be more impressed by what you play in a great song, not how fast you can play a 32nd note.

The Most Toxic Phrase Among Musicians
"Don't tell me how to play my instrument and I won't tell you how to play yours." — **Some Fragile Child Pretending To Be Mature Enough To Handle A Collaboration**

If there's one phrase I've heard uttered by countless musicians who make music no one wants to listen to, it's this one. On the contrary, I've never heard a successful musician utter this saying in even the most ego-filled musical environments. As much as you want to show off the awesome new technique you just learned, it's probably not the time or place. There are countless reasons someone needs to comment on your part. Every musician at some point can get lost in not challenging themselves enough or playing a part that's fun for them, but not quite right for the emotion of the song as a whole. You're not always the most objective judge of what your part is doing. **No one is immune to objectivity so cutting off comment on your performance you lose the ability to further your music.**

To write a good song, new ideas need to be welcomed, not shunned. By shutting down everyone's suggestions, you'll never know if you could have come up with a better idea. We need to remember that while music is an emotional expression, none of us are beyond reproach since we can lose our objectivity. Since we're judging music emotionally, it's entirely appropriate for someone to make a comment that what you're playing isn't emotionally appropriate.

Film producer Ron Howard screens his movies to audiences countless times. It's presumed these screenings are used to genetically modify movies into perfectly consumable products that make lots of money. Instead, Howard says it isn't to let the audience dictate the shape of the film, but to make sure what he's trying to communicate gets across. His objectivity is lost since he knows the details along with everything left on the cutting room floor. To get around his loss of objectivity, he has engineered a way to make sure the intent of a movie is working despite any changes made. In music, we can often get lost in the ideas that our intent isn't being communicated the way we think it is, so it's necessary for collaborators to comment on our work.

A truly great musician doesn't cherish their ideas, since they can easily come up with many ideas in a short amount of time that can work in a song. If you go on to success, there will be other times to use the idea you're being asked to abandon and it may be even better with further development in a song you write in the future.

Less Is More And Essays On Why A Part Works
Let's say you're working on a song and the MC is doing a line that has too many syllables.

You: Hey man, that line isn't working...
MC: It works because it's so savage!
You: Can we try something else?
MC: Bruh this line, like, *makes* the whole song!

Anyone who wants to get their way can talk endlessly about why a part works in theory terms. There are countless phrases like "less is more" or "it is what it is" that lazy morons use to justify their opinion that can be applied to a situation, whether or not these sayings truly are what's best for a song. Philosophizing why parts work as compared to hearing them back and giving them an open-minded emotional reaction ruins songs. **Any good communicator can parse words to justify why a part works, but it can never convince anyone to emotionally enjoy a song. "Less is more" has nothing to do with emotion; it concerns quantity, which is not an emotion.**

If a part isn't feeling right to a collaborator, that has to be cause for pause to try alternatives to see if the part can be improved. Odds are the part contradicts the intent of the song, so you need to find an alternative more in line with the intent. Taking a short time to try alternative ideas allows us to vet our ideas to make sure they're brought up to their highest emotional resonance. This vetting improves your ideas, even if you keep the original; you know that first idea was great after you hear alternative ideas that don't feel as good.

Using Examples To Get On The Same Page With Your Collaborators

One of the most important parts of collaboration is speaking a common language. Since music is so subjective, we constantly use words without clear definitions, so it's important to get on the same page with one another. Before I start any project where I'll be producing, I don't allow the project to start unless the band gives me a list of music they enjoy, so I can understand where they're coming from.

I primarily do this to have a tangible example to communicate with. When a guitarist tells me they want a "warmer tone," this can be very hard to interpret. If you ask five musicians what "warm" sounds like, you'll get five different examples. But if there are examples of tones that someone likes, it's easy to get on the same page. These examples can also help tell me what type of grooves they enjoy as well as if they like a more raw mix or a super polished one.

While I can hear demos and begin to understand them, they give me little-to-no clue about a group's tastes or their aspirations for their sound beyond the tools they have available to demo with. Most demos are demos since the musician doesn't have the tools to make the tones they want to hear. So I ask every band for a list of a few records, which tell me about the tones and productions that resonate with them for each instrument. This list may look something like this:

Drums:
Mars Volta - Deloused In The Comatorium (Drum sound)
Justice - Cross (Drum grooves while still being highly manipulated)
Glassjaw - Worship & Tribute (Drum intensity)

Vocals:
The 1975 - I Like It When You Sleep (Harmonies, backing vocals)
The Clash - London Calling (Use of different voices)
Bjork - Homogenic (Production)

Synthesizers:
Grimes - Art Angels (How unique the sounds are)
Anamanaguchi - Endless Fantasy (The emotional content of the tones)
PVRIS - White Noise (The way the synths play with the vocals)

Bass:
Death From Above 1979 - All (Tone)
Blood Brothers - Burn Piano Island Burn (Diversity of tones)
Tame Impala - Currents (Tone and arrangement)

Brainstorming Can Rain On Creativity's Day

One of the most common creative tools for a novice is the brainstorming session, which is commonly structured nearly identical to most musician's writing sessions. The idea being if everyone spitballs ideas, good ideas will come out and get the group closer to the decision at hand since, after all, a few heads are always better than one. Right?

The concept of brainstorming was invented by Alex Osborn of the esteemed ad firm BBDO. He's thought to be one of the inspirations for the character Don Draper on _Mad Men_. He popularized the idea of brainstorming in a series of business books he wrote throughout the 1950s. While you could point to years of creativity that occurred that followed his book's lead, the first rule he outlines for brainstorming seems to have been lost on nearly every one of the hundreds of bands I've ever attended a session of. This rule was that you're not allowed to criticize the ideas of others in the group.

Disobeying that rule has led to the toxic environments of latent resentment present in nearly every collaboration I know that's made more than one record. Osborn said that if the members of group feared negative feedback or ridicule, the sessions would fail. Anyone who's been to a band practice knows members are commonly reduced to having "stupid ideas" etc. When it comes to discounting creative instincts, a boundary needs to be established to make better art. But this balance is delicate, so fragile that Osborn called it a delicate flower.

While many musicians have a short temper for trying numerous ideas, Osborn found the best results came from allowing collaborators to think of the absurd while not being afraid to share the dumbest or most adventurous ideas. In fact, limiting the objective often gets better results, so if you want more imaginative results, you should ask for them. Quantity should come first and then, through evaluation, quality comes later. Once the well of contributing ideas runs dry, that's when editing should begin, just as we'll allow ourselves to perspire until we're empty, then begin to dissect.

Optimizing The Creative Environment Among Collaborators

One of the assumptions made about music is that if you put a bunch of the most proficient musicians in a room together, they're bound to make great music together. But anyone who's heard the majority of "supergroup" albums knows this isn't the case. There's a good reason for this — when the environment is toxic, even the best performers fail to make music anyone's excited about. Years ago, Google started Project Aristotle to discover what makes teams perform better. They discovered that teams operating in the right environment with mediocre players could outperform superstar players. The key to good collaboration is that if you get the right boundaries, teams perform better. Here are a few ideas they found as well as some of my own.

Psychological Safety - One of the keys to getting a good performance is psychological safety, which is the ability to speak your mind without fear of being punished even if you say a bad comment about your superior or the group as a whole. Just as we need to fail to get good ideas, honesty needs to be rewarded. There needs to be a conversation, not a dismissal even when it's questioning someone who's higher up the totem pole than you. The environment needs to be free of shaming where collaborators can say their innermost emotions since that's what's often being sung about. There can be no fear of ridicule or any expectations of being right all the time.

Being Heard - Whenever you get a group of collaborators together, some are bound to be more vocal than others. Humans vary in how precious they are with their words. It's important that everyone in a collaboration feels heard even if some collaborators take too long to say what they mean. To be sure everyone feels heard, try asking if anyone has anything left to discuss before closing comment on a song or a particular issue.

Group Norms - There will be bad moments in every collaboration. Whether it's caused by a lack of sleep or an impassioned objections, there's bound to be disagreement. Group Norms are the standard operating function of a group of collaborators. If your average day is filled with fights, your norms are tense, whereas if you're having a fun collaboration 13 out of 14 days, your norm is a good collaboration. Norms are important since everyone understands there's occasionally a bad moment, so if you operate well most days, a tense moment can be overlooked from time to time as long as the majority of the time you operate well. Trying to keep your norm as positive as possible enhances collaboration greatly to make up for inevitable bad moments.

Don't Assume Malice When A Lack Of Consideration Is Likely - One of the ways teams break down is the assumption of intent to hurt a member when the person didn't consider that this action would be hurtful. If someone is consistently being neglected or hurt, there should be a discussion to remedy the situation. Far too often we jump to the assumption of bad intentions when the person being accused of malice has their head and intentions focused elsewhere, making them oblivious to their hurtful behavior. It should always be OK to say you were hurt by someone else. On the other side of that coin, accusing someone of hurting you intentionally escalates situations needlessly when it's possible they were just inconsiderate. Try to confront these actions without accusation of malice.

Social Loafing - One of the downsides of large groups is the laziest collaborators will contribute less when they assume others will pick up their slack. Setting responsibilities and asking for comments can help to alleviate a lack of contribution. An expectation of results as well as contributions regularly keeps members creative ideas in practice.

Skin In The Game - Make sure collaborators see benefits that are on par with their expectations. Many songwriters do 50-90% of the work yet give those who help make the song better an equal cut of royalties so they'll have skin in the game and maintain a lifestyle that makes them feel rewarded for their other contributions like band business or handling other facets. Without benefits that are equal across the group of collaborators, animosity builds, leading to undermining power struggles.

Dealing With Personality Deficiencies

Ego Does Not Help Creativity

Ego is talked about as an incurable downside to working with proficient musicians. To make matters worse, most musicians don't understand what ego is, assuming it's whatever Kanye has said on his latest album instead of the toxic motivations behind some of their most crucial decisions. As someone who's worked with top session musicians and humongous rock stars, I can definitively say the personalities I've seen make the best work consistently put their ego aside for the sake of a song. Ego getting in the way of creativity can manifest itself in the following ways:

- Agreeing to hear other ideas while knowing you'll stick with your original idea because it's yours. Keeping your mind closed to others' ideas from a need to have your idea used, closes potential for improvement in favor of ego's gain.
- Defending that the part you're playing is as good as it possibly can get before you hear alternate ideas.
- Wanting "credit" for the work you did or taking the side of ideas that get you a greater share of "credit."
- Making decisions for songs based on what makes your own individual parts look best instead of the song itself.

When collaborators put their ego first, everyone knows it. While it may be an unsaid part of the process, deep down everyone is resentful towards those who put their ego before the good of the team.

Understanding your ego's flaws is an ongoing process for most of us. Some struggle less than others, but to get the best creative decision, you need to gain a perspective on where your ego fails you.

Silence Doesn't Kill The Ego - Some mixers try to alleviate ego struggles by not allowing a musician to comment on any part they played themselves. This practice sadly neglects the fact that a musician may see the nuances of their part better than any other member of the team. They see small but significant details in their work that need to be defended in order to make a song realized, as well as flaws that need tweaking. Keeping ego out of music isn't about silencing team members, it's about opening communication that's for the greater good instead of for selfish reasons.

Music isn't made better by restricting the discussion of instincts and emotion. Some people will silence commentary since they fear their insecurities will be exposed if others are allowed to comment on their work. They may even delude themselves that their ideas are as good as they can be, so no suggestion or challenge can ever improve upon what they do. No artist is beyond reproach, and anyone who tries to tell you this is how they work is hiding their insecurity.

When I mix a record, I tell bands to feel free to explore their every instinct since I'd rather look at a suggestion to make sure I can't optimize it than never have given a second look to a part that could be potentially strengthened. Egoless work is open to suggestion since it knows consideration gets to a better outcome. You cannot fear others' suggestions to protect an image of yourself.

You Want To Be Of The Right Opinion, Not Just Right - Ego prevents us from admitting we've changed our mind. Too many people think they need to look strong, trying desperately to avoid admitting their flaws for fear it makes them look weak. Everyone is human; no one thinks that you're immune to making mistakes, no matter how much they respect you. When you realize you're wrong about a decision, continuing to posture that you're right means you end up with a decision for your music that isn't as good as it could be. Changing your mind is a sign of strength, not weakness. It indicates maturity and someone who puts the purpose ahead of their image.

Try To Understand The Other Person's Perspective - You need to consider why someone feels the way they do for reasons other than them being selfish, evil or egotistical, otherwise you haven't properly considered their side. Far too often collaborators assume selfish motives instead of genuine concern or emotional intent when defending their opinion. Taking the time to consider the benefits of an idea and why it would work is the only way you won't be blinded by ego.

Getting Beyond The Power Struggle

In any relationship, whether it's a collaboration, friendship or sexual relationship, after the initial getting to know you period or the exciting honeymoon period, there's a usually a period called "the power struggle." In this struggle, collaborators will try to exert who will be the leader in various fields like business, planning, creative decisions, etc. As the politeness of initial meeting wears off, this struggle gets more and more apparent, often causing a breakup, years of strife or — in the best case scenario — it all falls into place, allowing for a symbiotic relationship to occur.

While some power dynamics easily settle into structure, others result in years of strife. For many collaborations, this becomes a passive-aggressive struggle that's never discussed or even realized by those involved. When experiencing strife, it's best to call it out and find a solution that gets this struggle over with to create a dynamic that works. Discussing the unsaid struggle to figure out a dynamic that works for both parties is the only way a collaboration can last.

Too Many Cooks In The Kitchen

Inevitably, right after I discuss having an open environment, someone chimes in that too many opinions are bad since "too many cooks in the kitchen spoils the meal." While I believe there are scenarios where there are too many cooks in the kitchen, most often this is used to silence collaborators by repeating an irrefutable cliché. When someone purposes too many opinions is the problem with the collaboration, the intended consequence is that someone has to stop saying their opinion. More often than not, this alienates a collaborator, causing them to withhold worthwhile contributions in the future. To understand how to navigate this dilemma, consider how a kitchen actually works.

In restaurants, there are valuable feedback mechanisms throughout their team. The wait staff tells the chef if there's a bad reaction to the food, like if the milk has turned, a recipe isn't right tonight or a cook on the line is botching an element. The management tells the chef if they're spending too much money or being too slow getting out meals to be profitable. The sous chef and cooks tell the chef if there are inconsistencies in the ingredients so they can contact another vendor. The chef is the person making the large creative decisions about these issues for as long as everyone else has confidence in their ability to do so.

Music often has a similar dynamic. The main songwriter is essentially the chef who comes up with the broad strokes of a song. Then there are collaborators to help execute what the songwriter cannot do on their own. With that said, it doesn't always mean that every collaborator's opinion should have the same weight on every issue. What makes the kitchen dynamic work is not being democratic, it's having each person serve a purpose. Music is trying to express an emotion, and the songwriter is usually the only person with the vision of that emotion. Effective collaborations often have roles that look over certain aspects of the process with one person having the majority of creative control.

The Need To Follow One Vision

Producer Dave Sardy, who has made many amazing records with bands like LCD Soundsystem, Slayer and Death From Above 1979, says this about the need to follow a single vision:

> "Anytime you have more than 3 or 4 people trying to get an idea across, I always think bands work best when one specific person in charge, the songwriter and if there's a band with more than one songwriter, whoever wrote that song needs to follow that vision through and everyone needs to get on board with what that vision is. I think films work the same way, when there's a strong vision, everything works well and when there's a lot of competing visions you get the movies we've all watched sometimes and think 'How the fuck did that get made?'"

Many times choosing how you handle fulfilling a vision before starting a project can alleviate many of the disputes along the way. It's effective to figure out the best assets of the group, giving them greater control over an aspect of the project. Democracy's purpose is to make decisions that make the majority of a country happy, but music's purpose is to make an emotion resonant, which is usually diluted by making the majority happy.

Democracy Isn't Always The Best Option
"Democracy is the worst form of government, except for all the others."
— **Winston Churchill**

While there's no clear course of action for every situation, if we want to make good decisions, I don't think democracy *always* gets us to the most resonant song. Now before you accuse me of being America-hating-liberal-hipster-scum, please hear me out. Too often when a decision comes up for a vote, the democratic process is corrupted by ulterior motives like focusing on an individual instrument or one member agreeing with other members due to power struggles within their dynamic. These democratic votes don't always lead to the best creative outcome. They can reflect the deficiencies in a team's dynamic with one another rather than a song that's resonant. Pleasing everyone is usually a way to compromise creativity that doesn't make a song as emotionally resonant as possible.

Instead, I've found that when a project has "too many cooks" it's best to discuss a course of action that'll get the best outcome. The team can take a vote to inform a <u>benevolent dictator</u> who has the overall decision power. Usually the main songwriter gets veto power over the emotional content of a song; the drummer will be in charge of groove and the producer is charged with veto power on sonic decisions. Whoever has the most understanding of the nuance of an aspect of the record will be charged with upholding its standard.

Instead of democracy, I think it's more helpful to think of your music the way a presidential cabinet works. The president makes the overall decisions on each choice as they were elected to oversee the intent of the country, but they use advisers who are experts in each field to help inform their ideas. If the president hears from the administer of beats, there's something wrong, they should probably take it seriously. However, if all the cabinet members think the beat administer is thinking selfishly, they'll ignore them.

The dictator may not be someone who has absolute control over all aspects of the project. Having a charter that dictates how disagreements will be handled that focuses on how to get the best creative outcome can not only help make better music, but it can save hours of strife in your life, as well as your studio bill. Especially when doing a second project with team members that had problems in the past, figuring out this charter can make your next go round far less painful. Having someone oversee different facets of the record that suit their strengths can eliminate distraction. These facets can be silly titles like "Minister of Groove," "Head of Tones" and "Captain Emotion."

While this title may not allow an absolute veto power, I may suggest their vote win unless all other members of the project disagree. For example, if we're arguing about a guitar tone and we know the singer usually has the best instincts about the guitar tone, we may give them two votes in a five-vote structure of four people. This way a tie can always be broken by the person who has the highest standards or best instincts.

Conversely, if it's known that the guitarist obsesses over details that don't make songs better, it may be better to decide a more rational person has the final say so the guitarist's neuroses aren't overly indulged. Producer Aaron Marsh of the band Copeland says it's his job to "find the innovator and let them innovate." Finding the member who can oversee a subject such as a feel, emotion or audio fidelity can lead to standards being upheld that may otherwise be decided by those who have no ear for it.

With that said, democracy might tell you that you need to give more consideration to your decision. If the majority is telling you that a bad decision is being made, it may be time to take pause to see if you've lost your objectivity, thinking with your ego or are blind to what they're hearing. I don't mean to say that democracy never leads to good results, especially when the vote is 4-1, but I do think it has its flaws in creative environments.

Eliminating Useless Opinions - In creative environments, team members without a strong opinion can be forced to vote on a subject that's rarely made about the problem at hand. They can't even hear the problem in question or feel no emotional resonance one way or another.

Eventually, pressure forces them to come down on a side that favors a strategic decision to play politics, one member vs. the other. This rarely benefits the song, so don't force these members to choose a side in a democratic vote. They'll usually vote for the member they feel closest with or some other idea that doesn't put the song's resonance first.

Always Judge With Heart, Not The Ego - The next way to make a good decision is to eliminate pontificating essays on why parts work and solely judge with the heart. If any decision is being made to satisfy someone's ego, most of the time it's a bad choice. Someone's opinion shouldn't be shut down since it benefits a part they played or their idea. Self-benefit is not the same as being egotistical; ego is focused on not wanting to be wrong or keeping your own contributions in a song in order to play a larger role. Make sure the song's emotional resonance is always considered first and other concerns last.

Mike Shinoda of Linkin Park has said that the group acts as a meritocracy where they put aside ego to allow the best ideas to win out. If someone in the group is uncomfortable, they'll experiment until that person feels the idea has been fully vetted enough to concede.

Debate Which Decision Furthers Your Intent The Most - The greatest hack to get to the heart of most decisions that come up for a vote in the studio is deciding which decision furthers the intent of the music. Commonly, the conflicts of creative interest get judged by ridiculous ideas instead of framing it on whether the intent is enforced or detracted by a part. If a part is conflicting the intent to make a sardonic, brooding song, judging whether it accentuates or detracts from that feeling should be the framing for its judgment.

The Dynamics Of Collaboration

Your Not So Perfect Match
"If you agree with everyone else you're collaborating with, the rest of the people are redundant." — **Rick Rubin**

One ineffective solution to the "too many cooks" dilemma is bandleaders who think they should stack their band with "yes men" or clones of themselves. The problem is ... this doesn't work. Brian Uzzi, a sociologist at Northwestern, extensively studied the teams that made the best musicals. Since musicals require so many different creators (lyricist, composer, director, etc.), this study was perfect to see a wide combination of collaborators. He discovered that the musicals that worked best had a group of collaborators that worked together a bit, but not too much.

When groups were mostly strangers or old pals, it seemed to lead to inevitable failure. This comparison wasn't a close race; it was very decided that a mix of familiar along with unfamiliar collaborators worked best. The conclusion was that old collaborators have a jovial way of critiquing each other, which creates an environment where new collaborators felt welcome to criticize with a fresh eye. An environment where there's questioning from a mild level of familiarity allows questioning that develops ideas into a greater work. The new connections also had new ideas that had an inspiring effect on the old collaborators.

Time and time again when observing great collaborations the members are individuals, not carbon copies of one another. They all have unique influences that contribute to the greater whole. Striving to find a perfect collaborator with the same taste as you is a futile pursuit that's detrimental to creativity. But that's the extreme case; a bad fit is a bad fit, so hiring someone who only listens to classical music for your hardcore band may not lead you directly to greatness. The questioning that comes from individuals' tastes should be seen as part of the vetting process that leads to better ideas.

Dissent is helpful since every study on the subject shows that dissent can help come up with better answers. So hating that your bassist doesn't always love your ideas can be the reason you make good songs. But that's not to be mistaken with saying "no" makes better creations. Figuring out how to augment the good by identifying its merits is just as important as saying no.

All too often musicians look for a collaborator who's a carbon copy of their influences, but what you see in most great bands is complimentary influences that brings depth to the table. In fact, study after study shows that creative outcomes are better when there are dissenting views in the room. Disagreements can't be constant or cripple the process, but dissent will usually help get to a better result by vetting ideas. While that can be taken to an extreme when ideas differ so much that you can't agree upon anything, a happy medium can be an ideal collaboration.

So what should you look for in a collaborator? I made an argument in my last book that when a musician is looking for a collaborator like a producer they should be looking for someone who fills in their blanks. If you're proficient in guitar solos and vocal melodies but are clueless about drum composition, you'll need a drummer that's highly proficient. A songwriter who enjoys parts that go on too long needs to be reigned in by someone with more concise tastes. Good collaborations come when expertise span the variety of disciplines needed to make music.

Obviously, if you're both not interested in making the same type of music, making it impossible to agree on a general direction, the collaboration won't last long. But when it comes to filling in blanks, this dynamic is what I see in most groups that work well together. If you're bad at harmonies, recording yourself or writing drum parts — finding someone with those skills can be much more important than the ridiculous details musicians put on help wanted ads.

Working With "Experts"

In collaboration, there's an odd dynamic when a more experienced collaborator comes to the project. This "expert" claims their opinion is more valid since they're an "expert," and they should have a dictatorship over a project. In most cases, this is used to silence others, which ruins songs. **No one can be an expert on the emotion you feel inside you.** As a record producer, I usually have to cede some control and efficiency to find the sound of a musician's vision since it's impossible for me to feel that emotion inside them until I hear it. I've seen countless instances of producers imposing their vision on an artist when they know exactly what they want and the producer vetoes that vision for the sake of their "expertise." Since a producer often makes more music than an artist, this dilutes the artist's intent to a more generic sound.

Conversely, the musician can often be wrong or so inexperienced that they need a large amount of guidance or an objective perspective on how they could more clearly communicate an emotion. When a producer tells you it's easier to get a result by employing a method of tracking they've done before, they have seen more than an artist. If an A&R guy tells you it's best to send the single to the label head after it's done since they'll be more likely to enjoy it, it's best to listen to them. If the engineer tells you your Stratocaster can't make the sound of a Les Paul, their expertise will supersede your knowledge of what you think may have been done on a record. Experts are often great at procedure or wisdom, but if they try to dictate direction on how the heart wants to express itself, they can burn down projects instantly.

Groupthink

Whenever you hear about the downfall of creators who were able to sustain great work for years on end, you'll hear the term "groupthink" thrown around. This phenomenon occurs when a group of collaborators becomes so insular that no one tells them what's going on outside their own world so they can no longer make good decisions. Everyone starts to think the same since they're only influenced by thoughts within the group. Thoughts from outside the group that are not shared by the larger majority are discarded. They become self-referential, thinking little can be learned from the outside, since what's happening within their group is superior to others outside of it. No one is ever questioning what they do since everyone thinks the same.

In psychology, they commonly discuss anxiety and paranoia stemming from a lack of "feedback," defined as criticism and the ability to bounce your ideas off of someone else. When a patient has been in solitude, their neuroses are compounded by having lost perspective from this feedback. When groupthink is present, this is exactly what happens. Ideas aren't vetted, so the lack of feedback causes a loss of objectivity to the outside world. This outside perspective makes them unable to make good judgments, ultimately leading them to their downfall.

Competition

Competition can either be lauded or derided depending on the type of personality experiencing it. Those who have seen competition motivate athletes and entrepreneurs to great heights can point to countless examples of it being a great motivator. Whereas introverted artists who fear competition by keeping their ideas to themselves are nearly infinite. Encouraging competitive types not to be that way is a worthless effort since, without some productive time on a therapist's couch or some deep soul searching, this need to compete is beyond curing. This can be very annoying for many of us who have to deal with them, but it's the only way to get them to focus on creating.

For new creators, competition is going to be detrimental. Before they have confidence in their field, it can discourage them. In fact, many personalities can shift as they become confident, whereas in their early days they feared all competition in fear of judgment. Teresa Amabile did a study that examined how reward affects creativity. In both her initial study along with countless follow-up studies, they found that being evaluated squelched creativity even if it had a reward in it.

She called this the intrinsic theory of motivation, which means that people will be most creative when they're challenged by the work itself. But there was an exception; this theory wasn't the only part of the equation with those who are experienced creators. These people are usually motivated by rewards as well as attention and financial gain. As creators gain success, they begin to believe in themselves and they feel they should be rewarded. Otherwise, they'll apply their skills elsewhere since they're functional enough to do many things with their skills.

The key to competition in creativity is to figure out what each person needs to nurture to bring out the best in them. If someone doesn't like being compared to others, be sure to avoid it at all costs as it'll often drive them to quit.

Humor Makes Collaboration Work Better

While we just discussed a whole lot of serious topics as well as scientific research into making your collaborations effective, *you should be having fun*. Creating takes a lot of thought, but if you take it so seriously that you have no fun, what's the point? Making music should be enjoyable, if you get around many of the creative roadblocks, it should make it easier to avoid the bad times so you can enjoy the process.

The good news is having fun also helps you to be more creative. At one point the insanely prolific author Isaac Asimov was asked to write a paper on creativity for DARPA in which he said, "for best purposes, there should be a feeling of informality. Joviality, the use of first names, joking, relaxed kidding are, I think, of the essence — not in themselves, but because they encourage a willingness to be involved in the folly of creativeness. For this purpose, I think a meeting in someone's home or over a dinner table at some restaurant is perhaps more useful than one in a conference room."

Studies have found that creativity tends to diminish when a project is done only for gain. Without an enjoyable part of the process, it's hard to pay attention; this is the reason many modern startups have ping pong tables along with other playful activities throughout their offices. John Cleese of the great comedy troupe Monty Python also agrees, stating: "Humor is an essential part of the creative process because if you're not having fun with it, the environment will get stressful and competitive."

In my tenure as a record producer, I've prioritized this skill as one of the highest in my record production skills. If the room is laughing, the person who stays negative sticks out like a sore thumb. All but the most sociopathic personalities are neutralized by everyone having fun while making progress on a project. Leaving time to have fun can be hard for some of the control freaks who are paying the bill for you to laugh at a "Bad & Boujee" remix, but if it makes the room laugh, you're earning a better collaboration.

Balancing Collaboration With Seclusion

The Hub And Spoke Method
In Cal Newport's _Deep Work_, he talks of a hub and spoke method of execution, where each person in a team will go back to their private office to develop an idea. They then vet the idea together in a collaborative environment. This method allows development to occur in private without the interruption of flow. Later, when the idea is fleshed out it, can be vetted by the group.

Even if you have a positive environment for developing songs that would make the happiest hippie kindergarten teacher give you a gold star, band practice is still not the optimal place for creativity to occur. Keith Sawyer, a psychologist at Washington University, talks about decades of studies that show brainstorming results in a worse creative outcomes. Instead, the best creative outcomes come when the individuals work alone and later pool their ideas.

Since we know being creative in front of others isn't the optimum environment, why is every startup employing an open office with no room to think alone? MIT's Building 20 is considered a mecca of creative achievements such as Noam Chomsky's linguistics department, which influenced both Pixar and Facebook's open offices being built around the hub and spoke idea. But unlike the open offices cheered throughout startups today, a small detail is left out of Building 20's history; it contained soundproofed offices for isolated work, unlike modern open office designs.

This allowed the creators to work alone in their own spoke but also meet with others in the hub. This model lets them think in private but then, when they'd leave their private soundproofed rooms, the building was designed to make serendipitous run-ins happen as often as possible, exposing them to other ideas outside their discipline. Put simply, the creators worked alone but were very likely to discuss with others what they're working on to gain both insight and objectivity into their work.

So if song development in groups is often toxic to creativity, how do we fix it? This model can be taken right back to many of the deficiencies of the band practice room or the modern day writing songs around a computer approach. Knowing what we know about creativity, it's usually best for one person to work by themselves when they feel inspired and then continually go back for collaborative vetting in the hub. In the modern band sense, this means working alone on a song privately and then taking it to the practice room or inviting collaborators to the studio to refine after you've gotten your creative burst out. When the collaborative environment gets stuck on a problem, it can be especially helpful to take the problem home to work in private.

Employing the hub and spoke method isn't always about going from your home demo studio to a collaborative band practice room. Chris Baio from Vampire Weekend talks about their band evolving from jamming in a room to now sending demos back and forth, with members adding their parts on top of what's already there in a DAW. The benefits of this practice are echoed in interviews I've done with members of Thrice and <u>Publicist UK</u> who, like Vampire Weekend, live in different cities, so to effectively collaborate, they have no other choice.

A hidden benefit to this method gets back to what we discussed when members of a group need to feel they're being heard and not shut down. By developing your idea on your own, you're free to build it until you're happy with it without criticism. The option paralysis of too many collaborators trying to get their ideas through at once can be paralyzing. Getting the initial idea as far along as possible in seclusion can allow a more clear mindset to avoid many pitfalls of creative obstruction.

Visionless people always defend the status quo. While I know most of our favorite songs were birthed in band practice sessions or sitting around a studio computer, this doesn't mean we can't reach greater heights by learning from this concept. But taking creative contributions out of the practice room for further development can help many musicians get to a much better creative place.

Chapter 13: Hearing And Giving Criticism

Hearing criticism is a skill that's learned slowly. All too often criticism is met with defensive statements like "well that's just your opinion" or "you're hating" in order to dismiss someone's opinion. Instead of evaluating what's actually behind the criticism, it's blocked and never considered for how it can help a creator to grow. By firing back reactionary retorts to criticism, the ability to grow from even the most negative of criticisms is shut down.

Instead of blindly defending yourself against every criticism, it's important to weigh the criticism against your intent to consider what can be learned from the critique. With practice, you can consider this criticism, gaining a healthy check on your intent to give you perspective so you can make the right decisions for your work.

It's easy to get flustered when hearing criticism, so getting some distance to evaluate what was critiqued is often necessary. Evaluating criticism brings you self-awareness as well as gives you strength to handle the consideration that's needed to create. Taking every critique you receive as a chance to grow by gaining further objectivity not only builds your strength as a human, but it's one of the best devices for growth in your mind.

The Toxicity Of Blaming The Haters

One of the worst reactions an artist can have is to dismiss all critics as "haters" when there's a lot you can learn from your critics. Today, if you want to hear criticism from the world, it's easier than ever with critique websites, blogs and social media comments. If you allow the comments to affect your creative decisions in some way, these critics are your collaborators. While that can be off-putting to some artists, it can be empowering if you put the right attitude towards this criticism.

Hearing criticism is usually met with resistance since it's a far easier path than measured analysis. All too often we assume anyone who doesn't like what we do is trying to bring us down, no longer supports us or being maliciously hurtful. While all of those traits can occur in criticism, they're misdiagnosed far too regularly. It's become easier for fragile egos to protect themselves from all criticism by categorically calling all negative critiques "haters" whose only motivation is to bring down their targets. Whether criticism is educated or worthwhile isn't even considered since it has to be brushed off entirely.

This approach to criticism is usually to protect ego out of fear of what would happen if you had to accept flaws that may be pointed out. While many criticisms are invalid or uneducated it's important to evaluate them in order to grow your self-awareness. Often in life, we hit a frustrating place where we're looking for answers on how to grow to make our lives better so we can further ourselves. Most of the time these answers lie in hearing a truth about ourselves we've yet to face. When you put your music out into the world, you open up an opportunity to hear about both your strengths and weaknesses. But this is only an opportunity if you allow yourself to give the comments on your music consideration.

Since I work on so many records every year, there are constant tweets, album reviews and social media comments about the work I've done. When I see a criticism of the production, I take it in while trying to consider what I can learn from it. Every project I do has intent, so I'm able to judge each criticism by whether that intent translates to outside ears. While we've exhaustively discussed making music for yourself first, others can advise you if your standards are translating properly. If someone called a production raw when I was going for a more polished production, I might have to rethink if I've lost touch with production standards.

Sometimes, a criticism may be intended to deride a song, but it's actually a compliment. It's always hilarious when I produce a record and someone says it is "too poppy" when that was exactly the plan — to make a record that was unashamed of how poppy it is. But hearing your record is sloppy or out of tune when you were going for a record that was meant to be precise and polished is helpful criticism that should lead you to reevaluate whether your standards are high enough.

If you get bad reviews, you should consider the reviewer's agendas. Usually a criticism is a reflection of how a reviewer wants to look to others, meaning if they say they like your music and you have a more mainstream sound, they could lose credibility in their world. If you're getting criticism from someone who doesn't even appreciate your style of music, the criticism may be purely out of a posture they need to take, making it worthy of dismissal.

Self-awareness is probably one of the most important qualities any of us can achieve, and hearing that we're "trying too hard" or our standards aren't on base can help us learn what we can gain more perspective on. With my last book, _Get More Fans_, I was told that the book's name was off-putting since it sounded like a self-help book, even though I thought it was a perfect title, which I labored over for months. But once readers cracked into the book they sensed its authenticity. Criticism can help us see the blind spots we all have. It's said we all have a note on our back that everyone else can see but we cannot see it ourselves. Being judged by the internet can help us become aware of what this note says to then consider and apply to our work.

It's hard to hear criticism at first as it's another muscle you need to build. Some artists need a filter at first by having a friend read them reviews to find what's useful and not malicious. In time they can grow to hear that not all of this criticism is valid. But calling everyone haters is the opposite of growth. Instead, take it in to begin building a muscle towards how to process it.

Advice From The Suits

Once you gain some success building a fanbase, suits will inevitably come knocking. These suits cannot help but comment on your music, so knowing when to take their comments to heart and when they're overstepping their bounds can be treacherous since keeping relations with them is an important part of growing a fanbase.

Suits often get a bad rap. No one ever pats them on the back when they tell an artist they can do better and that criticism leads to a successful record. Throughout my time engaging with suits (and even being one), the best practice I've seen is giving an objective opinion about how the artist can be the best they can be. Instead of forcing their creative direction on the musician, they give them feedback on how they can be the best version of who the creator wants to be.

Since musicians won't make good music if it's not what's emotionally resonant to them, suits' worst behavior is telling a musician to go in a direction they're not passionate towards. Telling an emo band they need to sound more like Massive Attack when they don't like their music, wastes time for both the suit and the artists when they make terrible music. It's good to offer advice like, "take a listen to Massive Attack to see if it influences what you do," but it's detrimental to their music to force an artistic agenda on a musician. A common trope of suits giving advice is to follow the latest trend, but if the musician doesn't like that trend, it always comes off as derivative, often leading to the death of that trend instead of helping the band. Nothing kills a trend faster than when 1,000 inauthentic imitators rush in with generic drivel.

While we've all heard the trials of art being shut down by suits that "don't hear a hit," there are cases where this has yielded great results as well as the oft-referenced utter failures. This advice has motivated many lazy musicians to exceed their artistic limits to craft a better song. But this advice has also come from a conformist-know-nothing-suit that's chasing trends instead of making trends that wouldn't know innovation if a sentient robot smacked them in the face. There's no better evidence of this than the debacle Wilco went through in their movie *I Am Trying To Break Your Heart* when the same company which rejected the record, later released it under a different imprint to much success.

When you read stories of the great artist developers, they impart influences along with standards upon artists. They tell stories of successful examples, but they don't exert their tastes on the artists. Telling a musician they can push their boundaries more or that they haven't found the right collection of songs is an opinion that allows an artist to analyze against their intent. If a musician is confident in their creative direction and knows what they want to express isn't aligned with a suit, it'll rarely end well in compromise. But often when a musician is less confident, they know that they can do better, so they'll take the comment to heart.

Just as the head and the heart are very different struggles, the suit and the artist are two different beasts that must coexist. Just like the head, a suit often overthinks concepts that ruin an artist's vision. But the artist can have too much heart, resulting in a loss of objectivity as they overly emote into a panic. Sadly, discussions of this struggle tend to be too black and white, where they either dismiss all of the advice from the suit or they trust the suit without sufficient consideration. **There's utility in suits' feedback if it avoids imposing inauthentic influence on artists.**

Who Do You Trust?

Throughout your creative existence, you'll be constantly inundated with unsolicited advice on how you could improve your music. It can be troubling to sort through, leaving artists enraged at some of the ridiculous unsolicited comments made on the internet. Figuring out whether this criticism is someone pursuing an agenda makes it even tougher to figure out. There are a few rules I've learned to figure out how I consider criticism:

How Does This Person Benefit? - Figuring out if someone's agenda is to pursue their own benefit can clue you into why they're giving this feedback. Consider if this feedback is only there to fuel a selfish gain for the critic, which should be taken with a grain of salt.

Is This Person Proficient In This Subject? - Producers and well-trained musicians are able to dissect small parts of sounds to tell you exactly why an element isn't working. They can also zoom too hard, getting too far into their own tastes to give you helpful advice for your intent. With that said if you're looking for feedback from a respected expert you admire, it can be helpful to process their criticism to weigh against your intent.

Uneducated Ears - Non-musician input is commonly written off when critiquing music. But I find the way non-musicians listen to music can be much more emotional than those who are constantly dissecting it from the bias of musical proficiency. Hearing emotional feedback or when an element sounds off from those who are uneducated can be a great alert to a problem. With that said, these uneducated ears can try too hard to find errors resulting in the silliest feedback you've ever heard. Just because someone has no music education doesn't mean they cannot feel emotion or tell you if your song feels as powerful as another song.

Confirmation Bias - When I get lots of feedback on a subject, I try to make sure I'm not suffering from confirmation bias. All too often when we hear criticism, we try to use it to find whatever is easiest or most convenient for our present state. I try to ask myself what's the hardest truth I'd have to consider from the criticism I receive about a song. This truth may be that I need to rewrite a whole section of a song or start a mix from scratch. Usually, the hardest truth is the one you have to face, since our minds try to convince us the easiest truth to execute will work.

The Public Has No Imagination And Will Rob You Of What Makes You Special

The majority of listeners have a limited vision of musical potential and only know how to imitate others. Anyone who has graduated kindergarten gets that there are psychological profiles of those who are leaders and followers. You'll hear tons of advice on how to make you more "commercial" or "accessible." Most of this advice comes from those who don't get that simply imitating what has already been done will get you nowhere. The world wants artists who have a unique character to their work, not another copy of a copy, but the advice you get is usually a coded message on how you can be a clone of a successful artist.

Finance blogger <u>Ramit Sethi</u> puts it like this: "The world wants you to be vanilla. They want you to be the same as everyone else. But the minute you are, they abandon you." This sentiment has been echoed by countless artists <u>including</u> Grimes. Most people are only able to tell you to imitate something else they enjoy or has received success. While this is great advice for athletes and those looking to figure out practices to get more successful, when it comes to your creative choices, this advice is largely useless.

Even worse, some advisers have intricate knowledge of one discipline but almost none of another. When it comes to how a painter can improve their work, I have nearly no vision on what to do with a finished painting, but with a half-done demo, I'll have hundreds of ideas. All of my advice comes from my experience in music and business, but is neglectful of the nuance of how you communicate art as a visual format.

If your critics are telling you to get rid of an aspect of your intent since it'll "help you get famous," you cannot give up on it. **The character and quirks you like about yourself are what others will criticize before you're successful and what they'll celebrate when you're successful.**

Giving Criticism

Just as important as hearing criticism is the ability to communicate your ideas effectively. There are a few practices that can make a world of difference in getting what you want as well as getting the most out of your collaborators.

Opening Up Creative Possibilities With Humility

If everyone is willing to hear comments on their work, you're on your way to bigger and better things. But let's not get too ahead of ourselves. On <u>my podcast</u> where I interview producers, there's a common trait that angers them. When a musician says, "can you turn the compressor off that snare?" when a compressor isn't even on a snare, it elicits an angry reaction from the producer as the musician is overstepping their boundaries.

Most people can smell from a mile away when someone is swimming out of their lane of expertise and into theirs. It's basic human nature to be a bit annoyed. While it's a bit silly these producers are angered by this — especially since the musician is trying to be happy with an album they may promote for the rest of their life — the producer is angered that you're not talking to them in a way that's helpful to achieve your goal. In order to get your goal across, restating the question as: *"Can we work on the snare a bit? Is it feeling a bit compressed maybe? I want it to be a bit more gentle."*

There are a few details to this technique to pay attention to: first, it's polite without offering a direct action that must be done. Secondly, it offers some solutions but doesn't give an imperative. It's also helpful to describe the emotional response you'd like it to be closer to. It can occasionally be hard to get on the same page using words like "gentle," but if there's an example of a record with the sound you'd like the snare to be closer to, you can usually get an engineer to get it closer to what you want.

The same criticism skills go for your band members; being super specific about what you want them to do can suck the creativity right out of them. While you may know you want your bassist to play an octave higher for the last bar of the chorus, it can be helpful to ask them for some other ideas on what they could do for that bar. Allowing them to come up with solutions makes them not only feel valued, but also helps them maintain their interest in the project. It also can lead them to come up with an idea that's better than what you thought of or can be combined with yours for an even better result. Even some of the least proficient musicians I've worked with will surprise me when I exercise this technique. If the musician is great at their instrument, they probably have a more advanced way of getting what you want if you communicate with them in a way that opens up possibilities instead of shutting them down with overbearing suggestiveness. If they don't come up with a better idea, you can always suggest that they go up the octave since you know that works.

Getting The Most From Outside Collaborators - When working with outside collaborators or studio musicians, there are a few ways you can maximize their contributions with a similar technique. I make them two mixes before a session; one contains the part the songwriter and I have composed for them to play on a MIDI instrument, along with another that doesn't include our example. I'll tell them to listen to the song without the part we wrote to come up with their own ideas. I'll get a few takes of their idea to see if they come up with anything better than what we already have. After that I get them to play the part we wrote, sometimes with some of the ideas they came up with added in. After they record the part we wrote, I then ask, "is there anything you can think of to improve this part?"

That single question is usually where the magic of the collaboration happens. The session player is often creatively stifled by following orders from those who don't understand their instrument, feeling both frustration and resentment. But given the chance to improve upon an already finished idea emboldens their expertise to find small inflections we overlooked that a proficient player understands. **Allowing collaborators to develop their own ideas while letting them feel like** the expert opens up creative potential. Even if you know exactly what you want, allow your ideas to be improved upon since there's little cost of time compared to the reward.

Constructive Criticism Is Often About Keeping A Conversation Going
"Rule of art: Can't kills creativity!" — **Camille Paglia**

In acting improvisation classes, there's a technique called "yes but" that allows a conversation to keeping going for your collaborators to work off of. When suggesting or criticizing a part of a song, this is helpful when you introduce "no but." Adding an alternative or a more descriptive part to your criticism allows a conversation to start, whereas only saying you don't like something leaves the conversation in an uncomfortable place. It's inspiring for collaborators to hear what you like or dislike since it offers a place to build from. Criticism is labeled constructive since you can build from it. Trying to make sure all of your criticism or affirmations have a description that inspires the next step helps keep the momentum going.

"Negativity is the enemy of creativity." — **David Lynch**

Leaving an open-ended solution to the problem that includes the person being criticized involved will always get a better reaction. After stating what you find wrong, offering a solution but not strictly stating that's the only way to do it leaves the door open. Simple statements like "what if we try___?" or " since you're good at this stuff, what do you think we could do to fix this?" can get an amazing reaction from collaborators.

If you do have to criticize someone, find anything nice to say first and your criticism will be met with much more open ears. I try to find anything — no matter how hard I have to try — I can compliment before giving a seriously harsh criticism when working with musicians. This tactic often leads to them accepting the criticism and openly evaluating it.

When To Be Detailed About What You Want
We just talked a lot about leaving things open for collaborators, yet there are times being overly descriptive can be extremely helpful. Just as you should leave your collaborators some wiggle room to be creative,

there are times to give a lot of direction. In short studio sessions, it can be hard for a collaborator to know what you want when you're not familiar with one another unless you're able to express what you're looking for in great detail.

As a mixer, I'm doing a process the musicians I work with have little knowledge about. When I receive mix notes from the musicians I work with, I tell them to explain their thoughts in as many words as possible. Usually, these musicians don't have the lexicon to easily describe what they want so encouraging them to go overboard can give me clues to what they're looking for. Detailed input on what you like whether it's tone, inflection, composition, etc. can be extremely helpful in getting your vision across, especially if there's a communication barrier.

Wait For The Idea To Be Realized

One of the most common disputes in collaboration is when someone critiques an idea before it's ready to be judged. Many ideas aren't able to be judged unless they've been developed for a few minutes or the proper context is presented. The fastest way to a fight during a song's drafting is to judge a person's idea before it's even been realized. Not only does this cripple the chance of the idea improving the song, but it also stifles the person who's idea it was.

Just as we discussed with brainstorming sessions in musical environments going wrong, we must remember one of the only ways collaborative environments work properly is by not criticizing others until the idea is fully developed. While this can seem like a waste of time, the momentum drained when collaborators feel hushed along with the bad environment it creates isn't worth the time spared.

Chapter 14: Gaining Creative Momentum

The hardest part of any project for most artists is to get started. At first, we see a mountain lined with fear and the potential for failure. We wonder if we're taking on the right task along with a million other thoughts that can cause us to avoid doing what we want to do. The good news is, resistance is usually all in our head, so we need to practice getting past it. The bad news is some of it's real, so you'll need to search within yourself to find how to overcome it to make the right decisions for your life.

Differentiating Self-Doubt, Self-Consciousness, Idea Doubt And Shame

"The worst enemy to creativity is self-doubt." — **Sylvia Plath**

A distinction that's often lost in creativity is the difference between self-doubt (also known as self-consciousness) and shame. Shame is the feeling that you, yourself or what you're creating aren't good enough and have decided you're untalented or dumb. You don't want to show yourself to the world since you feel unworthy of the attention. You're the problem, so by extension, all your ideas are unworthy of being shown to others. The problem with shame is it leaves nowhere to grow, whereas self-consciousness and doubt are temporary emotional setbacks.

"Self-consciousness is the enemy of creativity." — **Jarvis Cocker**

While some of the best nights of my life have been spent listening to his music, Mr. Cocker has this one wrong. Self-doubt is simply that you question whether your ideas are good enough. While I'll concede to Mr. Cocker that if you feel self-conscious about your ideas or being judged you may hold back your authentic expression or performances. But being self-conscious does have benefits. Any scientific study of great creators shows that the neurotic insecurity of self-doubt that leads to constant wondering if what you're creating is good enough is what often fuels great creators urge to reach great heights. They push past where many others would stop and work until they've made a work they feel is beyond reproach.

In addition to this, idea doubt is something totally different. It's important to recognize that ideas need to be developed. Often your doubts are a hint that your mind is finding a dissonance that needs to be more considered. This thought process finds the right approach to your idea or nixes it to find an idea that's more worthy of development. Trust your doubts and continue you to develop your idea, but don't see doubt as a sign you should give up until you feel it's been incubated fully. As a popular saying goes, "if you don't try the answer is always no, but if you do try it might be yes."

Why You Need To Start Now

Anyone older than 23 has heard someone say, "I learned more in my first month on the job than I did in four years of college." While this is a poor comment on academia in creative fields, there's a reason so many people say this. Going through the creative process teaches you more than you'll ever learn in school. Creating helps you learn what you want to do as well as gives you the practice you need to hit the bull's eye on what you're aiming for. You need feedback as well as experience which nothing can replace. You must go through the process to learn how to express what's inside of you.

One of the toughest realizations is that what you create when starting out won't be very good, so there'll be some work to do before it's great. Many musicians get frustrated when they first start creating since what they make is unlistenable. This is why it helps to start as a teenager since you haven't developed standards while having countless hours of unoccupied time to become proficient. But if you decide to start out later in life, remember your capacity to get good fast is way greater. Regardless when you do start, if you feel frustrated, Ira Glass of This American Life has great advice for you:

"For the first couple years you make stuff, it's just not that good. It's trying to be good; it has potential, but it's not. But your taste, the thing that got you into the game is still killer. And your taste is why your work disappoints you. A lot of people never get past this phase, they quit. Most

people I know who do interesting, creative work, went through years of this. We know our work doesn't have this special thing that we want it to have. We all go through this so if you're just starting out or still in this phase it's normal and the most important thing you can do is do a lot of work. Put yourself on a deadline so that every week you will finish one story. It's only by going through a volume of work that you will close that gap and your work will be as good as your ambitions."

Many musicians start out with music that's easy to compose so they don't overwhelm themselves. Pop punk, folk, minimalist techno and reggae all allow musicians without much technical proficiency to get started acquiring the skills to do better creations, even if they stay within these genres. As long as you can come up with good hooks that have heart, you can make acceptable music in these genres while you refine your skills.

Fear Of Failure And Rejection

Resistance most commonly comes in the form of fearing rejection. This feeling for most artists can only be conquered with a realization that it's part of the journey. Just as we need to make mistakes in the creative process, you need to fail to grow as an artist. Every artist that goes on to greatness has failed before, but they learn how to turn those failures into a callous that makes them stronger.

A great way of looking at this in practice is the attitude author Stephen King took towards failure. He hung up every rejection letter he got on a nail until it began to sag; he then got a second nail for all of them. His failure became a badge for his perseverance. Far too many artists quit when faced with any adversity before they can grow into being a great creator. Instead of seeing this rejection as a failure, you need to see this as badges of what you've overcome to get to where you want to go. Joan Jett famously got rejected by 23 different major labels before releasing her first record independently while on her way to becoming a legendary artist. Every band I ever managed asked a half a dozen times before I finally said yes. **"No" isn't always "no" forever. Failure and rejection are all a part of the path to doing great work, not a reflection of who you'll always be.**

When I do any project, I hit what many call the "point of despair." Fear overtakes you, allowing your doubts to get the best of you. The morning my last book was released, I had my first panic attack in a decade. An hour later, <u>the most important review I was waiting on</u> called it the best book for DIY musicians to read on the music business. I was humbled to realize no matter how many times I've given the "don't be scared" pep talk to the musicians I've produced, I wasn't immune. Our minds vet our ideas by applying questioning to them but occasionally go a bit too far and panic us. Push through and put yourself out there or you'll never know the many rewards of what happens when you put your ideas into the world.

You may have noticed that actors always say they took a certain role because they were afraid of it. The answer sounds so cliché, yet when you get to know the truth behind this saying, it's quite intriguing. They take the roles that make them feel least comfortable since they know it helps them to grow. The best creators know that fear is often a good sign since it means they may have to explore what they're scared of by leaving their comfort zone. When that risk is rewarded, it's one of the best feelings. A common trait of great artists is the way they get to great work is pushing past fear.

Musicians who push boundaries have to trust the part of a song that emotionally resonates with them but also makes them a little uncomfortable. Creatively, when there's some fear in what you're trying to do, that's usually a good sign you're about to make something more emotionally resonant than before. With that said, fear can also be a caution worth heading.

Compensating For Your Inner Monologue

When you talk to artists, they're all climbing a different mountain of emotional growth. Our inner monologue is usually a personality that's nothing like what we outwardly display, either overly complimenting us or being a negative roommate that puts us down. The roommate analogy is a great way to look at how you deal with this struggle. Figuring out how to balance this roommate's negativity or unrealistic view of your greatness is essential to being happy in your creative life. If we're lucky it's an honest critic of our work, but that often takes work through compensation and understanding after creating enough work to judge whether it nurtures or detracts from our process.

As we reach this awareness, we need to compensate for the deficiencies our inner monologue creates. If you tend to find that 99% of your friends tell you that you're too hard on yourself, it's time to take your inner-critic less serious and see where that gets you. Whereas if you're continually disappointed with your work, it may be time to listen to that voice when it tells you that you can do better. Just like a roommate you may have to do excessive work that feels like an unfair burden on you, but when you find peace with this roommate your head feels like a home instead of a hostile environment.

You Cannot Wait For The Right Equipment
"In my experience, poor people are the world's greatest entrepreneurs. Every day, they must innovate to survive." — **Muhammad Yunus**

There's a particular ailment of resistance that seems to inflict an ever-expanding amount of musicians. This being the "if only I had" form of resistance. Musicians commonly procrastinate on creating until they've fulfilled a fantasy equipment scenario that they believe will allow them to achieve greatness. Most of the time, this stems from a piece of equipment they assume a musician used to make a record they admire.

Today, having a laptop with a recording program's stock plugins and your instrument in hand will be a far more evolved palette than what many classic records were made on. The excuse that you'd be a great artist making amazing art if you had better equipment misses that you get to be an amazing artist by mastering terrible equipment. You need to start creating now to become proficient and learn from your mistakes, since you'll be making lots of them.

The best musicians usually start on the worst equipment possible, which later allows them to be proficient when they have amazing equipment since they've become so skilled at making bad equipment sound good. When you start off with poor equipment and later move to good equipment, it's intuitive to make great sounds with it. Eddie Van Halen famously started with the cheapest guitar around that would give him splinters all day. When he graduated to a great guitar, he was prepared to explore great musical heights, since it felt like a toy compared to what he started with. Take the challenge of creating in less than ideal circumstances and reap the benefits later. If you read about the early days of most of your favorite musicians, they usually did the same.

"Pick a format and get to work" — **Alan Douches**

Even worse than those who wish they had better equipment to create are those who already have sufficient equipment to create with but spend forever deciding whether a different DAW, mic preamp, guitar or some other equally trivial variable will finally be the key to making great music. Considering the equipment you use is very important, but far too many musicians deliberate this instead of spending time getting to know their equipment. It's not the $3,500 Les Paul that makes a guitarist sound great; it's what they're doing with it. The same goes for any other piece of equipment including DAWs and compressors. Creators who are proficient with their equipment are always those who make the best music, not those who spend more time swapping out pieces of gear than actually creating with it. **If you have the opportunity to create, taking the time to develop your skills is far more important than having an ideal set of tools.**

For years I suffered from always waiting for things to be perfect before I'd get to work. If I knew I'd have a new mic preamp in two weeks, I'd use it as an excuse to put off doing guitars on a song. Now I'm a different person. As I type this, my Mac laptop's screen is smashed after a cab drove off when I wasn't fully out the door. I could say it'll be too annoying to write on, so I should spend the day buying a new one and setting it up. But after years of going through this, I know I need to work with what I have in front of me. There will always be an analog synth that'll sound better. There will always be a day that it's better to edit your 20-minute guitar solo. Nothing will ever be perfect, so if the means are there, it's time to get to work.

An extension of this also goes for those who read books, blogs and attend workshops when they could be creating. Furthering your understanding of how to express what's in you is one of the most valuable uses of your time, *when you aren't able to create*. But if studying is the majority of what you spend your time on, put this book down and don't read this or another one again until you've expressed what you've been thinking about. The consideration of your creative process and tools should be a fraction of the time you spend getting inspired and perspiring or else you'll never express what's in you.

Writer's Block

Musicians regularly talk about having "writer's block" or "creative blocks." The confusion in this state is very real, but in my experience, there's never been a musician I couldn't coach out of it as long as they followed through on what we figured out. Let's first talk about the root of these blocks, being that the artist isn't happy with what's perspiring as they try to create. The creation isn't living up to their standards of what's worthy of further development. Since you need to trust your gut, this instinct should be taken seriously.

Emotional Evolution – It can be confusing since a creative block can come from being a different person emotionally than the last time you wrote songs. I, along with many other record producer friends, tell every musician that they should never stop writing since this is the most common cause of writer's block. When you go too long between batches of writing songs, skipping ahead can leave you confused about the emotions you're having at present. You felt one way in the past and now feel an entirely different way, so songs don't have the resonance they used to. Needing to express an emotion that's different than those you've expressed before can lead to your gut being unsure if the emotion is as resonant as possible.

But if you didn't follow the advice to never stop writing and are now in a block, that advice is of little help at this moment. What you now need to do is acknowledge you're a different person emotionally and figure out that if you're less fragile than you were during your last album, you may not want to rip your heart out when the right riff comes. You need to figure out what's currently inspiring you and perspire what you currently feel, accepting this may be a totally different emotion than what you used to express. For example, if you were listening to stoner rock while smoking a ton of pot on your last record but are now listening to folk music, those won't resonate in the same way. Acknowledge that and then figure out who you are today based upon what's emotionally resonating with you, by continuing to explore what you now feel. **Don't try to be the person you used to be; instead, pay attention to who you are now.**

Standards - A common cause for a block can be the standards we develop after hearing our ideas fully realized. After hearing how awesome your last record sounded once it was produced, mixed and mastered, hearing your ideas on Garageband can be pretty disappointing. You can be used to the emotion you got from hearing fully realized ideas; subsequently, barebones ideas don't resonate as strongly. It takes time to develop your ideas to be the level of emotional resonance you're looking towards. If you're experiencing an extended block, it can be helpful to bring a few songs to near completion to remember what that sounds like, even if you're not confident they're your best work. Even if you have to throw them out, by then, you'll have relearned what songs should sound like at certain points in the process, allowing you to make good decisions again.

Change Perspective - For less serious creative blocks where you're stumped on a small detail, it can be as easy as shaking things up in a small way. Simple changes in environment or interface, blindfolding yourself, playing your part on another instrument, standing up instead of sitting down, using a different hand or changing the octave you're in can all shake up the process enough to give you a breakthrough. Anytime you feel stumped, the best practice is to change small variables that give you another perspective until you break through.

Habits To Help Your Creative Output

Treating Your Creative Work As A Job

A common bit of advice you'll hear throughout the internet is you should "write one song a day" or treat your creative project as a job. This means that you should be devoting some time to this project 5-7 days a week. The most famous case of this is the author Stephen King, who writes 2,000 words a day whether it's a weekend, holiday or his birthday. While this is admirable, I think it neglects the details of what we should be doing with our time.

There are helpful hacks to this regimen, the first one being delegation. If I'm not feeling creative, I may do some librarian work, editing or some other simple work to get progress done. While Mr. King may write 2,000 words a day, this also means he has to set aside time outside of this practice to get inspired, do clerical work, edit and storyboard. You shouldn't measure your progress solely in what you perspire but instead as time spent towards making an output you're happy with. Each day you can allocate some time to being creative, doing any of the many jobs you have as a creator. Do some neatening of your space, be a better librarian of your ideas, read some interviews with those you admire, listen to some new records, work on getting more proficient at an instrument, learn more about recording and most of all do some drafting or writing.

The reason treating your creativity like a commitment is so highly praised is it helps discipline aloof artsy personalities. If it weren't for the forfeiture of deposits for studio time when musicians cancel a session, we would see half as many records made. Creators commit by saying what they're doing via release dates or bookings since it's the only way they'll stay disciplined. Making a commitment that keeps you on track for your goals is one of the only disciplines musicians seem to embrace.

"80 percent of success is showing up." — **Woody Allen**

One of the worst quotes thrown around about creative habits is that if you show up, most of the work is done. While this was the case in Woody's day when you had to get through so many gatekeepers to get a film done since DIY films were nearly non-existent, those days are long gone as the playing field for everyone to create gets lower and lower. Standing in total contrary to Mr. Allen's naive point is science. Hal Gregersen, a professor at INSEAD Business School, says "in fact, creativity is close to 80 percent learned and acquired." To be good at being creative, you do have to show up, but without finding the right inspiration, asking the right questions and analyzing your problems, you'll come up short.

The Consideration Of What's Holding You Back

While you should try to work every day you can, there are times when you need to give some evaluation as to why you don't feel like creating. We know the paralysis of doing nothing gets you nowhere, the usual advice is to push out some work whether it's terrible or not. If you're feeling more averse than usual to creating, there's probably a reason you're feeling this that can stem from the need to give further consideration on how your life and creative endeavor are intertwined.

Sometimes our bodies are telling us a message we need to hear. Not all resistance is toxic, but instead a symptom you need to explore further. Just like when you get a headache, your brain is trying to signal that you should pause to consider the source of a headache such as hunger, lack of caffeine or excessive drinking. Considering what's holding you back to remedy this resistance is often more effective than pushing out subpar work for the sake of productivity.

This is not to say you get to spend countless hours considering why your productivity isn't as good as your favorite artists, but if you're experiencing extreme resistance compared to your normal output, it's time to evaluate what's happening. With that said, when I start working it takes some time to get my momentum. I'll often feel resistance, thinking I'm too tired or should rest instead of creating. But if I push through for 15-30 minutes, I'll usually get some momentum for a few hours. If I still feel exhausted after an hour of work, I try to figure out what's wrong. Here are some common causes for why I feel resistance after pushing through it for a while:

Fear - I always try to figure out what I fear about a project. Years ago when I was working on my own album of dance material, I felt more resistance than normal as I tried to craft the record. My fears stemmed from not wanting to spend my life in dance clubs at 4 AM in my thirties. Once I figured this out, I abandoned the project to focus on my first book instead. I'm very thankful for this decision since the resistance I felt throughout the project was signaling I hadn't considered where this would take me in life.

I also feared how listeners would react to the music I put out. As someone known for producing punk records, when I wanted to follow my heart to make a dance record, it was scary. I realized that if I never did it, I'd regret it forever, but if I tried and failed it'd probably be good for me. I released a few songs to little reaction, moved on and am proud of what I did. One of those fears was necessary to explore to make a good decision; the other was fear that I needed to push through.

Exhaustion - I never know when to stop working if I'm excited about a project. So when my body feels too tired to create, I usually know it's time to watch an episode of *Mr. Robot* instead of pushing myself further. However, when feeling overwhelmed by a project, it can feel the same as exhaustion, so I need to give the problem of the project further evaluation. If I do some incubation on the project, the exhaustion usually disappears so I can create again.

The Need To Incubate - Author Neil Gaiman says he needs to get extremely bored to create. I often have a similar experience in that I need to watch TV, read books and browse the internet until I'm so bored that I'm hungry to create again. Feeling averse to creating is a signal I need to do more consideration since I know once an idea is considered, I always work diligently. It helps to observe your own patterns so you can interpret the signs your mind is giving you.

Health - I can feel "too tired to create" but if I drink some water and get some potassium I'm all of a sudden ready to work. If your body isn't receiving nutrition, it can be hard to motivate yourself, even when you're inspired. Many musicians compensate for this lack of health with energy drinks and coffee. While this can work for a while, it's no substitute for proper nutrition.

It Gets Better- Always remember resistance gets better. Once you start creating and push past the obstacle, it gets easier and more enjoyable. This is not to say there won't be more obstacles along the way. No one starts a project worth doing without resistance. Whether it's fear of how much time it'll take up, the stress of creation or how it's received, everyone has some resistance. Don't feel like a freak for having these feelings and know that resistance is normal. It's often getting you to consider your life choices and make sure you're ready for them.

Getting The Stress Out Of Your Head

It's very rare to be able to create without other obligations tugging at you. In my life, I have a startup business that demands I answer emails in a fast and productive manner. I find it extremely difficult to focus on being creative when there's a pending disaster. As much as I'd love to devote the time to my work, I know I'll be extremely blocked unless I write an email back and solve the pressing problem. Some artists have more trouble than others creating when they're stressed about a situation. While you should always try to work through it, if you cannot get through it, consider trying to arrange your calendar to create after you deal with the stress, if possible.

Morning Pages - Julia Campbell's _The Artist's Way_ talks about the technique of using "morning pages" where you do stream of conscious writing to clear your head of any stress. Anything that comes to mind should be written down to rid your brain of the burden of retaining it. Getting your stresses out on paper and then retaining it on a to-do list with a course of action can give you head space to create with less resistance. This technique can also lead you to write down thoughts that should be incubated and developed further.

Get It Out Before It's Gone - Stress isn't the only annoyance you need to get out of your head. One of the funny quirks about the brain is it's always looking to move on to the next idea. If you haven't retained your inspiration, your brain will eventually find new ideas to think about instead of the inspiration currently occupying space in your head. A common way to motivate yourself is to recognize that if you don't get inspiration out of your head, it may be gone forever. Just as we discussed with retention, every moment you wait to retain your inspiration it continually gets diluted, losing nuance with each passing moment. There's no time like the present to start perspiring.

Make The First Decision - Often, what's holding us back is the stress of a decision we need to make in our creation. Science shows that if you make the first decision you need to make, even if you edit it later, this gets us closer to getting into a flow state which gets us past resistance. We commonly over-contemplate decisions when we should be tinkering with them to get the momentum that we need to start creating.

Getting Creative Time Worked Into A Busy Life

Guard Your Creative Time
"Show me someone's calendar and I will show you their priorities."
— **Ramit Sethi**

One of the most effective ways to get past resistance is to make your creative project a higher priority. Merlin Mann has talked about that if your creative outlet is the most important priority in your life, your calendar should reflect that. He says: "Just as you wouldn't leave your best friend bleeding if they got hit in the face with a hockey puck, your creative life bleeds when you don't prioritize it." If you say your music is the most important thing in the world and you spend five more hours playing baseball or video games each week than you do on your music, that isn't factually true. While it may be true in your aspirations, this means you need to change your time delegation. This means you may need to cut down on the recreational league hockey and video games taking up your calendar to show that your music is indeed what's most important. It's essential to view your time as a pie chart where there's only a finite amount to give. When one commitment takes up more time, another commitment gets less.

Many artists talk about guarding their idea time and while they book time to execute their ideas like recording sessions or band practices, far too often they don't guard the time it takes to get inspired and create new ideas. **It's said that you don't find the time to create, you make the time to create.** Without making sure this time isn't interrupted, it will always get eaten up by other circumstances.

Paying The Bills While Being Creative

Figuring out how to balance paying the bills along with your creative endeavor is one of the hardest parts of life. As I write this, my job is both being a record producer five days a week and getting work done on my startup while finishing this book. One of the boundaries I can't get around is that despite my ability to work a 16-hour day recording bands with little resistance, trying to do two hours of writing after a ten-hour day of recording doesn't give me results I'm ever happy with. This realization led me to develop a schedule where I work at my recording studio for as long as possible so that I can take days off to write. Since my productivity is uninspired if I've expended my energy recording for long hours, I had to find a way to make this work, so I make progress on the book while still getting paid.

You may have experienced a similar case with your day job and, if so, you need to figure out ways to engineer your life to balance with paying your bills. Many artists do their creative work by waking up early before work. Others chill out for an hour or two after work and then begin to create. Figuring out a pattern instead of hoping for the best is the way most people find to be creative more often. It takes me a long time to wake up, so my best time to work happens from hour four to fourteen of being awake each day. This means I do chores, email and other boring work early in the morning so I can create at my ideal hours of the day.

Lifestyle Sacrifices

Musicians usually realize that if they want to fulfill their creative vision, they must sacrifice some parts of their life. It's no secret that musicians with fancy degrees will wait tables to have weekends free for their gigs and fund their recording expenses. I regularly talk friends through the decisions in life about sacrifice to fulfill their creative vision. While you cannot prescribe a course of action for every situation, there are some general life rules that commonly apply:

Living in Squalor - Many musicians are faced with the option of living with their parents, in roommate filled apartments or in their van to tour. Rents in creative havens like Brooklyn and San Francisco are hardly nurturing to allow free time to create. Living in less than ideal situations allows you to devote money and time to your creativity. While it's not always fun at the time, there are very few people who look back later in life regretting those times whether their music career was successful in their eyes or not.

Acclaimed writer Jonathan Franzen's early days were spent with him and his wife living in squalor to get by, eating out only once a year so that they could afford a lifestyle of writing eight hours a day and reading to get inspired the other hours of the day. My friend Ross Robinson lived in a rehearsal space to devote his recording budgets as a producer to nicer studios. When producing Korn's first record, he choose to do it at a studio where the band could live to get around this and get some rest during the record. Needless to say, the sacrifice worked as his career was solidified with this hack when the record went on to sell millions of copies. When writing my last book, I lived on a futon in my recording studio for months so I'd have less rent and be able to work less to get the book written. After the success of the book, I now sleep on an extremely comfortable bed.

Allocation - Far too many musicians set arbitrary budget limits on their creative endeavors. They never make small sacrifices to obtain the budget or time they would need to get the creative result they're looking for. Whether this is devoting another few hours a week to working on your songs or saving more money to go to a mixer who will help present your songs properly, figuring out how you best allocate your resources is crucial.

Using Science To Force You Into A Creative Habit

When developing creating into a habit we all too often get down on ourselves when we can't get into a routine. We begin to believe the resistance is too strong to overcome or that we're failures. This frustration is misdirected since no one teaches us how to get into good habits to create regularly. Charles Duhigg's book *The Power of Habit* illustrates what science has taught us about getting into good habits.

The first mistake creators make is to sneak in their project whenever they can instead of forming a routine. The first step is to establish a cue which tells you to start creating. Common cues are based on different indicators like location, time, an emotional state or upon finishing a duty like your day job. After the cue, you should go into your creative routine, whatever that may be.

After you complete your routine, you need to have a reward. For many of us the creative process is very rewarding, but for those experiencing resistance, it can be helpful to hold off on a reward until after the process is done. This reward can be a Netflix show, dinner, dessert or time with your loved ones. It can also help to establish long-term rewards. If there's a reward you'll get after creating that you crave such as praise, travel or money that will help motivate you, make sure you remind yourself of it or display it in some way. For many people having a reminder of the reward to motivate themselves is a great incentive. To motivate myself to write this book, I keep a calendar on my bedroom wall that tracks my progress to reminds me I can go to Japan once the book promotion is done.

Using Your Calendar To Force A Routine

Routine is a word met with disgust from musicians since it describes the horrible torture of being at a job you hate day in, day out. Especially for a group of people who are as opposed to discipline as musicians, often times tricking yourself into a routine is how you'll get what's in you out into the world. But a routine in your life can be helpful since it keeps you creating regularly. The idea of a routine is a prescribed action that takes place after a cue.

Motivating yourself can be about utilizing guilt. Jerry Seinfeld would try to make a chain of X's across a calendar where every day he'd put in the work of writing jokes, which symbolized not breaking the chain by doing his work for consecutive days. I employed a similar method writing this book where I tracked how many words I wrote each week to make sure I was keeping up with my deadlines. This method allows you to not only keep track of deadlines but also understand how much makeup work you'll need to do in order to have the work you're expected to have done on time.

Longer Sessions Don't Always Mean More Effective Days

When I talk with record producers on my podcast, a common conversation is that sixteen-hour days aren't the same as two eight-hour days. As you continually create, there's a temptation to make days longer to get more out of them. In time, there's a realization that there's an ideal session length that allows a full night of sleep so that you perform better the next day. Longer days don't necessarily mean twice the amount of work getting done. Instead, they result in sluggish, slow work that could be done in a more effective delegation.

There's a balance you need to strike with keeping momentum while taking sufficient breaks to make sure you keep a good headspace. I have a term I call "punch drunk", which is when I've punched in a part for too long. When punching in a track for too long, I'll feel a drowsy lack of clarity that, unlike being drunk, has no useful benefits. Sustained, focused work can be amazing for getting creative work done. But if you book two weeks of it, with no room for time off along with 14+ hour days, realize that a lot of that time may be spent being burnt out. You'll then spend a lot of this time doing forced work where you can't see straight or trying to get your composure.

Ear fatigue, ego depletion and a handful of other factors make it so that long days aren't always the answer to getting a higher output from your work. While on strict deadlines there can be no other choice. When working on tight deadlines, I try to make myself more present, by ignoring the phone, Twitter and my other addictions to stay focused, since I can't make my days longer, but can make them more effective.

Making Your Own Creative Process

There's a whole industrial complex pumping out content on how to optimize your creative process to get into better habits. Part of being a great artist is recognizing when there's a flaw in your system and then adapting to rid yourself of the flaw. Analyzing your process and where it breaks down is needed from time to time. For example, you may realize you aren't having enough ideas and have too many skeletons so have to start choosing some skeletons to dress up in flesh. Take the time to analyze where you think your creative process is failing and then make a plan to adapt. This reflection can be far more effective than reading another article on optimizing your creativity.

Finding Your Creative Cocktail

One of the other reasons a lot of advice on enhancing creativity falls short is everyone needs a different cocktail to get to where they feel right in the head. Everyone's brain is experiencing a different chemical reaction. To level off adverse effects or to enhance our effectiveness we turn to various chemicals to make our brains more optimal. Often, creators take a handful of different chemicals and dietary supplements to get the results they want. This combination is called a cocktail. Mason Currey's brilliant book _Daily Rituals_ examined many of the best creators' daily habits. Aside from the fact that it was stunning how many of them were on the strangest primitive drugs of their time, what you'll notice is everyone needs to find a cocktail of chemicals that works for them.

While you can buy the same amp as someone else you admire to get a similar tone, what works for one person's brain can have the opposite reaction in another. The only way to find an effective cocktail for you is by listening to your body to find a cocktail that helps you achieve the results you want. No two creators have the same habit in their cocktail intake. Some do it completely sober while others do it while taking more drugs than you can name off the top of your head, but the commonality behind all these great artists is they found a cocktail that works for them. But this is one part of creativity where imitating your idols won't always work since everyone's mind needs different chemical reactions to get the desired outcome.

Meditation

Meditation isn't for everyone, but if you've ever listened to <u>Tim Ferris' podcasts</u> where he interviews top performers in a wide variety of fields, you'll notice that about 90% of them have meditation in their cocktail. Unfortunately, until you've experienced the benefits of meditation, most people dismiss it. It's looked at as another burden that will take up time, despite its ability to make your life far easier. I went 36 years without effectively meditating, but in recent years the benefits I've seen from my irregular practice have been helpful.

<u>Leiden University</u> found that meditation could improve creativity by boosting the ability to think of new ideas. It's been found that meditation can allow you to see answers more clearly and concentrate better when faced with a tough problem. If you find it hard to focus for sustained sessions without turning to your phone or other distracting indulgences, regularly meditating can be helpful. If you find yourself unable to work without thinking of the ten thousand other things in your life, this can also be diminished with a regular meditation practice.

Sleep

While we get some of our best ideas when we're tired or barely awake, a lack of sleep is terrible for your health as well as your motivation. Look no further than your Facebook feed for an inspirational Arianna Huffington quote or a study shows that eight hours of sleep a day will improve memory, performance and concentration.

Because I need to be creative at least five days a week, I've made getting this sleep a top priority that I engineer my life around. This means sometimes being a party pooper by going home early when I'm out at a show having fun. If you regularly feel drained or unmotivated and don't regularly get eight hours of sleep, you need to adjust your life so you can get more sleep. This may mean changing jobs or the environment in which you create. Many creators pursue their projects in the morning since they know they're far too tired to be creative after a day of work and ego depletion, so going to bed even earlier is often the only route to creating. Sadly, this doesn't go well with musician lifestyles where you need to be at shows that regularly start at 10 PM.

Diet

Nothing is more boring than listening to a hipster from Brooklyn lecture you on how you should eat, so I'll keep this brief and scientific. Your diet affects your creativity since it greatly affects your motivation. If you're feeding yourself junk food, you'll have less energy. If you find yourself constantly procrastinating or giving up when faced with a hard problem, this is often due to a lack of energy. A simple way to get more energy is to eat better. If you don't know what eating better means, I'm sure there are ten friends who'll be happy to fill you with knowledge of how to get more kale in your diet and what you can drink that isn't soda.

I'd be remiss not to mention that the direction science is going is that your gut bacteria helps regulate brain plasticity. In layman's terms, if you're putting junk food into your system and it's having a detrimental effect on your gut bacteria you may be making it harder to have epiphanies which slows down your creativity. Aside from this, the "food coma" phenomenon is often from eating too many carbohydrate-based foods. As someone with a strong love of carbs, it pains me to say that before a day of creating, getting a meal that's low in carbs can help you be more energetic and attentive.

Caffeine - There's no doubt that caffeine has been a huge part of creating in nearly every discipline for centuries. It's a given as a tool musicians use to stay in the headspace to create. Many of them over-compensate with energy drinks that give an intense high and then a severe crash. With that said, the moderate use of coffee and teas in various levels of use are sustained during the creative process for nearly every musician. Science shows that the focus and improved mental clarity occurs with caffeine use that can help sustain creativity.

I drink coffee every morning and then matcha tea as the day progresses, which provides a calmer, more sustained caffeine buzz (I prefer MatchaBar's brand if you can get it). Many people are experimenting with coconut oil or MCT Oil in their coffee, which they find enhances brain clarity.

Hydration - Many mistake dehydration to be a small detail in your life. If you aren't drinking a minimum of 64oz of water daily, you aren't nurturing your body to do the tasks it needs to do at a basic level and this goes even more so for singers or those who drink lots of alcohol. Watering your body by keeping it hydrated gives you energy as well as mental clarity. Every bit of frustration you have throughout a day, as well as resistance, is easier to overcome when you drink enough water.

Drugs And Creativity

"I've never done heroin. I wouldn't recommend heroin. But it sure hasn't hurt my record collection." — **Bill Maher**

Drugs are a hard subject to broach since it's inarguable how many great musicians have used them and it's also impossible to refute that many of their lives have been ruined by them. Like the Bill Maher quote above, I have a hard time recommending anyone do drugs since I've lost over a dozen friends to cocaine, heroin and prescription drug overdoses. But I cannot also discuss creativity and music without ignoring this huge part of it.

So, to make this clear, I don't recommend anyone does drugs. I want to talk about what science says instead of anecdotal evidence about what has worked for a single person. All too often the stories we're told of drugs being the creative spark in great work doesn't hold up to any real testing to show it was the drugs that made them achieve a great height instead of lessening it.

Alcohol - The most popular creative drug and widely regarded as an ingredient to creative thoughts. It's been proven that small amounts of alcohol have a disinhibiting effect on the brain, allowing blocks to come down that were normally there and epiphanies to arise. There's a key word in that sentence — *small amounts* — since large amounts of alcohol slow your brain to a crawl and leave you exhausted the next day.

The disinhibiting effects of alcohol can allow you to stop being fussy about aspects of your creative process and move on to perspiring without self-doubt creeping in. There are very few studies on alcohol's effect on creativity, but the few there are say it can help incubation but not verification. This means alcohol can help you get a good idea, but you won't know whether it's good at the time. Just like drunken college antics with alcohol, what you wake up next to creatively in the morning can either be great or disastrous.

Marijuana - Putting marijuana near any other drug makes me uncomfortable since it's a false equivalency having it near drugs that kill people as opposed to one that occasionally makes some users a bit lazier. What most science shows is that certain groups of people — but not all — benefit from marijuana use by stimulating their creativity. Just like alcohol, Leiden University studies show that light use can help create new ideas, but too much marijuana use is detrimental to creativity.

Cocaine - Cocaine is an amphetamine that can focus you but also cuts down on the interaction between the creative parts of your brain. It may be tempting to engage in amphetamine use, but if you're looking for good ideas, this will hinder you. It does excite what scientists call the working memory where small connections can be made, but if you're looking for a large epiphany, this isn't where you're likely to find it.

A classic trope of musicians in a recording studio is blowing a line of cocaine the size of the mixing console. There are plenty of other ways to get that energy that won't potentially kill you, damage your brain permanently and drain your wallet while leaving you in a horrible comedown within 30 minutes of ceasing use. There are plenty of other options that are far less harmful to you.

Heroin - Heroin is a terrible drug that few would say the reward is worth the risk it poses to your life once you try it. Saying anything good can come of it will usually get you yelled at, like when Blur's Damon Albarn tried to convey this point. With that said, there's no study that I could find that links heroin use directly to creativity. Many scientists have hypothesized that it breaks down inhibitions like alcohol and that it can create an altered state that can be inspiring. Despite whatever inspiration it possibly provides, there's far better ways to get inspired that are much less dangerous.

LSD and Psilocybin - Thousands of creators cite LSD and Psilocybin as opening their minds to greater creative worlds. Science backs this up with even more scientific studies being done each year that shows controlled dosages of these drugs lead users to epiphanies, enhanced thought patterns and new evidence show it can even cure depression. Like alcohol, the key being "controlled dosages," since prolonged usage and extreme doses have ruined many minds. Experimentation can be extremely risky since it's hard to get a controlled dosage which makes these drugs dangerous with possibly irreversible effects.

Adderall - Adderall or the newer more fashionable relatives of it like Modafinil (aka Nuvigil) have yet to have extensive studies on their effect on creativity, but there are concerns that it may help execution but hinder imagination. With that said, there's no definitive information showing these drugs hinder creativity. While I've experimented with all of the above, they put me into too intense a state to work properly. I opt for a lighter nootropic that helps my focus like Onnit's Alpha Brain for an extra kick on writing days, which helps me think in a more concise way.

Anti-Depressants - Like Adderall, any research I could find wasn't determinative. But, what we do have is a lot of artists who say that it helped them be happy enough to be productive or that it left them feeling an uninspired nothingness. There are many artists who find their depression to be a color that gives their work life, while there are others who find it totally destructive. When considering anti-depressants for creativity, the only way to know if it'll be helpful is trying it yourself or forgoing the use of them while trying to make progress on your happiness without them.

Changing Your Cocktail

One of the toughest parts of gaining success in your creative endeavor is that some of the inspiration can come from the state of mind you were in at a previous time. Many musicians attribute their cocktail to why they had a creative height. One of my favorite directors Lars Von Trier famously told Politiken that he wouldn't be able to make good films anymore once he became sober: "Obviously, the parallel world has its price, but I got an enormous amount out of it. Just like all the artists I've respected the most. They've also wallowed in all sorts of mind-expanding drugs."

Many musicians live in fear of changing that cocktail since great ideas occur under that influence, but to think that way is to look at the countless artists who have changed their cocktail while continually creating great works. If you see your cocktail as being a culmination of your inspiration, daily lifestyle, habits and the epiphanies you've had, that's giving far too much credit to your cocktail. These variables are bound to change from record to record or even from song to song across a record, so being afraid to change ignores that these variables are always changing. With that said, when you find a healthy habit that helps you create better, it's deeply beneficial to nurture it by making it a part of your life.

If you do experience obvious creative diminishment after changing your cocktail, you can compensate in other ways. If you got most of your inspiration while drinking, try to find inspiration through more research or a new form of experimentation. If energy drinks helped you execute your ideas, eating healthier will give you the energy you used to have. You can always find a cocktail to give you an extra kick, but remember your cocktail isn't what makes you, it's just an enhancement.

The absence of an ingredient of your cocktail isn't a reason to avoid creating. All of these tips are small ways to make it easier to create, not an excuse that allows you not to do your work. Any cocktail ingredient allows you to enhance what you do, not take sole responsibility for the genesis of your creation. Many of the great creators have worked without any of these ingredients, and you can too.

Chapter 15: Engineering Your Environment For Creativity

If you have the time, ability and budget to control your environment you can make yourself more creative. There's a variety of choices that can help get distraction out of your life to help you be more creative. While some see these as essentials to creativity, they're really little tweaks that can give you additional momentum in your creative work.

Your Creative Space

Make It Easy To Create

When I attempted to make my solo record, one of the biggest barriers was how long it took to set up my home studio compared to my commercial studio. It was an extreme deterrent for me to create music knowing there'd be fifteen minutes of setting up and routing cables on one of my rare days off from doing that each day. The part of the brain that wants to create is very different than the practical one that does work like organizing DAW files. This is why it's important to route cables and make templates so you can capture ideas the second you're ready. Having the instruments you regularly use to create already setup can be the difference between capturing inspiration or losing it. Since you'll inevitably experience resistance, it's important there's not unneeded resistance that can be alleviated by making your workspace ready to capture ideas.

Navigating Comfort And Creativity

There are a plethora of articles online on what comfort does to your creativity that contradict one another. To understand this dynamic, let's figure out how to use comfort as a tool as well as understand when it's a deterrent. When I was a teenager, a successful A&R guy who had signed many of my favorite bands told me that he wouldn't work with a band that's "comfortable." He'd ask every potential signee if they liked being home more than on tour and if the answer was "yes" — no matter how good they were — he wouldn't sign them. He wanted to be sure this band would be out on the road touring to promote their music, not sitting at home on their couch. The comfort of their home would kill the promotion of their music when the go and gets tough; they'd return to their comfort zone.

This thought also applies to motivation. Artist David Choe <u>has said</u> "comfort kills creativity", so despite being extremely wealthy, he lives in an uncomfortable home so that he wants to be in his art studio creating all the time. After all, if your studio is the place you'd rather be, you'll be motivated to leave home to create as much as possible. But comfort does have a place in creativity. The statement can be seen another way: his studio is so comfortable that it nurtures his work. Having a comfortable chair as well as the tools you need to work is a comfort that can help sustain extended creative sessions. The reassurance in knowing you have tools that can be easily used to capture inspiration is an invaluable comfort that nurtures any artist's creativity.

While you can do many tweaks to optimize your creative environment to be more effective, you can never use your environment as an excuse not to create. Far too many artists use the fact that their environment must be perfect for them to work. This neglects that the environment is only there to help you capture yourself more effectively. A comfortable chair or a quiet space can help you to sustain creativity and flow. However, these tools only help make our environments more comfortable; they don't enable the creativity. This means you must do the work, even if these luxuries are unavailable.

The Messy Desk vs. The Sterile Studio

It's said that creative brains are trying to organize the chaos of the world, but if that's the case, then why are most of their working areas chaotic messes? Everyone loves to parade around the quotes from very smart creators about a messy desk, especially those who need to defend their rat's nests against significant others who are disgusted by their creative space. But like anything else, there's a balance to the chaos of the messy desk and not every mess can be justified by it being the way a master works. The benefits of a messy desk should be understood as most creators care less than others about keeping up appearances to be presentable. They care that their tools are close by so they can work when inspiration strikes.

As we talked about with compositing notebooks, keeping around a wide variety of tools and inspiration can stimulate creative juices. When the messy desk goes too far, you can never find anything you need to create due to a lack of organization. But the messy desk is defensible when you know where what you need to create is, but it's unsorted to the outside eye. It looks like a mess to the outside world, but the workspace has a function despite appearing chaotic to others.

Another reason for the messy desk is proficient creators would rather work than organize. The clutter doesn't bother them since they're focused on getting what's in their head out. Too many creators knoll to pretend they're making progress, but the more important task is perspiring. With that said, there are plenty of people who need neatness to create; this doesn't make them any less creative than those with a messy desk, just of a different discipline.

Some fancy recording studios make musicians uncomfortable. They're afraid if they "rock out" they'll break a piece of equipment that costs more than their car (or in the case of some mixing consoles, their parents' home) and are held back from feeling their music. Even worse, many expensive studios take down all the microphones and unwire the studio each day. This means whenever inspiration hits it may take hours to set back up to capture it. This neat organization can be aesthetically pleasing, but it's at the detriment to capturing inspiration. This organization is only helping the studios get likes on Instagram instead of creativity.

Drunk Tank Pink And Creative Blue

The book _Drunk Tank Pink_, is named after a finding that if police departments painted their drunk tanks an abrasive Pepto Bismol-colored pink, they could decrease the amount of fights within the drunk tank. The finding that discovered the calming effect of pink also found creativity can be enhanced using the color blue. A University of British Columbia study found that "through associations with the sky, the ocean and water, most people associate blue with openness, peace and tranquility which make people feel safe about being creative and exploratory." This is also a cue for your brain, which is why long walks outdoors can bring on new inspiration. The color red can also stimulate an attention to detail, so when looking to paint your creative environment, consider going beyond the normal white walls.

Distraction As Inspiration And Creative Deterrent

When we choose where to put our creative environment, the decision is often based on how much space we need from distractions in order to create effectively. If you listen to an interview with any creator on their space, they'll inevitably go into detail on how it either isolates them from distractions or it allows them to get inspired. The decisions of how we engineer our space are reflective of how we feel about distractions and our discipline. Engineering your environment to get into a flow state more easily will increase the quality of your output.

Distractions vs. Breaks

When we talk about our spaces, the cliché of the cabin in the woods comes up often as it's the most isolated space possible. One of the biggest issues with discussing this approach is a confusion between distractions and breaks. Distractions are unwanted elements that come into our creative place that break us out of our mindset. These can be alerts that come from your phone, others coming into your space or even seeing something outside the window that breaks your state of flow. They can also come in the form of temptations that are hard to resist. Distractions are largely destructive to our creativity since they take us out of flow states which make us lose our train of thought during creative bursts. They make us forget what we were even thinking of as we lose thoughts we may never have again. In _Deep Work_, Cal Newport talks of the need of long distraction-free sessions of work that allow your mind to go deeper into thought without the constant checks of social media. Instead, you want an environment that enables your mind's ability to go into deep thought on your work. Since reading his book, I've tried this technique in my own work and found it to be life-changing.

While it's great to welcome distractions while getting inspired and incubating thoughts, when it comes time to perspire, your ability to get into a flow state needs to be guarded. I put on headphones to seclude myself from the city I work in to be free of any distractions. My phone goes on airplane mode for hours at a time so that I only see alerts when

I'm out of a flow state. As a hyperactive multitasker who's addicted to their Twitter feed, I value my high-information diet, but it needs to be separated from when I perspire. It can be tough to depart from the connected world, but I've found that choosing which mode I'm in while guarding my perspiration against distraction has dramatically improved my work's quality. Newport puts it this way: "When you work, work hard. When you're done, be done."

Unlike distractions, breaks are useful and should be used whenever we feel overwhelmed or when we're not making the amount of progress we're used to. **Breaks help us incubate ideas and regain objectivity, so they should be welcomed and not seen as time taken away from progress, but as a nutrient towards further progress.** Psychologist Joydeep Bhattacharya says that the shower is good for epiphanies since you can finally hear the voices in your head talking. Taking a long walk is another great example of how to get some of this inspiration back. Recognize that an all work, no play attitude isn't the most effective approach. Far too many artists forget that whether their ticking clock is a deadline or a budget, time spent resting your brain is time earned in both efficiency and clarity towards your project. I often like to think of rest as a bow and arrow. If rest is how far back you pull the bow, greater rest allows the arrow to shoot faster and farther. Whereas if you barely rest, your arrow will shoot slower and travel a short distance.

If You Wanna Find Inspiration, Then You Know Where The City Is

Every major study on innovation has shown that cities yield greater inspiration for innovative work. If you're feeling uninspired and alone in your small town (as the cliché pop punk song goes), you're not alone; it can be pretty uninspiring and that's just science. For a wide variety of reasons, cities are more inspiring. The difference isn't small, either — a city ten times its neighbor's size isn't just ten times more creative, it's seventeen times more creative. Now with the widespread ability to learn and have an amazing network on the internet, I'm sure this can be hacked if you're using the vast world of the web to get inspired, but there's still sufficient evidence the benefits of living in a city add to creativity.

Steven Berlin Johnson's _Where Good Ideas Come From_ says that what leads to the greatest heights of creativity is interacting with creators of different backgrounds. When studying top innovators in many fields, they find they usually have a social circle where they interact with a wide variety of people of different disciplines. The chance that you'll interact with another person with insight or attend an inspiring event like a concert or art show is much more likely in the city. **Putting yourself around other creators and learning the parameters of their disciplines, as well as how they apply to yours, is proven to nurture better ideas.**

Because there's more possibility of possibility in a city, whether you're walking by or want to take in some culture, cities have more possibilities to inspire more possibility. There are thousands of bars, art spaces and restaurants where creators discuss their works every single night, so there's a likelihood of taking in inspiration there more than any concentrated area in the world. There are also writers and avid fans of music that can give you helpful insight to nurture you.

This makes a big case for why you see the vast majority of buzz bands coming out of the Brooklyn area I call home. Northwestern Brooklyn and a small part of lower Manhattan seem to turn out the majority of the buzz bands in American music. Even if the musician isn't from there, they at least spend some time here touring, recording, doing press or visiting friends. The total population of these neighborhoods is about half a million people, which is also the population of the whole state of Wyoming. But this area of Brooklyn is squeezed into under ten miles, which a river takes up about a mile of. Wyoming is just shy of 100,000 sq. miles, meaning it's 10,000 times the size. This environment is why I choose to make Brooklyn my home once I left my parents' house. While the seclusion of the country can give you the focus you need to create great art in an undistracted environment, the overwhelming scientific evidence says that you'll get more inspiration to achieve creative heights inside a city.

The Cabin In The Woods

But what about that creative haven the cabin in the woods? Many artists long for a distraction-free environment. This is why this scenario has been employed for as long as creativity has been discussed. Getting away from the distractions and obligations of being close to home, bills, friends and every other distraction from your creation can give your mind an immense amount of focus. Nevermind, that the only activities at your disposal are to create or go hiking.

There's a part of this approach that must employ a few techniques to be effective. While it's hard to call a book like *Walden* uninspired, we know cities are better for inspiration. Since we get more inspired by the possibility of possibility, the cabin life isn't very inspiring. Furthermore, <u>scientists find</u> when you have "leaky attention," you can get more inspired by distractions since it allows time for incubation. Now I'm sure if you have Spotify with 75 records on a playlist you've been dying to listen to, you can easily get inspired, but this isn't as effective as the natural incubator of the city. The city allows for more stimulation, distraction and serendipity, the cabin can be a bit too extreme if the discipline is all work and no play or distraction.

When the cabin in the woods technique works well, the artist is brimming with inspiration while ready to perspire. This scenario allows them to get all the inspiration out of their head without the world imposing its distractions upon them. This is often why you see commercial studios offer seclusion from the outside world. Since a commercial recording studio is mostly a space to execute ideas, I choose to keep my studio in a town outside of the creative hub I live in. Limiting unexpected drop-ins as well as the temptation to hit a great restaurant or a club helps keep work focused. But breaks, incubation time and other stimulation are needed even in the execution part of the process. Don't anticipate sixteen-hour days of perspiration once you arrive at a cabin. You need time to relax and get distracted to give more consideration to your creation.

Chapter 16: Sustaining Creativity

"One of the things we all constantly wonder is why people suck as they get older, if they're getting better at creativity why aren't they making better work. Well, some of this also comes down to the laziness of believing in yourself. Insecurity fuels a lot of hard work. Your ego can become an obstacle to your work. If you start believing in your greatness, it's the death of your creativity." — **Marina Abramovic**

It's extremely rare to find an artist who's able to do their best work continually for more than a few years. They rarely understand what made their work great or don't value figuring out how to sustain it. If you write down twenty of your favorite musicians, I bet it's less frequent they were able to sustain their creative peaks for more than a five-year period, never mind decades. It's uncommon to sustain this creativity since it's not a skill you acquire, instead it's another muscle that needs to be kept in shape. **It isn't only knowledge that allows us to sustain creativity, it's the habits to continually question yourself that sustains it.**

While it isn't up to us to judge whether someone is continuing to do their best creative work, since what matters is their own happiness with their work, many creators acknowledge their best work is behind them. Quentin Tarantino <u>says</u>, "A lot of people's work goes bad when they're working to live instead of living to work." With success, you get to quit your day job, but what comes that is the awful dilemma of whether to do what your heart tells you to do or what will be best for your wallet. Similarly, your priorities become spending more time with your family, significant other or on another pursuit instead of your music. This dilemma has sent countless musicians back to their day job when they make a poor choice or begin to prioritize their life outside of their creative pursuits.

Where Creators Fail

Arrogance Is Poison

While there are many reasons for creativity withering away, one of them is what Eric Weiner calls "creeping vanity," a concept where creators begin to believe their own hype while developing an arrogance that's beyond a healthy confidence. Weiner's book, _The Geography Of Genius_, says that every great culture began a different way, but they all suffer the same fate of death by arrogance. This arrogance leads them to become blind to the rest of the world while resting on their laurels thinking they don't need to put in the same work they've done in the past. **With each bit of success you receive, fighting back arrogance becomes one of the most important battles in your life.**

Far too often, once a creator receives success, they feel immune to criticism by believing their own hype. Outside criticism is invalid as they ignore the possibility of others' objectivity, since they see more than others (_remember the quote, "Talent hits a target no one else can hit. Genius hits a target no one else can see."?_), the rest of the world can't see the truth they see. This plagues countless unchecked egos, inevitably leading them to their demise. When we insult people by calling them egotistical, we find their confidence and bragging to be insufferable, but the true crime of ego is when arrogance creeps into their life. Thankfully, it leads to their downfall in due time.

Always Remain A Student Through Humility

There's a popular adage that you should always remain a student by remaining a perpetual amateur. If you're not continually growing by prioritizing the exceedingly difficult task of continuing to learn with the humility of a student, then your creative work will suffer. We do our best work when we admire others, knowing that we can learn from them. Just as arrogance is poison for creativity, when you stop learning you halt the pursuit of new ways to advance your knowledge. There's a common trend in humans that as we get older, we become less and less open to new experiences. But what we see with creators who can sustain great work is they fight off that mindset by continually exploring new possibilities of what they may enjoy.

Challenging Yourself - There's a rare breed of artists that can challenge themselves to not only research, but also create within any genre. This can be a heavy metal guitarist that finds a way to find the emotions of pop music resonant to them and express themselves in an unfamiliar genre. For these creators the thrill of creating is what inspires them. I know this type well, since it's why I enjoy producing so many different types of music. It's amazing how many people demean sampled music or EDM without ever experiencing how much intricate tweaking goes into it and how inspired they would be if they stopped blindly attacking a craft that's unappealing to them. As we discussed earlier, getting inspired by other disciplines is one of the best ways to get inspiration for your work. Some creators take on the mindset of trying to create without any instruction given by someone else. Taking on the challenge to create, even if it isn't what's most emotionally resonant to you, can be a great learning experience to bring back to the emotions you want to express in your own work.

I've Done That Before

        As you continue to create, one of the most difficult decisions is to know whether you're repeating yourself or if you're developing a "sound" or "style." This standard can be the driving force for some creators to attain great heights by constantly pushing themselves forward in an exploration of an emotion. For others, this crushes them creatively as they constantly throw away good ideas that are emotionally resonant in favor of trying to come up with fresh work.

        Many artists challenge themselves not to use clichés, especially in lyric writing. Holding yourself accountable to challenge a new emotional resonance is helpful, but there's also countless examples when musicians have eschewed this and gotten an emotionally resonant result by following their emotions no matter how cliché they may be.

        The balance of this standard is an under-discussed struggle of artists. Many musicians are satisfied making similar sounding songs that hit a similar emotional place for countless records, whereas others push past that out of being easily bored or a superfluous challenge to do something new. The creative balance is not to do this out of a need to do something new since other artists you respect always do something new. If you're creating songs that are emotionally resonant to you, trust that instinct. But if an element is feeling boring since you've done it before, it's also important to trust that instinct. While you can experiment with new ideas, if they don't feel as emotionally resonant as the songs that seem more generic, always remember that AC/DC and The Ramones made whole careers of hitting the same emotional and musical notes over and over again that still had emotional power.

Identity And Creativity

As people change, a struggle often occurs with their identity. As we grow, it can feel odd to continue to create under a name where you created music that doesn't feel the same emotionally. The urge to adopt a different identity or go solo can plague creators. This urge to perspire new emotions should be embraced since we should nurture any emotions that want to be expressed. Far too many creators feel guilt about expressing themselves when it becomes outside of what their audience expects of them. If you need to express new emotions that you feel the need to share, take on a new alias if that's what needs to be expressed.

Many musicians get mad about the press pigeonholing them and decide to take a "left turn" out of a rebellion. If you are making a creative decision to change for the sake of rebellion that isn't in line with what you emotionally feel, it rarely works out. **Identity and creativity align when you discover a more authentic expression of yourself, not just shape shifting into a new form for the sake of new form after being unhappy with how the world sees you.**

Don't Judge A Song By The First Impression

Just as we must research some things we may not enjoy, we sometimes need to give our inspiration more than a single chance. As we get older, inevitably it gets harder to connect with new music as we get less open to new experiences, but those who push past this tendency reap huge rewards. Inspiration in music isn't always easy to connect with at first since whether a song will be resonant to you upon first listen isn't a given. I greatly disliked many of my favorite bands on first listen, but upon further listens I found what was inspiring about them. The service Hit Predictor was started for record companies to predict whether a song could be a hit or not. They found that listeners can't accurately judge if they want to hear a song again until they've heard a song at least three times.

Far too many listeners become jaded by not giving music a chance to have an emotional impact on them by expecting a reaction immediately. We've all experienced not being impressed by a song upon first listen that later becomes a favorite of ours. Some of my favorite albums from groups like White Lung, Modern Baseball and The 1975 all sounded terrible to me on first listen, but on further listens I saw what made them so great. I'm often in a happy mood but hear a sad song, so I don't feel the resonance. If a recommendation comes from someone you trust, give it more than a single listen before you dismiss it. **As we get older, it's important that if we see someone is inspiring our peers or those we admire, we should give them more than one chance to understand what's inspiring about them. Stay open to new experiences by giving them more than one chance to resonate with you.**

The Traits Of A Creative Person

Highly creative people do have some commonalities, and the good news is most of them are traits you can work on growing into if you don't already embody them. It's important to remember that not only do you have to continue to develop these traits, you also have to defend them from withering away. Here are the common traits identified by the top minds in the field which you can work on developing to further your creativity.

Curiosity - The urge to find what makes things tick and explore ideas is the most imperative quality of a creator. Too many creators grow old and begin to think they know it all. They lose their urge to explore and rest on their laurels. While it gets harder to find creatively stimulating inspiration the higher your standards get, they pay off is greater, allowing you to continue to do exciting work.

Open To Experience - Being willing to try new things is crucial to growth. Those who are reluctant to try new things have a hard time finding good ideas. Many who study creativity argue this is the most important quality of a creator. This is why the term "jaded" gets thrown around synonymously with those who are no longer creating anything that sounds inspiring. They've become too closed off to get inspired.

Equipped With Organization Skills - While many creators are messy in their living spaces, they have the ability to organize when needed and do it at a highly functional level. The more time you spend in a mess dealing with inefficiencies, the less time you spend creating. A mess is only justified if it helps you create better.

Playfulness - Enjoying tinkering while immersing oneself in discovery is essential to getting to good ideas. Too many creators grow bored of the time it takes to create while wanting results too fast. Remembering that it takes time to develop and have fun with what you create is essential to the process.

Rebelliousness - Most great creators enjoy bucking trends. Finding what trends and models you disagree with to create a resonant work that shows why you disagree has been the start of great music throughout history.

Individualism - Great creators shun conformity and are proud of being unique instead of like everyone else. Creativity can often be traced back to a lack of inclusion at a young age and even extreme rejection (let's not try to count how many love songs that rejection has been the inspiration for). Contrary to the popular idea in how to treat children today by never telling them they do anything wrong, being rejected and feeling as if they're alone allows for an independent spirit. This allows them not to feel the need to conform to what everyone else does and births creations that aren't the same as everyone else.

Sensitivity - Good creators are sensitive to nuance and subtlety as well as overt and obvious traits in the world. Getting lazy with observation or being cynical and jaded may feel good, but it doesn't lead to good creativity. Feeling intense emotion keeps us feeling alive and those who feel more than others are often those who can communicate resonance effectively.

Persistence - A great artist has to keep pushing on in the face of adversity. There's very little low-hanging fruit left in creativity that'll be rewarding to create today that won't be tough. Sticking with our pursuits to get to what we're trying to express is essential.

Fluency - Increasing your understanding of commonly used instruments, recording them and exploring the options of how to treat them adds to your lexicon and ability to make the sounds that reinforce your intent is vital to expressing yourself authentically.

Elaboration - The ability to know how to develop ideas into elements that reinforce your intent. Practice finding more ways that align with the emotions you commonly have to find ways to reinforce them.

Confidence - Those who are confident create more effectively. Taking the time to explore what keeps you from feeling confident is time that helps your creative output.

Optimism - While the myth of the brooding, insufferably negative creative is prevalent through stories you hear, most creators are optimistic because they need to be to keep going and make great creations. They need the ability to see the light at the end of the tunnel.

Happiness - Both happiness and a good mood are found to enhance creativity. Since creativity can bring your life happiness along with a sense of purpose, it can help you be more creative just by creating more. This can often be a double-edged sword since being forced to sit at a boring desk job, restricted from your creative endeavors can bring on frustration and misery. Mark Beeman finds that those who score higher on a happiness test have an easier time creating. Finding out how to design your life so you're able to pursue your creative endeavors can get your creative motivation to a better place. Regardless, putting in effort to stay happy also will keep you happy.

Actions You Can Do To Be More Creative

Generate More Ideas - As we discussed with building a better album, the more abundant and better ideas you have, the easier it is to make them into great songs. Working to generate more ideas to then pick the best ones is one of the best skills you can develop.

Ask Better Questions - They always say geniuses ask better questions than others. Figuring out how to think about a question in a more nuanced way and how to take a more interesting route to an emotional expression can lead you to new places that are more resonant.

Put Yourself Near Other Great Creators - There are countless stories of the great creators of any age being inspired by talking to and collaborating with the best creators of their time. Get close to other creators and start a conversation.

Top Yourself - Don't settle for a downtick in your creativity. Continually top yourself and settle for nothing less.

Be More Present - Having your attention remain on what you're creating instead of being distracted by the thousand things vying for your attention today is a skill with great reward. Develop the ability to stay present and focused on your creation.

Look For Smaller Details - Find the small details that you admire in others and work on how you develop similar details.

Pattern Recognition - Look for patterns in what you enjoy and figure out how to incorporate those patterns into what you do.

Develop Proficiency - The more proficient you are in creating, the easier it is for you to express yourself and diagnose the flaws in your expression and repair them.

Go Deeper - While I've produced records for over twenty years, the research I did on this book made me feel as if I knew nothing about the subject until I made many of the epiphanies you just read. There's always another part of music you can learn more about that will increase the connections in your mind and allow you to take advantage of chance. Take the time to explore a subject you don't know about in order to improve your ability to understand how to communicate your emotions to get closer to your vision.

Take Risks - The more you read about both what makes for great creativity and what helps enhance flow states is pushing the boundaries of what you think you can do. Risk taking is an ingredient in most great creators work. Push yourself to see risk and push past it.

Last, But Most Importantly, PLAY! - I've gone on and on about tons of
very serious concepts, so it can be very easy to forget that you should
have fun. As I was finishing this book, Steven Berlin Johnson, who I cited
throughout this book, released _Wonderland_, which shows that nearly
everything great in this world has come from play. Have fun, take in the
lessons from this book but don't take it too seriously and take the time to
enjoy what you're doing. The most important way to make the music you
want to hear is to continue to play until you find what you're looking for.

Outro

If you enjoyed this book, there's more of it. The parts I cut from it (the B-sides) are free at processingcreativybook.com/extras including some tools I use to analyze songs. I love talking about creativity and do most of my discussions on Twitter @jessecannon.

Hopefully, after reading this, you will make emotionally potent songs which are by far the best marketing tool. If you do and want a guide on what to do with them, please check out my other book _Get More Fans: The DIY Guide To The New Music Business_. I update it every single year with the most thorough, honest and relevant information possible.

If you can help spread the word on this book especially if you borrowed, stole or illegally downloaded this book I would appreciate it. This book is self published on a small budget so please take the time and share it on your Instagram, Twitter, Facebook or write as many friends as you can think of that would enjoy it. Writing a review that takes a whole 60 seconds on Amazon helps authors more than you'll ever know. Thanks!

If you want help making the best record possible, I'm a co-founder of a company that does that called Noise Creators. We represent many of the best producers in music and can point you in the direction of someone who can help you make great music.

I wrote this book for many reasons, but one of them was to fill my life with interesting people. If you think we can do a cool project together or may be on the same page creatively, I'd love to talk. I love producing, mixing and mastering records and working on other outside-of-the-box projects. I don't judge people's work, I just try to figure out how I can help them. Find me at JesseCannon.com.

Thanks for reading!

Further Reading

I wrote this book since I don't think musicians study creativity as much as they should and spend an insufficient amount of time researching it. When we talked about inspiration, I suggested figuring out who your favorite musicians were inspired by so I did the same for this book. The following is a list of who inspired this book. If you want to dig deeper on creativity here are some books I drew from that I recommend.

A Whole New Mind by Daniel Pink - A great book on thought exercises you can use to change the way you think for the better.

Bird By Bird by Anne Lamott - An interesting discussion on writing and creative process through the lens of an author.

Catching The Big Fish by David Lynch - Lynch's poetic thoughts on creativity.

Creative Intelligence by Bruce Nussbaum - A detailed discussion of what makes up creative intelligence.

Creativity by Mihaly Csikszentmihalyi - A thorough exploration of creativity research by one of the originators of creativity research.

Creativity Inc. by Ed Catmull - A fun read on Pixar's origins with discussions on their creative mistakes and how they fixed them.

Daily Rituals by Mason Currey - A fun and interesting read on the ways many famous creators worked and their cocktails.

Daring Greatly by Brene Brown - If you don't understand how vulnerability connects you to others and how it can help your music, I suggest reading this.

Deep Work by Cal Newport - A fantastic book about concentrated work and why you need to work in a more isolated environment.

Ego Is The Enemy by Ryan Holiday - An enlightening discussion I recommend for anyone who has trouble putting their art and greater good before their own glory.

Explaining Creativity by Keith Sawyer - The definitive textbook on creative science.

Flow by Mihaly Csikszentmihalyi - The formative book on flow and why it's so important.

Getting Things Done by David Allen - A must read for anyone who wants to get better at getting things off their to-do list and clearing their mind to have more focused thoughts.

Group Genius by Keith Sawyer - The deepest exploration of collaborations and how to do them well.

How Music Works by David Byrne - A thorough discussion on Byrne's creative decisions throughout his career.

Musicophilia by Oliver Sacks - A great look at music's effect on the brain.

On Writing by Stephen King - King's thoughts on how he's developed his craft over the years.

On Repeat: How Music Plays The Mind by Elizabeth Hellmuth Margulis - A scientific look at how hearing repetition in music affects the brain.

Smarter, Faster, Better by Charles Duhigg - A enlightening book on collaboration and productivity.

Song Machine by John Seabrook - A fun look at the history of how pop songs get created in the music business.

Songwriters On Songwriting by Paul Zollo - Amazing thoughts from songwriters on the creative process.

Sparks of Genius by Robert & Michelle Bernstein - A deep scientific discussion of creativity.

Steal Like An Artist by Austin Kleon - A fun book on inspiration and how it figures into the creative process.

The Artist's Way by Julia Campbell - A discussion on how to improve your creative output.

The Creative Brain By Nancy C. Andreasen - A psychological perspective on creativity and science.

The Creative Habit by Twyla Tharp - A unique discussion of the routine and thoughts that go into developing art through the lens of a wise ballerina.

The Geography Of Genius by Eric Weiner - A fantastic book exploring the rise and fall of the great creative societies through time.

The Paradox of Choice by Barry Schwartz - A detailed discussion on option paralysis.

The Power Of Habit by Charles Duhigg - If you want to learn how to get into better habits and use science to help get you there, this is the most entertaining while informative book on that subject.

The War Of Art by Steven Pressfield - The definitive book on resistance.

This Is Your Brain On Music by Daniel J. Levitin - A phenomenal book on how music affects your brain.

Where Good Ideas Come From by Steven Berlin Johnson - My favorite book on the subject of creativity. A fun and interesting read on innovation and the origin of ideas.

Unlocking Creativity by Michael Beinhorn - Beinhorn, being one of the best producers in rock, gives insightful thoughts on creativity and record making.

Zig Zag by Keith Sawyer - An interesting perspective on the creative process with a deep science backing.

There were also a few sources outside of books I gained a great deal of insight from regularly:

99U - A great site that regularly discusses creativity from a design perspective.

Brain Pickings - An amazing site that goes over books and explodes some of the better thoughts inside them.

Fight Mediocrity - A site that makes great YouTube videos and book summaries.

Party Smasher Inc. - A great blog, discussing creativity in the punk, metal and hardcore world.

Song Exploder - A fantastic podcast that takes a song and interviews its creators about the thoughts and methods behind it.

The Punk Rock MBA - A great blog and discussion forum on creativity in business.

The Talkhouse - A website where artists talk to other artists about their work and what they admire in others.

CPSIA information can be obtained
at www.ICGtesting.com
Printed in the USA
BVHW071113010421
603929BV00002B/140

9 780988 561335